Teacher's Edition

WORLD ENGLISH 1

Real People • Real Places • Real Language

Kristin L. Johannsen

HEINLE
CENGAGE Learning

Australia • Brazil • Japan • Korea • Mexico • Singapore • Spain • United Kingdom • United States

HEINLE
CENGAGE Learning™

World English 1 Teacher's Edition
Real People • Real Places • Real Language
Kristin L. Johannsen

Publisher: Sherrise Roehr

Managing Editor: Berta de Llano

Senior Development Editor: Margarita Matte

Development Editor: Michael Poor

National Geographic Editorial Coordination:
  Leila Hishmeh

Technology Development Manager: Debie Mirtle

Director of Global Marketing: Ian Martin

Director of US Marketing: Jim McDonough

Product Marketing Manager: Katie Kelley

Marketing Assistant: Jide Iruka

Senior Content Project Manager/Art Direction:
  Dawn Marie Elwell

Senior Print Buyer: Betsy Donaghey

Cover Designer: Page 2 LLC

Cover Photo: Colin Monteath/Minden Pictures/
  National Georgraphic Image Collection

Compositor: Nesbitt Graphics, Inc.

International Edition:
World English 1 TE ISBN 13: 978-1-4240-5113-7
World English 1 TE ISBN 10: 1-4240-5113-4

U.S. Edition:
World English 1 TE ISBN 13: 978-1-4240-6299-7
World English 1 TE ISBN 10: 1-4240-6299-3

Heinle
20 Channel Center Street
Boston, MA 02210
USA

Cengage Learning is a leading provider of customized learning solutions with office locations around the globe, including Singapore, the United Kingdom, Australia, Mexico, Brazil, and Japan. Locate your local office at:
international.cengage.com/region

Cengage Learning products are represented in Canada by Nelson Education, Ltd.

Visit Heinle online at elt.heinle.com

Visit our corporate website at www.cengage.com

Printed in Canada
1 2 3 4 5 6 7 13 12 11 10 09

CONTENTS

DESTINATIONS

1. Do you know the names of these places? Where are they?

2. Do you enjoy traveling? Why?

UNIT GOALS

Talk about past vacation trips
Exchange information about vacations
Use *was/were* to describe a personal experience
Talk about a discovery from the past

62

63

Warm-up questions stimulate students' previous knowledge and life experiences while providing teachers with useful leveling information.

Striking photographs from around the globe introduce students to the unit theme.

Clearly defined goals provide students with a "blueprint" that helps them visualize their learning.

A clear and practical goal is presented, practiced and mastered every two pages in each unit.

A   GOAL 1   TALK ABOUT PAST VACATION TRIPS

Vocabulary

A. Match the photos to an activity from the box.

visit places of interest ____	take photos____
take a bus tour ____	pack/unpack suitcases ____
check into the hotel ____	buy souvenirs ____
rent a car ____	

1.   2.   3.

4.   5.   6.   7.

B. Which of these do you do *before* and *during* your vacation?

Before _____
During _____

C. Take turns. Tell a partner what other things you do before or during a vacation.

Grammar: Simple past

Simple past tense

Statement	He **rented** a ca...
Negative	I **didn't have** a...
Yes/no questions	**Did they go** to...
Short answers	Yes, they **did**. N...
Information questions	Where **did** you...

*We use the simple past tense to talk about complet...
*Some verbs are regular in the simple past tense. They have an *-ed* ending.

learn — learned	travel — traveled	buy — bought	leave — left
arrive — arrived	want — wanted	fly — flew	say — said
play — played	need — needed	know — knew	see — saw
ask — asked	help — helped	go — went	take — took

64   Destinations

A. Complete the sentences. Use the simple past tense form of the verb in parentheses.

1. Last year, we _____ (visit) Machu Picchu in Peru.
2. We _____ (not, like) the hotel.
3. We _____ (buy) some interesting souvenirs.
4. When _____ (you arrive) at the airport?
5. We _____ (go) to Paris and Rome last year.

B. Unscramble the words to write questions and answers.

1. **Q:** to Europe Did you go year? last

   _____

2. **A:** to we No, went America.

   _____

3. **Q:** did buy you those Where souvenirs?

   _____

4. **A:** them bought in We Egypt.

   _____

Real Language

You can use the following expressions to show interest.

Informal ————————————→ Formal

Wow!   Sounds cool.   Really!   That's interesting.

Conversation

A. Listen to the conversation. How long did Maria stay in Cuzco?

Track 1-25

Christine:	Hey, I love that <u>poncho</u>, Maria. Where did you b...
Maria:	I bought it in <u>Peru</u>. We went to Peru for our vaca...
Christine:	Wow! Sounds cool. Did you go to <u>Lima</u>?
Maria:	No, we flew directly to <u>Cuzco</u>. We wanted to see... <u>ruins at Machu Picchu.</u>
Christine:	How long did you stay there?
Maria:	We stayed for <u>five nights</u>.
Christine:	Lucky you!

...tice the conversation with a partner. Switch roles and pra...

...tice the conversation again and change the underlined words using ...information in the chart.

Country	Italy	United States	Great Britain
Capital	Rome	Washington, DC	London
Other City	Venice	Orlando	Edinburgh
Place of special interest	Doge's Palace	Disneyland	The Castle

Frequent **Conversation** activities motivate students to practice natural language themselves after practicing with a model dialog.

Real Language information boxes in every unit focus students' attention on frequently used phrases and how to use them.

✓ **Goal 1**   **Talk about past vacation trips**

Take turns with a partner telling about a vacation you took.

Lesson A   65

T-4

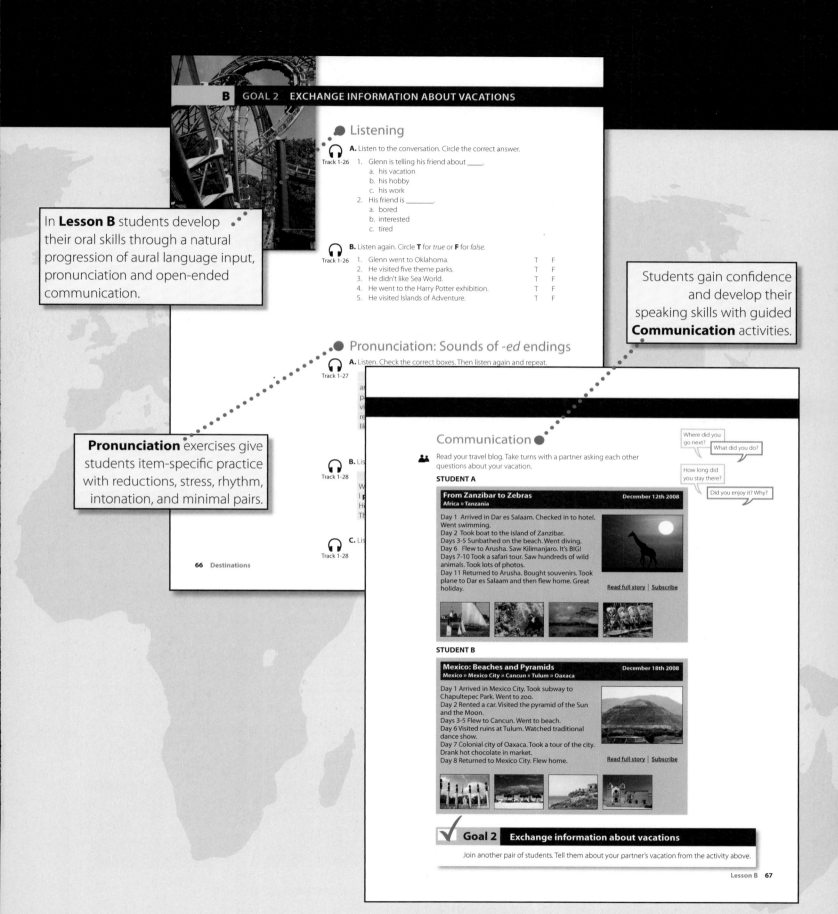

B GOAL 2 EXCHANGE INFORMATION ABOUT VACATIONS

Listening

A. Listen to the conversation. Circle the correct answer.

Track 1-26

1. Glenn is telling his friend about _____.
   a. his vacation
   b. his hobby
   c. his work
2. His friend is _____.
   a. bored
   b. interested
   c. tired

B. Listen again. Circle **T** for *true* or **F** for *false*.

Track 1-26

1. Glenn went to Oklahoma.	T	F
2. He visited five theme parks.	T	F
3. He didn't like Sea World.	T	F
4. He went to the Harry Potter exhibition.	T	F
5. He visited Islands of Adventure.	T	F

In **Lesson B** students develop their oral skills through a natural progression of aural language input, pronunciation and open-ended communication.

Pronunciation: Sounds of -ed endings

A. Listen. Check the correct boxes. Then listen again and repeat.

Track 1-27

Pronunciation exercises give students item-specific practice with reductions, stress, rhythm, intonation, and minimal pairs.

B. Lis

Track 1-28

C. Lis

Track 1-28

66 Destinations

Students gain confidence and develop their speaking skills with guided **Communication** activities.

Communication

Read your travel blog. Take turns with a partner asking each other questions about your vacation.

Where did you go next?
What did you do?
How long did you stay there?
Did you enjoy it? Why?

STUDENT A

From Zanzibar to Zebras   December 12th 2008
Africa » Tanzania

Day 1 Arrived in Dar es Salaam. Checked in to hotel. Went swimming.
Day 2 Took boat to the island of Zanzibar.
Days 3-5 Sunbathed on the beach. Went diving.
Day 6 Flew to Arusha. Saw Kilimanjaro. It's BIG!
Days 7-10 Took a safari tour. Saw hundreds of wild animals. Took lots of photos.
Day 11 Returned to Arusha. Bought souvenirs. Took plane to Dar es Salaam and then flew home. Great holiday.

Read full story | Subscribe

STUDENT B

Mexico: Beaches and Pyramids   December 18th 2008
Mexico » Mexico City » Cancun » Tulum » Oaxaca

Day 1 Arrived in Mexico City. Took subway to Chapultepec Park. Went to zoo.
Day 2 Rented a car. Visited the pyramid of the Sun and the Moon.
Days 3-5 Flew to Cancun. Went to beach.
Day 6 Visited ruins at Tulum. Watched traditional dance show.
Day 7 Colonial city of Oaxaca. Took a tour of the city. Drank hot chocolate in market.
Day 8 Returned to Mexico City. Flew home.

Read full story | Subscribe

✓ **Goal 2**   **Exchange information about vacations**

Join another pair of students. Tell them about your partner's vacation from the activity above.

Lesson B **67**

Language Expansion sections focus on specific areas that help learners' to build language strategies and become more competent users of English.

C GOAL 3 ASK ABOUT LIFESTYLES

▲ mouth-watering fruit

Language Expansion: Compound adjectives

A. Match the compound adjectives to their meanings.

1. mouth-watering ___
2. homemade ___
3. heart-warming ___
4. lifelong ___
5. stress-free ___
6. homegrown ___
7. overworked ___
8. low-calorie ___

a. works too much
b. delicious
c. without worries or problems
d. not high in calories
e. makes you happy
f. produced in your own garden
g. all your life
h. not made in a factory

B. Complete the sentences. Use the adjectives from exercise **A**.

1. Kevin and I went to kindergarten together. We are _____ friends.
2. When I was a child, my father had a vegetable garden, so we ate lots of _____ fruit and vegetables.
3. I have to work long hours and I'm always tired. I think I am _____.
4. My grandmother makes the best _____ chicken soup in the world! It's absolutely _____.

▲ homemade pie

Grammar: Questions with *how*

Grammar presented in the unit is practiced through a variety of activities, each designed to reinforce students' knowledge of how the language works and assure them accuracy and appropriateness in their use of English.

How much exercise do you do?
How many cigarettes do you smoke?
How old is your father?
How long did your grandfather live?
How often do you go to the gym?
*We use **how much** to ask about the quantity of non-countable nouns.
*We use **how many** to ask about the quantity of countable nouns.
*We use **how old** to ask about age.
*We use **how long** to ask about length or a period of time.
*We use **how often** to ask about frequency.

A. Match the questions and the answers.

1. How often does Ian go swimming? ___
2. How old is Akuru's grandmother? ___
3. How much junk food do you eat? ___
4. How long do you think you will live? ___
5. How many cigarettes does Mario smoke a day? ___

a. She's about 95.
b. Until I'm 80.
c. About 15.
d. Not much.
e. Once a week.

D GOAL 4

Reading

A. Answer the questions.

1. Do you think the author enjoys travelling? _____
2. Why should you check the expiration date of your passport? _____
3. Why should you tie a sock to your bags? _____

Word Focus boxes provide definitions of additional vocabulary, useful collocations, and special usage.

Real Language

We use the expression *share some pointers* to say *give advice.*

Word Focus

expiration date = The *expiration date* of a document is the date it comes to an end or can no longer be used.

⌂ Smart Traveler

EXPERT OPINION

_____ _l, *Mike Connelly,* **shares some pointers** on
_____ *easy!*

___UMENTS Make sure you have all your documents:
___ort, visas, tickets, traveler's checks, etc. You should always
___ck the **expiration date** of your passport. Many countries
___n't let you enter with less than six months left on your
___assport. Don't forget to buy medical insurance. Medical bills

can be very expensive, especially in the United States and Europe. Finally, you should make copies of all your important documents and credit cards and keep them in another bag.

■ **PACKING** My advice is—always travel light! I hate to carry heavy bags. Just take the minimum. There is an old saying: *Breakfast in Berlin. Dinner in Delhi. Bags in Bangkok!* So, don't pack anything important in your check-in bag; put important things in your carry-on bag. You don't want to arrive home without your house keys. Another tip—don't use expensive suitcases. People don't steal dirty old bags. Finally, here's a good little tip—tie a sock or brightly colored string to your bags. Why? So you can quickly see your bag on the airport carousel.

■ **THE AIRPORT** My first piece of advice is that you should always carry a good book. It helps to pass the time as you wait for your delayed flight. Don't forget to take a sweater or a jacket on the plane. It can get very cold on a long night flight. And then there is airline food. Take a snack (cookies or fruit) with you. Sometimes the food is late, sometimes it doesn't arrive at all, and it's never very good.

Writing activities reinforce the structures, vocabulary and expressions learned in the unit.

B. Circle **T** for *true* and **F** for *false.*

1. You need a lot of documents to travel. T F
2. You need to take a lot of clothes in your bag. T F
3. Bags can be hard to identify at the airport. T F
4. Flights are never late. T F
5. Airplane food is always good. T F

Writing

Write some travel tips for your country. Think about the following topics:

• transportation
• how to carry money
• Can you drink the water?

Thailand is a safe country and the people are very friendly. But, like most places, you should be careful. Here are some tips:

• Taxis are cheap, but ask the price first.
• Many tourists use *tuk tuks.* However, they are dangerous. Be careful.
• Don't use the buses. They are slow and crowded.
• Don't carry a lot of money with you. Most shops accept credit cards.
• The water is not safe to drink, so you should buy water in bottles.
• Don't go out alone at night.

Have a nice stay!

✓ **Goal 4** **Share special travel tips with others**

Read your travel tips to a partner. Then share them with the class.

Magazine-style readings are a springboard for opinion sharing and personalization, and provide opportunities for students to use the grammar and vocabulary presented earlier in the unit.

Florida, U.S.

Before You Watch

A. Look at the photos. Do you have working dogs in your country? How do these dogs help us?

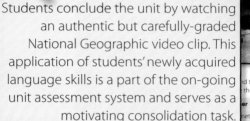

▲ guide dog   ▲ sheepdog

▲ police dog

...d the sentences. Then read the video summary. Use the
...the text.

...er illegal

...netimes they carry **disease**.
...e quiet. I'm trying to work. You're **bothering** me.
You can't park your car there. It's not allowed. It's **illegal**.

Video summary
Airline passengers sometimes carry food, for example fruit, that may bring
_____ into a country. Detector dogs can find this fo...
smelling the passengers' bags. Brent Heldt is training a dog called Stoc...
to be a detector dog. Stockton has to find the _____
but also he must not _____ the passengers.

36 Going Places

While You Watch

A. Watch the video. Circle the names of things you see.

uniform	apples	suitcase	passport
gun	orange	mango	beef jerky

B. Watch the video again. Circle **T** for *true* and **F** for *false*.

1. Brent and Stockton play before they start work.   T   F
2. Detector dogs look for meat.   T   F
3. Stockton does not find the meat.   T   F
4. Stockton eats the meat he finds.   T   F
5. Stockton is learning slowly.   T   F

After You Watch

In the video we saw that dogs can be very useful in airports. Work with a partner
to write a list of possible problems with dogs in airports.

Communication

Role-play the following situations.

Situation 1
Student A is a dog handler.
Student B is a passenger. The dog is sniffing your bag. You don't like
dogs. In your culture dogs are dirty. Complain to the dog
handler.

Situation 2
Student A is a passenger. The dog finds some fruit in your bag. It is a gift
for your mother.
Student B is the dog handler. Explain that the passenger shouldn't bring
fruit into the county. Take the fruit.

Video Journal 37

BONUS COMMUNICATION ACTIVITIES

Activity 1

Look at the picture. Discuss the questions.

a. Where is Carmen from?
b. How old is she?
c. Can you read her writing?
d. Are there any mistakes?
e. Is she worried?
f. Do you make mistakes with your English?
g. Are mistakes important?

Activity 2

Work with a partner.

STUDENT A
Describe Nakshatra's clothes to a partner.

STUDENT B
Describe Meghana's clothes to a partner.

Discuss these questions together.

a. Do you think Nakshatra likes Meghana's
   clothes? How do you know?
b. Do you think young people should wear
   traditional clothes? Give your reasons.

▲ Nakshatra Reddy and her daughter Meghana

146 Communication Activities

Students conclude the unit by watching an authentic but carefully-graded National Geographic video clip. This application of students' newly acquired language skills is a part of the on-going unit assessment system and serves as a motivating consolidation task.

The video can be watched in class from the **Classroom DVD** or students can watch it individually on the **Student CD-ROM**.

Bonus Communication Activities that offer students additional opportunites to develop their oral skills are provided at the back of World English Student Books 1 and Intro.

This **World English Teacher's Edition** is designed to make your preparation as simple as possible, allowing you to maximize actual classroom teaching time. It features page-by-page suggestions on how to teach the course, answer keys to the Student Book and Workbook, culture notes, extension activities, audio scripts of listening passages not printed in the Student Book, and video scripts.

A snapshot from the course **Scope and Sequence** provides a quick reference as the teacher presents the new unit to students.

The **Unit Theme Overview** provides teachers with all the background information that they will need as they work through the unit. It also gives them a quick preview of the type of activities the students will do throughout the unit.

Step-by-step teaching suggestions are provided on every page of the unit.

Detailed **Grammar** explanations are provided for teacher reference in Lessons A and C.

An additional **Grammar Practice** activity can be used when necessary for re-teaching and review.

Goals		Language Focus
UNIT 1 People	• Talk about people	*Her/his name is ____ .* *S/he's from ____ .* *S/he's a(an) ____ .*
UNIT 2 Work, Rest, and Play	• Describe an unusual celebration • Share your ideas with the class	*It's called ____ . It's for ____ .* *People always . . . on ____ .*
UNIT 3 Going Places	• Deciding what to take on a trip • Limiting travel needs to one suitcase	*I think we should take . . .* *Don't take . . .*
UNIT 4 Food	• Completing a menu • Ordering meals at a restaurant	*Do you have . . .* *Would you like . . .*
		I think . . . *prefer*

This Teacher's Edition provides additional Communication and Writing practice through classroom materials that can be photocopied. **Communication Activities** include information gap, group work, interview worksheets, simulations and role-plays.

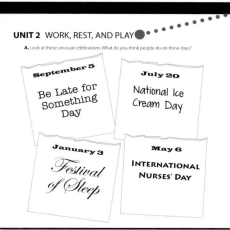

UNIT 2 WORK, REST, AND PLAY

A. Look at these unusual celebrations. What do you think people do on these days?

September 5
Be Late for Something Day

July 20
National Ice Cream Day

January 3
Festival of Sleep

May 6
INTERNATIONAL NURSES' DAY

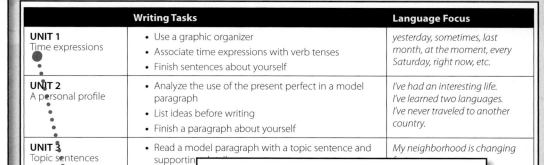

	Writing Tasks	Language Focus
UNIT 1 Time expressions	• Use a graphic organizer • Associate time expressions with verb tenses • Finish sentences about yourself	*yesterday, sometimes, last month, at the moment, every Saturday, right now, etc.*
UNIT 2 A personal profile	• Analyze the use of the present perfect in a model paragraph • List ideas before writing • Finish a paragraph about yourself	*I've had an interesting life.* *I've learned two languages.* *I've never traveled to another country.*
UNIT 3 Topic sentences	• Read a model paragraph with a topic sentence and supporting... • Choose th... • Write you...	*My neighborhood is changing*

The **Writing Program** reinforces and complements the lessons in the Student Book. Writing gives students a chance to reflect on the English they've learned and to develop an indispensable academic skill.

UNIT 6 DESTINATIONS
DESCRIBE A PLACE

A. How was your life when you were a child?

When I was a child . . .
1. I wanted ____
2. I didn't want ____
3. I went ____
4. I didn't go ____
5. I learned ____
6. I didn't learn ____

✓ Take turns. Ask a partner questions about the sentences above.

What did you want when you were a child?

What did you not want when you were a child?

B. When you were a child, what was your favorite place to be? (e.g. your family's kitchen; a park near your house; your grandmother's farm; etc.) Answer these questions about that place.
1. What was your favorite place? ____
2. Why did you like that place? ____
3. How did you get there? ____
4. What did you do there? ____
5. What did you see, hear, and feel in your favorite place? ____

✓ Write about your favorite place when you were a child. Use some of the information above.

My Favorite Childhood Place

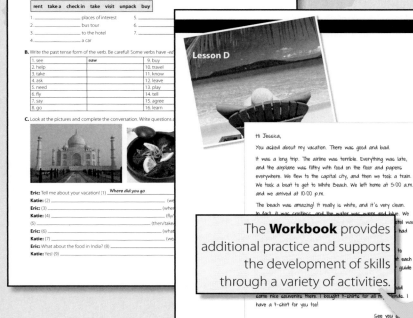

DESTINATIONS **UNIT 6**

Lesson A

A. Complete the expressions for vacation activities.

rent	take a	check in	take	visit	unpack	buy

1. ____ places of interest
2. ____ bus tour
3. ____ to the hotel
4. ____ a car
5. ____
6. ____
7. ____

B. Write the past tense form of the verb. Be careful! Some verbs have -ed

1. see	saw	9. buy	
2. help		10. travel	
3. take		11. know	
4. ask		12. leave	
5. need		13. play	
6. fly		14. tell	
7. say		15. agree	
8. go		16. learn	

C. Look at the pictures and complete the conversation. Write questions a

Eric: Tell me about your vacation! (1) ____ Where did you go
Katie: (2) ____ (we
Eric: (3) ____ (wher
Katie: (4) ____ (fly/
(5) ____ (then/take
Eric: (6) ____ (what
Katie: (7) ____ (we
Eric: What about the food in India? (8) ____
Katie: Yes! (9) ____

Lesson D

Hi Jessica,

You asked about my vacation. There was good and bad.

It was a long trip. The airline was terrible. Everything was late, and the airplane was filthy with food on the floor and papers everywhere. We flew to the capital city, and then we took a train. We took a boat to get to White Beach. We left home at 5:00 a.m. and we arrived at 10:00 p.m.

The beach was amazing! It really is white, and it's very clean. In fact, it was spotless, and the water was warm and blue. We ... hotel was

... had

to

... at each

... guide

... had

... ome nice souvenirs there. I bought t-shirts for all m ... iends. I have a t-shirt for you too!

See you ...

Amy

The **Workbook** provides additional practice and supports the development of skills through a variety of activities.

Circle the correct answer.
1. Amy stayed at ____.
   a. the capital city   b. a beach   c. a small town
2. Her trip to White Beach was ____.
   a. easy   b. hard   c. short
3. The hotel was ____.
   a. big   b. dirty   c. fascinating
4. The food wasn't ____.
   a. healthy   b. interesting   c. delicious

What did Amy think about these things? Check ✓ her opinions.

	☺	😐	☹
1. her vacation			
2. the airplane			
3. the beach			
4. the hotel			
5. the food			
6. the bus tour			
7. the souvenirs			

You took a vacation in London. Look at the vacation information. Write a letter to your friend about it.

Your London Tour
... port
... rants
... ndon
... the Thames River
... ouvenirs i... amous department stores

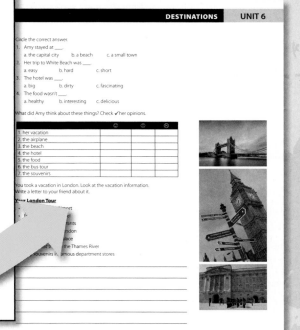

Overview

World English uses rich, engrossing National Geographic text, photos, art, maps, and videos to involve students in learning about real people, real places, and real language.

Each unit is divided into four two-page lessons and a two-page Video Journal.

A concrete objective at the beginning of every lesson focuses students' attention on what they will be learning. At the end of the lesson, a personalization activity gives students an opportunity to apply what they've learned and lets both teachers and students check student progress.

Unit Opener

Each unit opens with a two-page spread of striking photos. These have been chosen both to illustrate the unit theme and to provide material for discussion. Before beginning the unit, teacher and students can describe the pictures, name as many things as they can in them, and make guesses about when and where the photos were taken. The two discussion questions then lead students into the topic and introduce several key vocabulary items.

In this Teacher's Edition, a Unit Theme Overview is provided to orient you to the scope of the unit and to give additional information that may be useful in discussing the unit theme. Throughout the lesson notes, For Your Information boxes contain additional facts about the topic of a listening passage, reading, or video.

Vocabulary

Lessons A and C both begin with a short activity presenting lexical items related to the unit theme. In Lesson A, the vocabulary section introduces the core words that students will need to discuss and learn about the unit topic. These are presented in context, with text or pictures to aid students in understanding. After completing the exercises in this section, students have a written record of the meanings of the words, which they can refer to later. The lesson notes in this Teacher's Edition contain a Word Bank of supplementary vocabulary that can be used in activities or taught as enrichment.

Grammar

World English features an explicit grammar syllabus, with individual grammar points tied to the unit theme. Two different grammar points are taught in Lesson A and Lesson C. They are used in the opening presentation of the lessons along with the vocabulary items and then explicitly presented in a box with examples, rules, and usage notes.

Students first do controlled practice with the structure in writing, then freer production in writing, and finally use the structure in controlled speaking practice. Every grammar point is followed by a Conversation section that gives further practice in the use of the structure.

The lesson notes in this Teacher's Edition contain a brief summary of each grammar point for teacher reference, as well an additional Grammar Practice Activity.

Conversation

Lessons A and C contain model conversations highlighting both the vocabulary and the grammar for the lesson. Students first listen to the conversation with their books closed and answer one general comprehension question. Next, they listen again while reading the conversation. They are then ready to practice the conversation, taking turns with both roles before making their own conversations based on the model and incorporating specified information along with their own ideas.

Listening

Lesson B starts off with a listening activity. After a warm-up to introduce the subject of the activity, students listen to a conversation, radio program, or interview multiple times, completing a series of written tasks of graded difficulty. The first time, they are asked to listen for the gist or main ideas; subsequent activities ask them to find numbers, details, or further information. A post-listening task helps students to explore and personalize what they've heard.

Audioscripts for all listening activities begin on page T-155.

Pronunciation

The pronunciation component of **World English** emphasizes stress, intonation, reductions, and other features to make learners' English more natural and comprehensible to a wide international audience. Students first learn to recognize a feature of English pronunciation and then to produce it. Examples are presented on the audio recording in the context of the unit theme. Students begin by listening, then repeat with the audio recording, and then practice freer production of the features while interacting with a partner.

If a particular pronunciation point is especially challenging for your students, it can be practiced in a number of ways. You can have the entire class repeat the items in chorus, then the two halves of the class, then rows or columns of students, and finally you can call on individual students to pronounce the items. When students practice in pairs, circulate around the room listening and correcting.

Communication

In contrast to the controlled speaking practice in the Conversation sections, the Communication activities give freer practice with the structures and vocabulary that the students have learned. These activities are designed to allow personal expression, but still within a controlled field of language, so that all students can feel confident of success. While students are doing these activities, you should circulate around the class to help with vocabulary and ideas as needed and to make note of errors and interesting responses to discuss with the class after the end of the activity.

The lesson notes in this Teacher's Edition include one Expansion Activity per unit for further discussion around the theme of the listening passage. For classes where more practice of free communication is desired, this book also contains 12 Communication Activity Worksheets, which may be photocopied, one for each unit. The activities, which require 15 to 30 minutes of class time each, reinforce the vocabulary and structures from the unit while giving students another opportunity to express their own ideas in English.

Language Expansion

The first part of Lesson C is a Language Expansion activity that is meant to broaden students' vocabulary around the unit theme by introducing a closely related group of lexical items. These are presented in context and are used immediately in writing and then speaking, giving students more options when doing the Grammar and Conversation activities that follow in Lesson C.

Reading

Lesson D is centered around a reading passage. All of the reading passages in **World English** are abridged and adapted from authentic articles in National Geographic publications. To help students read for interest and enjoyment, unfamiliar vocabulary is explained either with glosses in a Word Focus box or in a picture dictionary illustration.

The lesson notes in this Teacher's Edition include a Web search activity and a suggestion for a simple project that can be done as a follow-up for each reading passage.

Writing

The writing activities in Lesson D of **World English** flow from the subject of the reading passage and are always preceded by an exercise in which students discuss and explore the topic further. This generates ideas and forms a natural prewriting sequence. Writing tasks are short and simple and range from writing single sentences in the lower levels, through writing groups of sentences, on up to writing an entire paragraph.

The writing activities in the units emphasize helping students put their ideas into written form. Where a more structured approach to writing is desired, this Teacher's Edition contains a complete Writing Program, which may be photocopied. These optional writing worksheets, one for each unit, provide instruction and practice in a sequence of writing skills graded to the level of the course.

Video Journal

Each unit of **World English** concludes with an authentic National Geographic three- to four-minute video, with a voice-over that has been specially edited for language learners. The video segments recycle the themes and language of the main unit, bringing them to life in colorful locations around the globe. A Before You Watch activity presents new words that students will hear and gives information about the setting of the video. Students watch the video several times while completing While You Watch activities that ask them first to find general themes and then to locate specific information. They give their response to the video in an After You Watch activity.

Each unit concludes with a Communication activity that draws all the strands of the unit together and allows students to demonstrate what they've learned.

Special Features in the Student Book

Engage! These questions challenge students to personalize the topic by expressing their own experiences, opinions, and ideas. They can be answered in a whole class, in groups, or in pairs.

Real Language This feature highlights high-frequency expressions from everyday language that will make students' speech sound natural and confident. To present them, point out their use in the activity and discuss other situations when they might be useful. If desired, have students work in pairs to create conversations using the expressions.

Word Focus These boxes present and explain additional vocabulary used in an activity, as well as introduce commonly used collocations.

Bonus Communication Activities At the end of student books Intro and Level 1, six activities present students with the opportunity to practice the language and structures that they have learned in a guided oral format as they discuss stunning photographs with a partner.

WORLD ENGLISH 1

Real People • Real Places • Real Language

Martin Milner

HEINLE
CENGAGE Learning

Australia • Brazil • Japan • Korea • Mexico • Singapore • Spain • United Kingdom • United States

HEINLE
CENGAGE Learning™

World English 1
Real People • Real Places • Real Language
Martin Milner

Publisher: Sherrise Roehr

Managing Editor: Berta de Llano

Development Editor: Margarita Matte

Development Editor: Michael Poor

National Geographic Editorial Liaison:
  Leila Hishmeh

Technology Development Manager:
  Debie Mirtle

Director of Global Marketing: Ian Martin

Director of US Marketing: Jim McDonough

Product Marketing Manager: Katie Kelley

Marketing Assistant: Jide Iruka

Senior Content Project Manager/Art Direction:
  Dawn Marie Elwell

Senior Print Buyer: Betsy Donaghey

Cover Photo: Colin Monteath/Minden Pictures,
  National Geographic Image Collection

Compositor: Nesbitt Graphics, Inc.

Library of Congress Control Number: 2008937885

International Edition:
World English 1 ISBN 13: 978-1-4240-5015-4
World English 1 ISBN 10: 1-4240-5015-4
World English 1 + CD-ROM ISBN 13: 978-1-4240-5102-1
World English 1 + CD-ROM ISBN 10: 1-4240-5102-9

U.S. Edition:
World English 1 ISBN 13: 978-1-4240-6336-9
World English 1 ISBN 10: 1-4240-6336-1

Heinle
20 Channel Center Street
Boston, MA 02210
USA

Cengage Learning is a leading provider of customized learning solutions with office locations around the globe, including Singapore, the United Kingdom, Australia, Mexico, Brazil, and Japan. Locate your local office at:
international.cengage.com/region

Cengage Learning products are represented in Canada by Nelson Education, Ltd.

Visit Heinle online at elt.heinle.com

Visit our corporate website at www.cengage.com

Printed in Canada
1 2 3 4 5 6 7 13 12 11 10 09

CONTENTS

✓ Unit Goals	Grammar	Vocabulary	Listening	Speaking and Pronunciation	Reading and Writing
UNIT 1 **People** page 2 • Meet people • Ask for and give personal information • Describe different occupations • Talk about people and their occupations	Review of present tense: *to be* *Be* + adjective (+ noun) Possessive nouns	Occupations Countries Nationalities Descriptive adjectives	Focused listening: Personal introductions	Asking for and giving personal information Contractions: *–'m, –'re, –'s*	"People from Around the World" Writing about a person and her occupation
UNIT 2 **Work, Rest, and Play** page 14 • Talk about a work day • Talk about free time • Describe a festival or a celebration • Compare different festivals	Review: Simple present tense Adverbs of frequency	Daily activities Party words	Focused listening: A radio celebrity interview	Talking about daily schedules and free time Verbs that end in *–s*	"Carnival: One Festival, Many Faces" Writing a descriptive paragraph
UNIT 3 **Going Places** page 26 • Identify possessions • Ask for and give personal travel information • Give travel advice • Share special travel tips with others	Possession Imperatives and *should* for advice	Travel preparations and stages Travel documents and money	General listening: Conversations at travel destinations	Giving personal information for travel forms Rising intonation in lists	"Smart Traveler: Expert Opinion" Writing travel tips
UNIT 4 **Food** page 38 • Talk about food • Order a meal • Talk about diets • Discuss unusual and favorite foods	Count and noncount nouns: *some* and *any* *How much, how many* with quantifiers: *lots of, a few, a little*	Food Diets	General and focused listening: In a restaurant	Role-play: purchasing food at a store Ordering from a menu Reduced forms: *Do you have . . .* and *Would you like . . .*	"Bugs as Food" Writing a favorite recipe
UNIT 5 **Sports** page 50 • Talk about activities happening now • Compare every day and present time activities • Talk about favorite sports • Discuss adventure holidays	Present continuous tense Stative verbs	Doing sports Team sports Individual sports	General and focused listening: Every day activities vs. today's activities	Talking about what people are doing now Discussing favorite sports Reduced form: *What are you . . .*	"Climbing the Dragon's Spires" Writing an email
UNIT 6 **Destinations** page 62 • Talk about past vacation trips • Exchange information about vacations • Use *was/were* to describe a personal experience • Talk about a discovery from the past	Simple past tense Simple past tense: *to be*	Travel activities Emphatic adjectives	General listening: A vacation	Comparing vacations Describing personal experiences Sounds of *–ed* endings	"The City of Machu Picchu, the Cradle of the Inca Empire" Writing a postcard

	Unit Goals	Grammar	Vocabulary	Listening	Speaking and Pronunciation	Reading and Writing
UNIT 7	**Communication** page 74 • Talk about personal communication • Give and write down contact details • Describe characteristics and qualities • Compare different types of communication	Verbs with direct and indirect objects Linking verbs	Communication Electronics The senses	Focused listening: A radio call-in program	Asking for contact information Describing sights, sounds and other sensations Endings –ty and –teen	"The Secret Language of Dolphins" Writing a text message
UNIT 8	**The Future** page 86 • Talk about plans • Discuss long and short term plans • Make weather predictions • Discuss the future	Be going to Will for predictions	Plans Weather conditions	General listening: A talk show	Talking about weekend plans Discussing the weather Reduced form of going to	"Future Energy" Writing statements about the future
UNIT 9	**Shopping for Clothes** page 98 • Make comparisons • Explain preferences • Talk about clothing materials • Understand and describe a process	Comparatives Superlatives	Clothing Descriptive adjectives Clothing materials	Focused listening: Shoe shopping	Talking about clothes Shopping—at the store and online Rising and falling intonation	"Silk—the Queen of Textiles" Writing about favorite clothes
UNIT 10	**Lifestyles** page 110 • Give advice on healthy habits • Suggest ways to improve bad habits • Ask about lifestyles • Evaluate your lifestyle	Modals—could, ought to, should, must, have to Questions with how	Healthy and unhealthy habits Compound adjectives	General listening: Personal lifestyles	Discussing healthy and unhealthy habits Giving advice for improving habits Should, shouldn't	"The Secrets of Long Life" Writing a paragraph about personal lifestyle
UNIT 11	**Achievements** page 122 • Talk about today's chores • Interview for a job • Talk about lifetime achievements • Discuss scientific achievements	Present perfect tense Present perfect tense vs. simple past tense	Chores Lifetime achievements	Listening for general understanding and specific details: A job interview	Interviewing for a job Catching up with a friend Reduced form of have	"Uncovering the Mysteries of the Universe" Writing an email to catch up
UNIT 12	**Consequences** page 134 • Talk about managing money • Make choices on how to spend your money • Talk about how our actions can have positive consequences • Discuss ways to prevent habitat destruction	Real conditionals (also called the First conditional)	Personal finances Animal habitats	Listening for specific details: At a travel agency	Making decisions about spending money Talking about important issues Sentence stress	"Habitat Destruction" Writing a letter to the editor

Get To Know

Arizona, United States
Stress is part of life in the modern world. What can you do to control it? *The Science of Stress*

Brockworth, England
An unusual 200-year-old tradition from England. Chasing a ball of cheese down a very steep hill. *Cheese-Rolling Races*

Orlando, Florida, United States
Join man's best friend as he looks for illegal food in American airports. *Beagle Brigade*

Hawaii
Find out more about the famous Hawaiian dance. *Hula*

Cuzco, Peru
Tourists come from all over the world to see the Lost City of the Incas. But is tourism destroying Machu Picchu? *Machu Picchu*

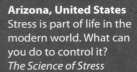

Your World!

Florence, Italy
Visit the last factory in Florence to make silk by hand. *Traditional Silk Making*

Japan
The puffer fish: ugly, poisonous, and expensive. So, why do people like to eat it? *Dangerous Dinner*

Cheju Island, Korea
A group of women from Korea go diving every day to find seafood. Are they the last? *Korean Women Divers*

North Africa
Learn how to use the sun's heat to cook your dinner. *Solar Cooking*

Tanzania, Africa
The snows of Kilimanjaro are disappearing. Find out why. *Missing Snows of Kilimanjaro*

South Africa
How do African Bushmen communicate with conservationists? Is it working? *Wild Animal Trackers*

= Sites of the video clips you will view in *World English 1*.

- Introduce the theme of the unit. Tell students that in this unit, they will meet real people from many different places.

- Direct students' attention to the pictures. Go over the questions with the class. Tell students there are no right or wrong answers for this activity—they should guess and compare ideas.

- Allow time for students to look at the pictures individually and consider their answers.

- Have students work with a partner to compare ideas about the pictures.

- Compare answers with the class. Compile a list of ideas on the board.

- Follow up with these questions, asking them orally or writing them on the board for students to answer in pairs:

  1. Which person is like you? Why?

  2. Which person is not like you? Why?

- Go over the Unit Goals with the class, explaining and/or translating as necessary.

PEOPLE

1. Who are these people? Share your ideas with a partner.
   a. What are their names?
   b. How old are they?
   c. Where are they from?
   d. What do they do?

2. Are they like you?

UNIT GOALS

Meet people
Ask for and give personal information
Describe different occupations
Talk about people and their occupations

2

	Unit Goals	Grammar	Vocabulary	Listening	Speaking and Pronunciation	Reading and Writing
	• Meet people • Ask for and give personal information • Describe different occupations • Talk about people and their occupations	Review of present tense: *to be* *They're Thai.* *He's not a dancer.* Be + adjective (+ noun) *It is an easy job.* Possessive adjectives	Occupations Countries Nationalities Descriptive adjectives	Focused listening: personal introductions	Asking for and giving personal information Contractions: *-'m, -'re, -'s*	"People from Around the World" Writing about a person and his or her occupation

UNIT 1

Unit Theme Overview

- Students begin their work in **World English** Book 1 by considering some of the things people have in common and looking at the kinds of information we often exchange with other people when we first meet them.

- In English-speaking countries, one common topic of conversation when people first meet is occupations and the work people do. It is considered a relatively neutral subject at social and business events (asking about a new acquaintance's family, which is appropriate in some cultures, is considered too personal). People ask questions about a person's occupation and if the person enjoys it. Learning how to ask questions is also a very good strategy for lower-level learners, because it helps to maintain conversation in a natural way.

Meet People

Vocabulary

- Direct students' attention to the map. Tell them they are going to meet people from these places. Go over the names of the countries, pronouncing them for students to repeat.

- Then introduce the names of the occupations listed in the box. Pronounce them for students to repeat and explain as necessary. Point out that *police officer* is a word for both *policeman* and *policewoman*.

A • With the class, look at each photo and fill in the answers.

- Alternatively, for stronger classes, have students work individually to complete the sentences. Then check answers with the class. Note that in #4 and #8 students need to answer with a nationality + noun.

Answers: 2. teacher, Peru, 3. police officer, Ireland, 4. French photographer, 5. engineer, Jordan, 6. travel agent, Bahrain, 7. doctor, Thailand, 8. Australian pilot

Engage!

- Discuss this question in pairs or as a class. List students' ideas on the board.

B • Point out the expression in the Real Language box.

- Read through the conversation with the class. Model a conversation about Norma from exercise **A**.

- Match students with a partner and have them make new conversations about the other people pictured in exercise **A**.

- Call on pairs of students to present their conversations to the class.

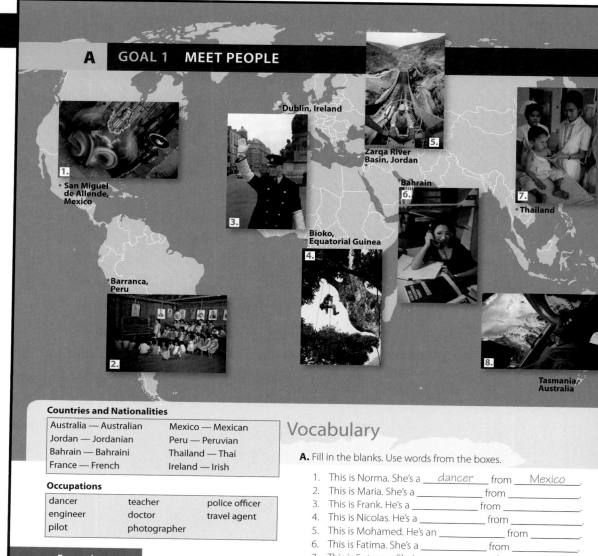

A   GOAL 1   MEET PEOPLE

Dublin, Ireland
5.
Zarqa River Basin, Jordan
1.
San Miguel de Allende, Mexico
Bahrain
6.
7.
• Thailand
3.
Bioko, Equatorial Guinea
4.
Barranca, Peru
2.
8.
Tasmania, Australia

Vocabulary

Countries and Nationalities

Australia — Australian	Mexico — Mexican
Jordan — Jordanian	Peru — Peruvian
Bahrain — Bahraini	Thailand — Thai
France — French	Ireland — Irish

Occupations

dancer	teacher	police officer
engineer	doctor	travel agent
pilot	photographer	

A. Fill in the blanks. Use words from the boxes.

1. This is Norma. She's a __*dancer*__ from __*Mexico*__.
2. This is Maria. She's a _____ from _____.
3. This is Frank. He's a _____ from _____.
4. This is Nicolas. He's a _____ from _____.
5. This is Mohamed. He's an _____ from _____.
6. This is Fatima. She's a _____ from _____.
7. This is Sutanee. She's a _____ from _____.
8. This is David. He's an _____ from _____.

B. Work with a partner. Talk about the people in the pictures.

Norma is from Mexico.

Oh, she's Mexican. What does she do?

She's a dancer.

Engage!

Which occupations do you think are the most difficult?

Real Language

We say *what does she/he do* to ask about a person's occupation or job.

4   People

Word Bank: Occupations

nurse	artist	reporter
office worker	government employee	scientist
pharmacist		salesperson
computer programmer	writer	secretary
electrician	professor	homemaker
accountant	architect	
	firefighter	

Grammar: *Be*

Statements with *be*			
Subject pronoun	*be*	Negative	
I	am		
You/We/They	are	not	a dancer.
He/She/It	is		

Yes/no questions			
Be	Pronoun		Short answers
Are	you/they		Yes, I am.
			No, I'm not.
Is	he/she/it	Mexican?	Yes, they are.
			No, he isn't.

Subject pronoun + *be*		Be contractions	
I am		I'm	
		You're	
You/We/They are		We're	
	Thai.	They're	Thai.
		He's	
He/She/It is		She's	
		It's	

A. Match the questions and the answers.

1. Are you a doctor? ____
2. Is she Korean? ____
3. Is Ben British? ____
4. Are you American? ____
5. Are Mario and Teresa students? ____

a. Yes, he is.
b. No, she isn't. She's Japanese
c. Yes, they are. They come from Argentina.
d. No, I'm not. I'm a nurse.
e. No, I'm not. I'm Canadian.

B. Fill in the blanks with a pronoun and the correct form of the verb *be*.

1. _____ from Japan. I'm from Thailand.
2. _____ from Indonesia? Yes, I am.
3. Where _____ from? They're from China.
4. _____ an architect. He's a doctor.
5. _____ from Canada? No, we're from the United States.

Conversation

 Track 1-2

A. Listen to the conversation. Where is Sean from?

Sean: So, Claudia, where are you from?
Claudia: I'm from Chile.
Sean: So, you're Chilean, eh. Sounds cool. Are you from Santiago?
Claudia: Yes, I am. And you, Sean? Where are you from?
Sean: I'm Canadian.
Claudia: Wow! Canada. I'd love to go to Canada. Which city are you from?
Sean: I'm from Toronto.

CANADIAN JET AIRLINES
Issue Date 2008 NOV 12
Expiration Date 2011 NOV 11
Captain Sean Brown
Toronto, Canada
ID# 256778A

 B. Practice the conversation with a partner. Switch roles and practice it again.

✓ Goal 1   Meet people

Work with a partner. Create new personal IDs. Use the conversation above to meet each other.

Grammar: *Be*

The verb *be* presents difficulties for learners whose languages do not have a similar structure. They may produce incorrect sentences such as ~~He Chinese~~ or ~~She a doctor~~. If necessary, explain to the class that every English sentence must contain a verb (a word for an action) and that *be* is a verb.

Grammar Practice

With the class, make a list of six to eight famous people from other countries. Then have students write sentences about their occupations and nationalities. For example,

David Beckham: *He's a soccer player. He's English.*

Grammar

- Review statements with *be*. Tell students, *I am a teacher. What about you?* Elicit, *I am a student/a secretary/a doctor.* Ask several students.
- Go over the information in the box and elicit more examples.
- Review short answers. Then go over the information in the box and elicit examples.
- Review *yes/no* questions. Go over the information in the box.
- Match students with a partner. Tell them, *Ask three questions.* Encourage them to use short answers.
- Go over the formation of contractions with *be*.

A • Have students work individually to match the columns.
- Check answers.

Answers: 1. d, 2. b, 3. a, 4. e, 5. c

B • Have students complete the sentences with pronouns and *be*.
- Check answers.

Answers: 1. I'm not, 2. Are you, 3. are they, 4. He isn't, 5. Are you

Conversation

A • Have students close their books. Write the question on the board: *Where is Sean from?*
- Play the recording. **(CD1 T2)**
- Check answers.

Answer: Canada/Toronto

B • Play or read the conversation again for the class to repeat.
- Practice the conversation with the class in chorus.
- Have students practice the conversation with a partner and then switch roles and practice it again.

✓ Goal 1

- Have students work individually to make an ID for an imaginary person on another piece of paper.
- Then have them make a new conversation based on the information in the ID.

Ask For and Give Personal Information

Listening

- Tell students they are going to hear part of a TV game show. Ask them what usually happens at the beginning of these shows (the players are introduced). Tell them they are going to hear this part of the show.

A • Match students with a partner. Have them look at the pictures and read about the people, then talk about the missing information.

B • Tell students to listen and write the missing information. Play the recording. **(CD1 T3)**

C • Tell students to listen again and finish their answers.

- Play the recording one or more time. **(CD1 T3)**

- Check answers.

Answers: 1. Japanese/engineer,
2. Colombian/Colombia/doctor,
3. Canadian/Canada, 4. Brazilian/Brazil

- If desired, play the recording one more time, pointing out the answers as they are heard. **(CD1 T3)**

- Ask, *Do you like game shows? Which ones? Who is usually on game shows?*

Listening

A. Look at the pictures. Talk to a partner. Guess the missing information.

B. Listen to the TV game show. Fill in the blanks with the correct information.
Track 1-3

1. **Name:** Kyoko Hashimoro
   Nationality: _____
   City: Tokyo
   Country: Japan
   Occupation: _____

2. **Name:** Luis Gomez
   Nationality: _____
   City: Bogota
   Country: _____
   Occupation: _____

3. **Name:** Jim Waters
   Nationality: _____
   City: Coldstone
   Country: _____
   Occupation: Farmer

4. **Name:** Bianca da Silva
   Nationality: _____
   City: Rio de Janeiro
   Country: _____
   Occupation: Musician

C. Listen again. Check your answers.
Track 1-3

6 People

For Your Information: Game shows

Game shows are extremely popular in countries around the world. On them, people must answer questions or participate in activities to win money or prizes. On some game shows, contestants compete alone, while others involve teams or playing with celebrities. Countries as diverse as Argentina, Bulgaria, Iceland, Iran, Macedonia, Pakistan, South Africa, and Venezuela all have game shows among their most popular TV programs.

Pronunciation: Contractions of *be*

A. Listen and repeat.

Track 1-4

1. I am	I'm
2. you are	you're
3. he is	he's
4. she is	she's
5. it is	it's

B. Listen. Circle the verb or contraction you hear. Then listen again and repeat.

Track 1-5

1. (I am)/I'm a teacher.
2. He is/he's an engineer.
3. She is/she's not a nurse.
4. They are/they're interesting.
5. You are/you're welcome.

Communication

Student A chooses a card. **Student B** guesses the card by asking questions.

B: Are you 28 years old?	**A:** No, I'm not.
B: Are you a doctor?	**A:** Yes, I am.
B: Are you Argentinean?	**A:** No, I'm not.
B: Is your name Helen?	**A:** Yes, it is.

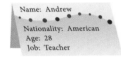

Name: Andrew
Nationality: American
Age: 28
Job: Teacher

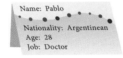

Name: Pablo
Nationality: Argentinean
Age: 28
Job: Doctor

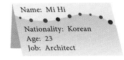

Name: Mi Hi
Nationality: Korean
Age: 23
Job: Architect

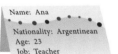

Name: Ana
Nationality: Argentinean
Age: 23
Job: Teacher

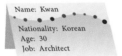

Name: Kwan
Nationality: Korean
Age: 30
Job: Architect

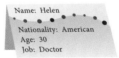

Name: Helen
Nationality: American
Age: 30
Job: Doctor

 Goal 2 | **Ask for and give personal information**

Interview some of your classmates. Ask their name, their age, and the job they do or want to do.

Expansion Activity: What's my name?

Divide the class into groups of four or five students. Model the activity. Say, *I'm a famous person. I won't say my name. Ask me yes/no questions to guess my name.* Model some *yes/no* questions students can ask: *Are you a man or woman? Are you (Japanese/foreign)? Are you on TV? Are you from (Tokyo)?* etc. After they guess your "identity," have them play the game in groups, taking turns choosing a famous person.

Pronunciation

- Review the idea of contractions. Explain that we use contractions in fast or informal speaking.

A • Tell students to notice the difference in pronunciation between the separate and contracted forms.

- Play the recording one or more times. **(CD1 T4)** Call on rows or columns of students to pronounce the pairs.

B • Tell students to listen to the sentences and circle the pronunciation they hear. Play the recording one or more times. **(CD1 T5)**

- Check answers.

Answers: 2. He's, 3. She's, 4. They are, 5. You're

- Have students read the sentences to a partner, using both the regular and contracted forms. Walk around checking for correct pronunciation.

Communication

- Explain the activity to the class. Model the example for the class.
- In pairs have students play the game. Walk around helping as needed.

Note: People from Argentina are also called *Argentine*.

☑ Goal 2

- Tell students they are going to get information from their classmates. Review the questions they will ask: *What's your name? How old are you? What do you do?* (For younger students, have them ask *What do you want to be?* and answer *I want to be (a scientist).*
- Tell students to take their notebooks and pens, stand up, and walk around the class to interview three classmates.
- When all students have finished, have them sit down. Ask for information about each student by pointing and saying, *Tell me about this student.* Elicit, for example, *His name is Yong-Jun. He's 25. He's an office worker.*

Describe Different Occupations

Language Expansion

- Introduce the idea of adjectives—words that describe a noun (a **big** house, a **good** book). Present the pairs of adjectives in the photos. Elicit more examples for each adjective (for example, *Who's a rich person? What's a boring job?*).

A • Have students work individually to classify the words.

- Check answers.

Answers: Good: rich, interesting, safe, easy; Bad: poor, boring, dangerous, difficult

B • Ask students if they know what a helicopter is. Why do people fly in them?

- Have students work individually to write adjectives. Compare answers with the class.

Suggested answers: rich, dangerous, interesting, good, safe, unhappy

Word Focus

- Ask students, *Which jobs have a good salary?* Write a list on the board.

Grammar

- Go over the information in the first box and elicit more examples from the students. Say *Tell me about your job/your classes/this school* to elicit sentences like *My job is interesting/My classes are difficult/My school is big.*

- Then go over the information in the second box and repeat the questions, but have students tell you instead, *It's an interesting job/They're difficult classes/It's a big school.*

Language Expansion: Descriptive adjectives

▲ easy

▲ difficult

▲ happy

▲ unhappy

▲ boring

▲ interesting

▲ rich

▲ poor

▲ safe

▲ dangerous

A. Write the words in the correct column.

Good	Bad
happy	unhappy

B. Fill in the blanks with adjectives.

Mrs. Green is _____, but she is not happy. Why? Her husband's job is _____. He is a helicopter pilot.

Mr. Green says, "I like my job. It is an _____ job and the **salary** is _____. It's not dangerous. In fact, it's very _____." But Mrs. Green is still _____.

Word Focus

salary = money earned by the work you do

Grammar: *Be* + adjective (+ noun)

Subject	Be	Adjective		Subject	Be	Article	Adjective	Noun
My friend	is	rich.		It	is	an	easy	job.
His job	is	dangerous.		Your friend	is	an	interesting	person.
I	am	not happy.		It	is	a	difficult	life.
My brother's job	is	interesting.						

Word Bank: More descriptive adjectives

large	small
popular	unpopular
new	old
young	old
modern	traditional
important	unimportant
worried	calm

A. Circle the correct word or phrase in the parentheses.

1. My father's job is (interesting/an interesting).
   He is a newspaper photographer. It's not (easy/
   an easy) job but he enjoys it.
2. I am a teacher. The salary isn't very (good/an good).
   I'm not (rich/an rich).
3. John is an engineer. It's (difficult/a difficult) job but
   it's (interesting/an interesting) job.

B. Unscramble the words to write sentences.

1. job   friend's   is   My   dangerous.

   _____

2. is   person.   interesting   Kim's   friend   an

   _____

3. your   brother   happy?   Is

   _____

4. rich   is   not   a   My   father   man.

   _____

5. Chile.   friend   John's   from   is

   _____

> ### Possessive Adjectives
>
> This is **my** friend.
> Is that **your** brother?
> **His/her** friend comes from Uruguay.
> **Their** parents are nice people.
>
> *Possessive nouns are formed with an apostrophe (') + -s.
> Laura**'s** friend is from London.

Conversation

Track 1-6

A. Listen to the conversation. What does Graham do?

Graham: What do you do, Elsa?
Elsa: I'm an engineer.
Graham: An engineer! That's interesting.
Elsa: Yes, but it's difficult work. And you, Graham?
       What do you do?
Graham: I'm a policeman.
Elsa: A policeman! Is it dangerous?
Graham: No, in fact, sometimes it's boring.

B. Practice the conversation with a partner. Switch roles and practice it again.

✓ Goal 3   Describe different occupations

Work with a partner. Take turns. Choose an occupation and say
two things about it.

Grammar Practice: Possessive adjectives

Sit with the class in a circle. The teacher begins by saying, *My name
is _____.* The student on your right then says, *His/her name is
_____. My name is _____.* The next student says the names of
all of those that have come before (using complete sentences). If a
student forgets a name, he or she starts over again with *My name
is . . .* Play until all students have had several turns and have learned
most of the names.

Grammar: Adjectives

Adjectives generally do not cause
difficulty for learners. However,
students may occasionally add an
s to adjectives that describe plural
nouns (*they're interestings books*).

- Review the possessive adjectives.
  Hold up your book and say, *It's
  my book.* Pick up a student's
  book, hand it to the student,
  and say, *It's your book.* Point to
  a female student, point to her
  book, and say, *It's her book.* Point
  to a male student, point to his
  book, and say *It's his book.*

A • Have students work individually
  to choose the correct answers.
- Check answers.

Answers: 1. interesting, an easy.
2. good, rich, 3. a difficult, an
interesting

B • Have students work individually
  to write the sentences. If
  necessary, ask, *What do you
  know about the first word of a
  sentence?* (It has a capital letter.)
- Check answers.

Answers: 1. My friend's job is
dangerous. 2. Kim's friend is an
interesting person. 3. Is your brother
happy? 4. My father is not a rich man.
5. John's friend is from Chile.

C • Have students close their books.
  Write the question on the
  board: *What does Graham do?*
- Play the recording. **(CD1 T6)**
- Check answers.

Answer: He's a policeman.

B • Play or read the conversation
  again for the class to repeat.
- Practice the conversation with
  the class in chorus.
- Have students practice the
  conversation with a partner and
  then switch roles and practice
  it again.

✓ Goal 3

- Have students work with a
  partner taking turns to talk
  about an occupation, one from
  the previous lessons or another
  one they know about. Model for
  the students: *My friend is a bus
  driver. It's boring and sometimes
  dangerous.*

Talk about People and Their Occupations

- Introduce the topic of the reading. Tell students they are going to read about people in four different countries.

A
- Tell students to read the article the first time and find the people's jobs. Tell them to circle any words they don't understand.
- Check answers.

Answers: Angutikavsak: hunter; Peter: farmer; Tanya: student, musician; Rimii: actress; Alan: policeman;

- Go over the article with the class, answering any questions from the students about vocabulary.

B
- Have students read the article again to mark the statements *true* or *false*.
- Check answers.

Answers: 1. F, 2. T, 3. F, 4. T, 5. F

C
- Tell students to read the article a third time to find the information.
- Check answers.

Answers: 1. She's from Boulder, Colorado, in the United States. 2. He's Peter's dog. 3. It's not boring, and he likes helping people. 4. He's a hunter. 5. It's difficult work. The salary is good.

Reading

A. Look at the pictures. What do these people do?

B. Circle **T** for *true* and **F** for *false*.

1. Peter is a pilot.   T   F
2. Rimii Sen is Indian.   T   F
3. Alan Kirby's job is boring.   T   F
4. Angutikavsak's life is not easy.   T   F
5. Tanya is an actress.   T   F

C. Answer the questions.

1. Where is Tanya from? _____
   _____
   _____

2. Who is Shep? _____
   _____
   _____

3. Why does Alan like his job? _____
   _____
   _____

4. What does Angutikavsak do? _____
   _____
   _____

5. What does Rimii say about her job? ___
   _____
   _____

People from Around the World

Angutikavsak is from Greenland, and he is a hunter. All his friends are hunters too. "It is a difficult life here. In winter, it is very cold. We are not rich, but we are happy." he says.

Peter Elworthy is from New Zealand. He is not a pilot; he is a farmer! His farm is very big, so he uses an airplane. Peter's dog, Shep, is also in the plane.
"Is Shep frightened in the plane?" I ask.
"No, he's happy. He loves flying."

For Your Information: Greenland

The English name of Greenland comes from the name given to it by Scandinavian settlers in the Middle Ages. When they landed at the southern tip of the island, the climate was warmer than it is now, and the land was green with vegetation. Greenland is controlled by Denmark and has a population of about 57,000 people, of whom 88 percent are native Inuit people and the rest are Europeans. Although most Inuit families in Greenland today have at least one person working for money, hunting is still an honored and important occupation there. People still eat traditional foods like seal and walrus meat, and they wear clothes made of polar bear and caribou skins. In many families, one woman works at a job to earn money to pay for electricity, guns, ammunition, and other needs, so that the men can continue to hunt full-time.

Rimii Sen is an actress. She is Indian, and she is from Mumbai. "People think an actress's life is exciting, but it is difficult work. However, the salary is good!"

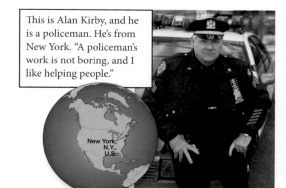

Tanya Rogers is from Boulder, Colorado, in the United States. She is a student, and she is also a musician. "I love my music, but it's very cold here in winter."

This is Alan Kirby, and he is a policeman. He's from New York. "A policeman's work is not boring, and I like helping people."

Writing

Write about Angeline and her occupation.

_____
_____
_____
_____
_____
_____

✓ Goal 4 | Talk about people and their occupations

Work with a partner. Talk about a friend or family member and their occupation.

Writing

- Tell students to look at the picture and the map and write about Angeline's job, like the descriptions in the reading.
- Have students exchange papers with a partner. Ask students to mark corrections and suggestions for improvements on their partner's paper.
- If desired, have students rewrite their papers, to be collected for marking.

✓ Goal 3

- Match students with partners. Have them take turns telling about a friend's or family member's occupation.
- Call on students to tell the class about the person's occupation.

After Reading

Have students bring in a newspaper or magazine photo of a person doing his or her job. Divide the class into groups of four or five students, and have the students take turns showing and describing their pictures. Discuss the most interesting/unusual pictures with the whole class.

Video Journal

Before You Watch

- Have students look at the pictures, and talk about what, if anything, they know about Korea and Cheju Island. Tell students they are going to hear about an unusual occupation.

- Go over the words in the box. Have students complete the sentences.

- Check answers.

Answers: divers, seafood, tour guide

While You Watch

A • Tell students to watch the video the first time and write the missing information. Play the video.

- Check answers.

Answers: Sunny Hong: Korean, tour guide; Ms. Hong: Korea, diver, 63

E | VIDEO JOURNAL *THE LAST OF THE WOMAN DIVERS*

Before You Watch

Fill in the blanks. Use the words in the box.

| tour guide   divers   seafood |

In Korea, there is a group of women _____. They go to the sea every day to catch _____, like octopus and shellfish. Some of the women are not divers. One of them works with tourists. She is a _____.

While You Watch

 **A.** Watch the video and fill in the blanks.

Name: Sunny Hong

Country: Korea

Nationality: _____

Occupation: _____

Age: 28

Name: Ms. Hong

Country: _____

Nationality: Korean

Occupation: _____

Age: _____

12   People

For Your Information: Cheju Island

Cheju Island (also spelled Jeju) is an area of Korea that developed its own distinctive culture and customs because of its isolation. It has a much warmer climate than the rest of the country and produces citrus fruit. One unusual feature of Cheju's culture is that traditionally women have had roles of authority in the family, because they earned a lot of money, especially through diving. Today, tourism is the biggest industry in Cheju. People come to the island for its scenery (a volcanic mountain with numerous waterfalls), warm climate, and beaches.

 B. Watch again. Circle **T** for *true* and **F** for *false*.

1. Diving is difficult and dangerous.   T   F
2. The water is cold.   T   F
3. The divers can stay underwater for 10 minutes.   T   F
4. Sunny Hong is a diver.   T   F
5. The women sell the seafood.   T   F

After You Watch

 Sunny Hong speaks English. She is a tour guide. She is not a diver. She says, "I am lucky." How can speaking English help *you*?

Communication

1. Write jobs in the chart.

Jobs women do well	Jobs men do well

 2. Work with a partner. Compare your lists. Are they the same? Do you agree with your partner?

B • Tell students to watch the video again and answer *true* or *false*. Have them read the statements. Play the video.

• Check answers.

Answers: 1. T, 2. T, 3. F, 4. F, 5. T

After You Watch

• Have students answer the question with partners.

• Discuss the question with the whole class. Compile a list on the board. Which things are most important for the students?

Communication

• Have students work individually to write jobs in the chart. If necessary, have them refer back to earlier lessons for the names of occupations listed there.

• Match students with partners and have them compare lists.

• Discuss the different jobs that students listed, and see whether the class agrees with their opinions. Point out, *The divers in Cheju Island are women. What about divers in other countries? Are the women in Cheju good divers?*

Teacher Tip: Correcting writing

You can save a lot of time in marking student papers by using peer correction. Before students turn in a paper, have them exchange their work with a partner and mark any mistakes or problems they see on their partner's paper. Then have them make the corrections on their own papers before handing them in to you for marking.

- Introduce the theme of the unit. Ask students, *When do you work? When do you rest? When do you play?*

- Direct students' attention to the pictures. With the class, look at each picture in turn, and have students name things they see in each one.

- Have students work with a partner to match the words with the correct pictures.

- Check answers.

Answers: (left to right) 1. work day, 2. celebration, 3. festival, 4. weekend

- Have students talk with a partner about which of these activities they would like to be doing.

- Compare answers with the class, compiling a list on the board.

- Follow up with these questions, asking them orally or writing them on the board for students to answer in pairs:

  1. *What do you do on working days?*
  2. *What do you do on weekends?*

- Go over the Unit Goals with the class, explaining and/or translating as necessary.

WORK, REST,

1. Which word or phrase describes each photo?
   a. work day
   b. weekend
   c. festival
   d. celebration

2. Where do you want to be? Why?

UNIT GOALS

Talk about a work day
Talk about free time
Describe a special celebration or festival
Compare different festivals

14

	Unit Goals	Grammar	Vocabulary	Listening	Speaking and Pronunciation	Reading and Writing
	• Talk about a work day • Talk about free time • Describe a special celebration or festival • Compare different festivals	Review: simple present tense *Alison* **catches** *the bus at five thirty.* Adverbs of frequency *We* **always** *give presents at Christmas.*	Daily activities Party words	Focused listening: a radio celebrity interview	Talking about daily schedules and free time Verbs that end in -s	"Carnival: One Festival, Many Faces" Writing a descriptive paragraph

AND PLAY

UNIT 2

15

Unit Theme Overview

- In this unit, students will learn to talk about regular, repeated activities, using the simple present tense. The sequence of topics discussed moves from the more familiar and universal, to the unique and more specific.

- Students begin by discussing their daily activities on a work day, which are fairly similar around the world with some important cultural differences (for example, most North Americans like to take a shower in the morning, to start their day feeling clean and fresh, while Japanese people generally bathe at night, to wash away the cares of the day and go to bed relaxed).

- They next consider their free-time activities, which show more individual variation, before considering festivals in their country. Finally, they learn how the same festival or Carnival is celebrated in very different ways in three different countries. Throughout the lessons, they are practicing the language used for the recurring events that make up the fabric of our lives, wherever in the world we live.

Talk about a Work Day

- Introduce the topic. Ask, *What do you do on a work day?* Compile a list on the board.

A • Present the vocabulary in the box by miming or explaining.

- Have students work individually or with a partner to label the pictures. Tell students they will use the boxes later.

- Check answers.

Answers: read the newspaper, eat breakfast, go to bed, catch the bus, go to the movies, eat out, take a nap, watch TV, visit friends, start work, get up, take a shower

B • Have students circle their daily activities.

- Compare answers with the class. Read the activity and ask for a show of hands from those who do it every day.

C • Have students number their circled activities in the order they do them.

- Call on students to read their list to the class.

D • Introduce/review the use of *first, next, then, finally* to talk about a sequence of events. Give an example from their daily routine in class: *First, we check our homework. Next, we read the lesson. Then, we practice speaking. . . .*

- Have students talk about their daily routines with a partner.

- Call on students to explain their daily routines to the class.

Vocabulary

A. Label the pictures. Use phrases from the box.

read the newspaper
get up
eat breakfast
go to bed
take a shower
catch the bus
go to the movies
take a nap
watch TV
visit friends
start work
eat out

a. _____ b. _____ c. _____

d. _____ e. _____ f. _____

g. _____ h. _____ i. _____

j. _____ k. _____ l. _____

> **First** I get up, **then** I take a shower, **next** I get dressed . . .

B. Circle the activities in exercise **A** that you do every day.

C. In what order do you do these activities? Number the pictures.

D. Describe your daily routine to a partner. Use *first, next, then, finally*.

Word Bank: Daily activities

catch the train/ subway	eat lunch
drive to work/school	do chores
sign in/punch in (at work)	cook dinner
go to class	take care of children
take a break	clean the house
	wash the dishes

Grammar: Simple present tense

The simple present tense is used for repeated, habitual actions (*I eat vegetables every day*) and for statements of fact that are always true (*The sun rises in the east*).

Common errors to watch for include omitting the *-s* with the third person singular (*He go to work*); adding a form of *be* to the verb (*He is go to work every day*); and forming negative sentences with *no* (*He no go to work every day*).

Grammar: Simple present tense

Simple present tense

Statements	Negative
I/you **start** work at eight o'clock.	I/you **don't start** work at eight o'clock.
Alison **catches** the bus at five-thirty.	Alison **doesn't catch** the bus at five-thirty.
We/They **go** to the movies every Saturday.	We/they **don't go** to the movies every Saturday.

Yes/no questions	Short answers	
Do you **start** work at eight o'clock?	Yes, I do.	No, I don't.
Does Alison **catch** the bus at five-thirty?	Yes, she does.	No, she doesn't.
Do we/they **go** to the movies every Saturday?	Yes, we/they do.	No, we/they don't.

*We use the simple present tense to talk about habits and things that are always true.

Complete the exchanges (questions and answers) with information from the date book.

1. **Q:** What time do you _____?
   A: I get up _____ seven o'clock.
2. **Q:** _____ you watch TV in the morning?
   A: No, I _____ watch TV in the morning.
3. **Q:** What time _____ start work?
   A: He starts work _____.
4. **Q:** Do they _____ at ten o'clock?
   A: No, they go to bed _____.

Prepositions of time

on	in	at
on Saturday(s)	in the morning	at eight o'clock
on the 4th of July	in the afternoon	at night
on Valentine's Day	in the evening	

Conversation

A. Listen to the conversation. Does Mia work on Saturday?

Track 1-7

Chris:	So, Mia, you're a secretary.
Mia:	That's right.
Chris:	What time do you start work?
Mia:	At nine o'clock.
Chris:	Do you work on Saturday?
Mia:	Yes, I do, but we finish work at twelve o'clock on Saturdays.
Chris:	What do you do in the evenings?
Mia:	I watch TV or read the newspaper.

B. Practice the conversation with a partner. Switch roles and practice it again.

✓ Goal 1 Talk about a work day

Talk with your partner about your work day.

Grammar: Prepositions of time

Generally speaking, *in* is used with broader periods of time: *in the twentieth century/1976/ winter/April/the morning.*

On is used with shorter periods of time: *on Wednesdays/New Year's Day/March 15th.*

At is used with points in time: *at 7:30/noon.*

Grammar Practice: Simple present tense

Have students interview each other about their usual daily activities. Then have each student write five sentences about his/her partner's activities. Call on students to read an interesting sentence to the class.

Grammar

- Go over the formation of present tense statements, reminding students that they must add -s with *he/she*.
- Ask a student to tell you three things he/she does every day. Then ask the class, *What does (Akiko) do every day?*
- Go over the formation of negative sentences. Ask a student to tell you three things he/she doesn't do on Sundays. Then ask the class what the student doesn't do.
- Go over the formation of *yes/no* questions and short answers. Ask students a series of questions about their daily activities. Elicit short answers.
- Go over the prepositions of time in the box. Ask students, *When do you do your homework/take a shower/see your friends/watch TV?* and elicit answers with the prepositions of time.
- Have students work individually to complete the conversations.
- Check answers.

Answers: 1. get up, at, 2. Do, don't, 3. does he, at, 4. go to bed, at eleven o'clock.

Conversation

A
- Have students close their books. Write the question on the board: *Does Mia work on Saturday?*
- Play the recording. **(CD1 T7)**
- Check answers.

Answer: Yes.

B
- Play or read the conversation again for the class to repeat.
- Practice the conversation with the class in chorus.
- Have students practice the conversation with a partner and then switch roles and practice it again.

✓ Goal 1
- Match students with a partner and have them take turns telling about a usual work (or school) day.

Talk about Free Time

A • Tell students they are going to hear an interview with an actor about his activities. Have them read the question.

• Play the recording one or more times. **(CD1 T8)**

• Check answers.

Answer: b

B • Tell students to listen again to the interview and answer the questions. Go over the questions with them.

• Play the recording one or more times. **(CD1 T8)**

• Check answers.

Answers: 1. b, 2. a, 3. a, 4. b

• Tell the class, *Bob Hardy is famous. Is his Sunday like yours? Do you think famous people do usual things? Why, or why not?*

Pronunciation

A • Remind the class that with *he* or *she*, verbs in the simple present tense take *-s* at the end. Point out that the *-s* has different pronunciations (*/s/* after a voiceless sound, */z/* after a voiced sound, and */iz/* after *ch, sh, s,* or *z* sounds). Tell them to listen to the pronunciations. Play the recording. **(CD1 T9)**

• Point out the differences in pronunciation. Play the recording again and have students mark the sound they hear. **(CD1 T9)**

• Check answers.

Answers: starts /s/, comes /z/, catches /iz/, watches /iz/, gets /s/, eats /s/, goes /z/

B • Tell students to listen again and repeat the words. Play the recording. **(CD1 T9)**

• Have students practice reading the words to a partner. Walk around the class checking for correct pronunciation.

B   GOAL 2   TALK ABOUT FREE TIME

Listening

Track 1-8

A. Listen to the interview with Bob Hardy. What is Bob talking about? Circle the correct answer.

    a. his daily routine
    b. his free time
    c. his work

Track 1-8

B. Listen again. Circle the correct answer.

1. On Sundays, Bob gets up at ___.
    a. eight o'clock
    b. nine o'clock
    c. ten o'clock
2. In the morning he ___.
    a. reads the newspaper
    b. visits friends
    c. goes to a movie
3. What does he do at one o'clock?
    a. He has lunch.
    b. He takes a nap.
    c. He visits friends.
4. What does he do in the evening?
    a. He watches TV.
    b. He goes out for a meal.
    c. He reads.

Pronunciation: Verbs that end in *-s*

Track 1-9

A. Listen and check (✓) the correct column.

	Ends with /s/	Ends with /z/	Ends with /iz/
starts			
comes			
catches			
watches			
gets			
eats			
goes			

Track 1-9

B. Listen again. Repeat the words.

18   Work, Rest, and Play

For Your Information: Leisure activities

Free time is spent in different ways in different countries and cultures around the world. In the United States, a recent survey showed that reading was the #1 free-time activity. This was followed by watching TV, then spending time with family. In a U.K. survey on leisure-time activities, watching TV and videos was the most popular pastime; listening to the radio came second. In a similar survey conducted in Japan, the most popular free-time activity was eating out. The second most popular activity was driving. Karaoke, which ranked fourth, was more popular than watching videos, which came fifth. Listening to the radio or music ranked sixth.

Communication

 Work with a partner. Fill in the date book with your information. Then fill in your partner's information. Ask questions like:

What do you do in the evening?

What time do you have breakfast?

Me

Sunday

Morning

Afternoon

Evening

My Partner

Sunday

Morning

Afternoon

Evening

✓ **Goal 2** | **Talk about free time**

Talk with a partner about your free time.

Communication

- Introduce the idea of a date book—a small book where you plan your activities every day. Ask students if they have a date book.
- Have students work individually to fill in their usual Sunday activities. Help them with vocabulary as needed, writing the additional items on the board for other students to use.
- Go over questions for asking about other people's activities. Write on the board,

  What do you do in _____?

  What time do you _____?

- Match students with a partner and have them ask questions to complete the page for the partner's activities.
- Ask, *Who heard something interesting? What does your partner do on Sundays?*

✓ Goal 2

- Have students change partners. Have them tell their new partners about what they do in their free time and when they usually do it.

Expansion Activity

Have students work with a partner to prepare an imaginary date book page for a famous person, giving his or her activities on a Saturday or a Sunday. Then combine pairs to form groups of four students and have them ask and answer questions to fill out a date book page for the other pair's famous person.

Describe a Special Celebration or Festival

Language Expansion

A • Have students work individually to read the text about celebrations.

• Ask, *What countries does the text talk about?* (India, the United States, Italy, Spain) *What are the celebrations there called?* (Diwali, Independence Day, Carnival, San Fermin)

• Go over the meanings of the words in blue.

B • Have students work individually to fill in the correct words.

• Check answers.

Answers: 1. fireworks, 2. fun, 3. costumes, masks, 4. celebrate, 5. decorate, presents

Grammar

• Direct students' attention to the line with percentages. Tell the students, *I always get up early. What about you?* Elicit, *I sometimes/never/usually get up early.* Continue with *eat lunch at home/go to bed late/watch TV in the morning*, etc.

• Tell the class, *I am never late for class. What about you?* Elicit answers from students.

• Go over the information in the chart.

▲ In the United States, Americans always end their Independence Day celebrations with **fireworks**.

▼ In Venice, people wear **costumes** and cover their faces with **masks** to celebrate Carnival.

Language Expansion: Party words

A. Read the text. Pay attention to the words in **blue**.

All around the world, people need to **celebrate**. During the week we work, on weekends we rest, but we also need to have fun. Festivals are special celebrations. During festivals people dance, sing, wear different clothes, eat special food, and give **presents** to friends and family.

◄ People in India enjoy Diwali, the Festival of Lights. They **decorate** streets and houses with lights of many colors.

◄ On the feast of San Fermin every year, Spaniards and tourists run with the bulls in Pamplona. It is very dangerous, but they say it's **fun**.

B. Complete the sentences with the words in **blue** from exercise **A**.

1. We watch the _____ on New Year's.
2. I love parties. You can dance and sing. It's _____!
3. At Halloween, children wear _____ and _____ to cover their faces.
4. We _____ Christmas on the 24th and 25th of December.
5. At Christmas, we _____ a tree with colored lights and put _____ under it for friends and family.

Grammar: Adverbs of frequency

0% _____ 100%

never   sometimes   often   always

For Your Information: Famous festivals

Fallas (Valencia, Spain): Huge paper figures and scenes are built on the streets and then burned on March 19.

Hogmanay (Edinburgh, Scotland): People celebrate New Year's Eve with parades, fireworks, and noisy parties.

Jidai Matsuri (Kyoto, Japan): People dressed in costumes from all eras of the city's history parade through the streets.

Calgary Stampede (Calgary, Canada): The city sponsors a huge rodeo with cowboy competitions, food, and music.

Songkran (Thailand): People celebrate the Thai New Year by throwing water on each other in the streets.

Dragon Boat Festival (Hong Kong): Dragon-shaped boats filled with rowers and drummers have races.

Camel Fair (Pushkar, India): Thousands of camels and their owners gather to race and celebrate.

Word order

Subject	Adverb of frequency	Verb	
We	always	give	presents on Christmas.
We	never	dance	in the streets at Christmas.
Subject	***Be***	**Adverb of frequency**	
Christmas	is	always	in December.
Carnival	is	usually	in February or March.

*We use adverbs of frequency to say how often we do something.
*Adverbs of frequency come **before** the verb.
*Adverbs of frequency come **after** *be*.

A. Unscramble the words to make sentences. Write the sentences.

1. always   We   have   a   on   Christmas   turkey.

_____

2. Valentine's Day.   never   I   send   cards   on

_____

3. sometimes   on   visit   our   We   neighbors   New Year's.

_____

4. Alan   his   forgets   wife's   sometimes   birthday.

_____

5. go   They   the   movies   often   to   on   the   weekend.

_____

 B. Take turns. Tell a partner what sentences in exercise **A** are true for you.

Conversation

Track 1-10

A. Listen to the conversation. Does Carol have a family meal on New Year's?

Neil: What do you do on New Year's Day?
Carol: Well, we sometimes go downtown. They have fireworks. It's really pretty. Other people invite friends to their house and they have a party.
Neil: Do you give presents to your friends and family?
Carol: No, we never give presents on New Year's.
Neil: Do you have a meal with your family?
Carol: No, we do that on Christmas. On New Year's we just party!

> **Real Language**
>
> We say *we party* when we have fun with friends.

 B. Practice the conversation with a partner. Switch roles and practice it again.

 Goal 3   **Describe a special celebration or festival**

Talk with a partner about your favorite celebration or festival.

A • Have students work individually to write sentences. Remind them that adverbs come after *be*, but before other verbs.
• Check answers.

Answers: 1. We always have a turkey at Christmas. 2. I never send cards on Valentine's Day. 3. We sometimes visit our neighbors at New Year's. 4. Alan sometimes forgets his wife's birthday. 5. They often go to the movies on the weekend.

B • Have students work with a partner to talk about the things in exercise **A** that they do (or don't do).
• Compare answers with the class.

Conversation

A • Have students close their books. Write the question on the board: *Does Carol have a family meal at New Year's?*
• Play the recording. **(CD1 T10)**
• Check answers.

Answer: no

B • Play or read the conversation again for the class to repeat. Point out the Real Language box. Explain that *we party* (using *party* as a verb) is informal language that we use with friends.
• Practice the conversation with the class in chorus.
• Have students practice the conversation with a partner and then switch roles and practice it again.

☑ Goal 3

• Have students change partners and then talk about what they do for their favorite celebration or festival.

Grammar: Adverbs of frequency

Adverbs modify (give more information about) the action in the verb of a sentence. Frequency adverbs answer the question, *How often?*

The most common error to watch out for is in word order: *He* ~~gets up sometimes~~ *early. I* ~~never am~~ *late.*

Grammar Practice: Adverbs of frequency

With the class, make a list of festivals and celebrations in the students' countries, including birthdays. Tell each student to choose one celebration they enjoy and one celebration they don't enjoy very much. Have them write five sentences about what they do for each celebration, using adverbs of frequency. (Give examples: *I don't like New Year's Eve. I always stay home. I usually go to bed early!*) Call on students to read one of their lists to the class. What are their favorite celebrations? What are their least favorite?

Compare Different Festivals

Reading

- Introduce the topic of the reading. Ask students what, if anything, they know about Carnival (a holiday that traditionally marked the beginning of the Christian season of Lent, when people had to pray a lot and eat very plain food).

A • Have students look at the pictures and try to guess the locations.

- Have students read the article to check their guesses. Tell them to circle any words they don't understand.

- Check answers.

Answers: Trinidad, Brazil, United States

- Go over the article with the class, answering any questions from the students about vocabulary.

Additional words in the reading:
paint = something we use to make things a different color
fantastic = very surprising
take control = say, "Do this. Don't do that."
mud = dirt and water
serious = very important
competition = a game to win

B • Have students work individually to answer *true* or *false*.

- Check answers.

Answers: 1. T, 2. T, 3. T, 4. F, 5. F

Reading

👥 **A.** Look at the photos. Guess the country.

▲ The costumes often take a year to make and cost thousands of dollars.

▶ Samba schools compete in the *Sambadrome*.

📖 **B.** Circle **T** for *true* or **F** for *false*.

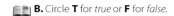

1. People often wear costumes for Carnival.　　　　T　　F
2. The writer comes from Trinidad.　　T　　F
3. In New Orleans, people dance in the street at Carnival.　　T　　F
4. Carnival is in May.　　　　　T　　F
5. There are Samba schools in Venice.　　　　　T　　F

22 Work, Rest, and Play

☐ Trinidad and Tabago

Carnival: One Festival, Many Faces

Trinidad and Tobago

A girl throws yellow paint in my face. I'm not angry. I laugh and I throw paint at her. This is fun! This is Carnival—Trinidad style.

Carnival is a festival that takes place before the Christian season of Lent, 40 days before Easter. The date changes every year, but it is usually in February or March. It is the last chance to have some fun before Lent begins.

▲ More than 300,000 tourists come to New Orleans for Carnival. And they spend half a billion dollars!

For Your Information: Carnival

Carnival is a holiday celebrated in Catholic and Orthodox Christian countries around the world. It originally started as a preparation for the season of Lent, during which no parties could be held and no meat could be eaten. Some aspects of Carnival are older than Christianity and originated in ancient Greece and Rome. The most famous traditions, including parades and wearing masks, began in Italy and spread from there to Germany, Spain, and the New World. Today it has become a nonreligious festival, and it lasts anywhere from a few days to many weeks.

Around the world people celebrate Carnival in different ways. In New Orleans, musicians play jazz and people dance in the streets. In Rio de Janeiro, samba schools spend a year making fantastic costumes for the Carnival parade. In Venice, they wear beautiful masks. In some parts of Germany, for one day the women take control of the town and cut off men's **ties**. Here in Trinidad, people party!

It is two o'clock in the morning on *Dirty Monday* and we are having a street party. People get dressed in old clothes and throw mud and paint at each other. But tomorrow the serious celebrations begin. People spend the whole year making costumes and writing songs for Carnival. Tomorrow is their big day. There is a competition for the best costumes and songs. The winners get money and a car. It's serious business.

So, why don't *you* come to Trinidad to celebrate Carnival?

Word Focus

tie = a long piece of cloth worn around the neck; usually worn by men.

Writing

Write about a festival in your country. Answer these questions.

   a. What is the name of the festival?
   b. When do you celebrate the festival?
   c. Why do you celebrate this festival?
   d. What do you do?

> Songkran is a very important festival in Thailand. It is the Thai New Year and we celebrate it from the 13th to the 15th of April.
>
> We celebrate it to say goodbye to the old year and to welcome the new year.
>
> Traditionally, at Songkran we visit old people to pay respect. And many people clean their houses. But the best part of Songkran is when we throw water at other people in the street. We even throw water at strangers, but they do not get angry. It's just good fun.

 Goal 4 | **Compare different festivals**

Share your writing with a partner. Tell your partner how your festival is different from Carnival.

Writing

- Tell students to choose a festival in their country and write about it. They should write at least one sentence about each question. If necessary, brainstorm a list of festivals with the class and write them on the board for students to choose from.

☑ Goal 4

- Match students with a partner and have them read their papers to each other. Then have them talk about differences between their festivals and Carnival.
- Compare ideas with the class.

After Reading

Have students work individually or in pairs to search online for information in English about a festival in their country. What do foreign visitors like to do at the festival? Have them tell the class what they found.

Video Journal

Before You Watch

A • With the class, look at the pictures and discuss the different types of dance and where they are from: hula, from Hawaii; ballroom dancing, from Europe and North America; flamenco, from Spain; and Balinese dance, from Bali in Indonesia.

B • Go over the words with the class. Then have students work individually to complete the sentences.

• Check answers.

Answers: 1. surprised, 2. legends, 3. missionary, 4. waves, 5. judge

E VIDEO JOURNAL *HULA*

Before You Watch

A. Where are these dances from?

B. Study the words and definitions. Use the words in the box to complete the sentences.

legends = stories about the past
waves = movement on water
missionary = a person who brings a new religion to a country
surprised = when you don't expect something
judge = a person who decides which person is the winner

1. Juan and Maria are together again. I'm _____!
2. Old people tell _____ to young children.
3. My uncle is a _____ in Africa.
4. It is dangerous to swim here. The _____ are very big.
5. The _____ is wrong! I am the winner.

For Your Information: Hula

Hula is a traditional dance from the Hawaiian Islands that was developed by people from Polynesia who settled there many centuries ago. It is accompanied by singing and traditional instruments. Traditional hula was religious and used local instruments, such as drums made from gourds and coconut shells. Female dancers wore only a skirt and no blouse. After the islands were taken over by the United States, hula was driven underground, and when it began to be performed in public again, costumes and music were changed to fit foreign tastes. Instruments such as guitars were brought in. Today, both forms of hula, traditional and modern, can be seen in Hawaii.

While You Watch

A. Watch the video. Number the sentences in the correct order.

___ But some Hawaiian people dance the hula in secret.
___ The hula starts 300 years ago.
___ The missionaries tell the queen of Hawaii to stop the dance.
___ The hula dancers take part in a festival every year.
___ Today there are special schools where people learn the hula.

B. Watch the video again. Circle the correct answer.

1. The hula is ___ years old.
   a. 300
   b. 3000

2. The girls in the legend copy the ___.
   a. waves
   b. trees

3. The missionaries were ___.
   a. surprised
   b. interested

4. The dancers have to practice for many ___ before they can perform.
   a. days
   b. hours

5. The judges look at the dancers' ___.
   a. hair
   b. costumes

After You Watch

Talk with a partner. What traditional dances do you have in your country? What is your favorite dance?

Communication

Describe the pictures to a partner. Talk about the following.

a. Where are the dancers from?
b. Are the people happy?
c. Which dance do you like most? Why?

While You Watch

A • Tell students to watch the video the first time and number the ideas in the order the video talks about them. Read the sentences together. Play the video one or more times.

• Check answers.

Answers: 2, 3, 1, 5, 4

B • Tell students to watch the video again and find the correct answers. Have the students read the statements. Play the video.

• Check answers.

Answers: 1. a, 2. a, 3. a, 4. b, 5. b

• Talk to the class about what surprised them most about the hula.

After You Watch

• Match students with partners. Have them talk about types of dance in their countries and dances they like to watch or do.

• With the class, talk about the types of dance the students enjoy watching or doing. Which kinds are popular in their countries?

Communication

• Have students work with a partner to discuss the pictures.

• Compare answers with the class.

Teacher Tip: Starting and ending group and pair work

To make group and pair work go smoothly, it's helpful to use clear signals for beginning and ending the task.

• Write starting and ending times on the board (Group work starts: 10:15. Group work ends: 10:25.)

• Tell your students that group work ends when you clap your hands three times.

• Train your students that when they see you raise your hand, they should also raise their hands and stop talking. The room will fall silent without you interrupting.

- Introduce the theme of the unit. Ask students, *What are some ways to travel?* Elicit ideas like *airplane, bus, train, car*.

- Direct students' attention to the pictures. Ask, *Where is this?* (an airport) With the class, look at each picture in turn, and have students name things they see in each one.

- Have students work with a partner to match the words with the correct pictures.

- Check answers.

Answers: (from left to right)
1. check-in desk, 2. baggage carousel, 3. security, 4. immigration

- Have students discuss the question with their partner. If many students are unfamiliar with airports and flying, talk about the question with the class.

- Follow up with these questions, asking them orally or writing them on the board for students to answer in pairs:

  1. *Where are big airports in our country?*

  2. *How do you usually travel?*

- Go over the Unit Goals with the class, explaining and/or translating as necessary.

GOING PLACES

1. Which word best describes each picture?
   a. immigration
   b. baggage carousel
   c. check-in desk
   d. security

2. What do you do at these places?

UNIT GOALS

Identify possessions
Ask for and give personal travel information
Give travel advice
Share special travel tips with others

26

Unit Goals	Grammar	Vocabulary	Listening	Speaking and Pronunciation	Reading and Writing
• Identify possessions • Ask for and give personal travel information • Give travel advice • Share special travel tips with others	Possession *It **belongs** to Ali. It's **his**.* Imperatives and *should* for advice *Take a sweater.* ***Should** I take a taxi?*	Travel preparations and stages Travel documents and money	General listening: conversations at travel destinations	Giving personal information for travel forms Rising intonation in lists	"Smart Traveler: Expert Opinion" Writing travel tips

UNIT 3

27

Unit Theme Overview

- Travel is one of the world's largest industries, and it's growing larger every year. In the year 2000, over 1.4 billion passengers traveled by airplane alone, and it's virtually impossible to say how many used trains, ships, and other modes of transportation. Travel can provide English learners an opportunity to use their new language skills. Even learners who stay at home are more and more likely to encounter foreign travelers who use English as a language for international communication.

- In this unit, students learn vocabulary pertaining to international travel, especially air travel. They talk about travel preparations and learn how to give advice about travel, while gaining information that may be useful to them on future trips.

Identify Possessions

Vocabulary

A • Go over the phrases, explaining the vocabulary as needed.

• Have students work with a partner to number the pictures in order. If many students are unfamiliar with air travel, have them do the exercise in groups, or do it together as a whole class.

• Check answers.

Answers may vary.
Suggested answers: Top row: 3, 2, 10, 5, 1; Bottom row: 7, 9, 8, 4, 6

B • Have students work individually to fill in the sentences with expressions from exercise **A**.

• Check answers.

Answers: 1. go through customs, 2. go through security, 3. check in, 4. buy duty-free goods, 5. board the airplane, 6. claim your baggage

---

A GOAL 1 IDENTIFY POSSESSIONS

Vocabulary

👥 **A.** In what order do you do these things? Number the pictures.

 ▲ take a taxi

 ▲ pack your bags

 ▲ go through customs

 ▲ go through security

 ▲ buy your ticket

 ▲ board the airplane

 ▲ claim your baggage

 ▲ go through immigration

 ▲ check in

▲ buy duty free goods

B. Complete the sentences. Use a phrase from exercise **A**.

1. After you _____, you can leave the airport.
2. Do I have to take off my shoes when I _____?
3. At the airport, the first thing you do is _____.
4. Many people _____ like perfume and chocolates at the airport.
5. When you _____ you can only take a small bag.
6. Make sure you don't take the wrong bag when you _____ at the carousel.

Word Bank: On the airplane

overhead bin	beverage cart
seat	in-flight movie
tray table	aisle
seat belt	emergency exit
flight attendant	lavatory
captain	passenger

Grammar: Possession

English shows possession in a number of ways. Three are presented here: Possessive adjectives modify a noun (*my/his/your bag*). Possessive pronouns take the place of a noun (*mine/his/yours*). *Belong to* + object pronoun is a verb showing possession. (*The dog belongs to them.*) In addition, there are possessive nouns (covered elsewhere), which are formed with *'s.* (*That's Mark's car.*)

Grammar: Possession

Possessive adjective	Possessive pronoun	*Belong to*	
my	mine		me.
your	yours		you.
his	his		him.
her	hers	It **belongs to**	her.
our	ours		us.
their	theirs		them.

Real Language

To ask about possession we can say *Whose____ is this?*

A. Complete the conversations. Use a word or phrase for possession.

A: Excuse me. Is this _____ bag, Karen?
B: No, it's not _____.
A: Is this Anna 's bag?
B: No, _____ is green.
A: _____ ticket is this?
B: I think it _____ Shawn.

B. Answer the questions using *belong to* and a possessive pronoun.

1. Whose passport is this? (Ali) It belongs to Ali. It's his._____
2. Whose keys are these? (my keys) _____
3. Whose camera is this? (my sister's) _____
4. Whose bags are these? (John and Lucy's) _____
5. Whose tickets are these? (Logan's and mine) _____

Conversation

Track 1-11

A. Listen to the conversation. Who does the bag belong to?

Anna: Whose bag is this?
Bill: It's not mine.
Anna: Maybe it's Jim's. Is this your bag, Jim?
Jim: No, mine is black.
Anna: Well, whose is it?
Bill: Maybe it belongs to this woman. Excuse me, does this bag belong to you?
Woman: Yes, it's mine. Thank you so much.

B. Practice the conversation in a group of four students. Switch roles and practice it again.

✓ **Goal 1** **Identify possessions**

Work with a partner. Use the conversation for ideas to ask about different possessions.

Grammar Practice: Possession

Have students bring scissors and old magazines with pictures (fashion, technology, sports, cooking, etc.) to class, to be cut up and shared. Divide the class into groups of three or four students and give them five minutes to look through the magazines and cut out pictures of 10 things they would like to own (for example, a pair of shoes, a camera, skis). Have each group put all their pictures in a pile, mix them, and then work out whose picture each one is, using possessive pronouns: *Is this yours? No, it's his. That's not mine*, and so on.

Grammar

- Present/review the possessive adjectives. Hold up your book and say, *Here is my book.* Pick up a student's book, hand it to the student, and say, *Here is your book.* Point to books and call on students to form sentences.

- Present/review the possessive pronouns. Hold up your book, and say, *It's mine.* Call on students to form similar sentences.

- Introduce *belong to*. Hold up various items and say, *It belongs to me/you/him/her*, etc. Then hold up students' possessions and say, *Whose book/bag/ dictionary is this?* to elicit, *It belongs to him*, etc.

A • Have students work individually or in pairs to fill in the spaces.

- Check answers.

Answers: your, mine, hers, Whose, belongs to

B • Have students work individually to write sentences.

- Check answers.

Answers: 2. They belong to me. They're mine. 3. It belongs to my sister. It's hers. 4. They belong to John and Lucy. They're theirs. 5. They belong to Logan and me. They're ours.

Conversation

A • Have students close their books. Write the question on the board: *Who does the bag belong to?*

- Play the recording. **(CD1 T11)**

- Check answers.

Answer: the woman

B • Play or read the conversation again for the class to repeat.

- Practice the conversation with the class in chorus.

- Have students practice the conversation in groups.

☑ Goal 1

- Have students work with a partner to make a new conversation like the one they just practiced.

- Call on students to present their conversations.

Ask For and Give Personal Travel Information

Listening

A • With the class, look at each picture and talk about what people do in each place.

• Tell students they are going to hear three conversations. They should listen and find the place for each conversation.

• Play the recording one or more times. **(CD1 T12)**

• Check answers.

Answers: 1. check-in counter, 2. immigration, 3. hotel reception

B • Tell students to listen again to answer the questions. Have them read the statements.

• Play the recording one or more times. **(CD1 T12)**

• Check answers.

Answers: Conversation 1: 1. T, 2. F, Conversation 2: 1. T, 2. F, Conversation 3: 1. T, 2. F

C • Tell students to listen to all three conversations and find the conversation that contains each question. Have them read the questions. Play the recording twice. **(CD1 T12)**

• Check answers.

Answers: 2. 1, 3. 2, 4. 3, 5. 2, 6. 1, 7. 2, 8. 1

Pronunciation

• Explain that in English, when we say a sentence containing a list of things, our voice rises when we say each thing on the list, and falls when we say the last thing on the list.

A • Tell students to listen to the sentences and read along in their books. Play the recording. **(CD1 T13)**

• Tell students to listen again and repeat the sentences. Play the recording one or more times.

• Call on rows or columns of students to repeat the sentences. Then call on individual students to repeat the sentences.

Listening

A. Listen to the conversations. Where do the conversations take place?

Track 1-12

Conversation 1 _____

Conversation 2 _____

Conversation 3 _____

▲ hotel reception

B. Listen again. Circle **T** for *true* and **F** for *false*.

Track 1-12

Conversation 1

1. The man books a window seat.   T   F
2. The man has two bags.   T   F

Conversation 2

1. This is the woman's first visit to the United States.   T   F
2. The woman is staying in the United States
   for three weeks.   T   F

Conversation 3

1. The man is staying at the hotel for one night.   T   F
2. The man has one bag.   T   F

▲ immigration

C. In which conversation did you hear these questions? Listen again and check your answers.

Track 1-12

1. Is this your first time in the United States? _2_
2. Can I see your U.S. visa, please? ___
3. Where are you staying? ___
4. Is this your bag? ___
5. Can I see your passport, please? ___
6. Can I see your ticket and passport, please? ___
7. What is the purpose of your visit? ___
8. Window or aisle seat? ___

Pronunciation: Rising intonation on lists

A. Listen and repeat the sentences.

Track 1-13

1. I'm going to London, Paris, Rome, and Madrid.
2. I've got my camera, cell phone, laptop, and Palm™.
3. You can take a taxi, the shuttle bus, or a rental car.

▲ check-in counter

B. Practice these sentences with a partner.

1. We want to travel by bus, train, plane, and taxi.
2. I need to pack a sweater, a jacket, a scarf, and a warm hat.
3. Let's visit Argentina, Brazil, Chile, and Peru.
4. When I get to the hotel, I need to check in, take a shower, and change my clothes.

Communication

 Take turns. Ask a partner questions to fill out the immigration form below with his or her information.

Department of Immigration PERMISSION TO ENTER
1. First name
2. Middle name
3. Family name
4. Date of birth
5. Place of birth
6. Nationality
7. Country of residence
8. Principal destination in this country
9. Hotel and/or street address
FORM 12a/PTO (Revised08) [Pursuant to Section 211(d)(3) of the IPA]

✔ **Goal 2** — **Ask for and give personal travel information**

Work with a partner. Plan a trip. Tell your partner where you want to go, what you need to do before you travel, and when you want to travel.

B • Have students work with a partner to mark the rising and falling arrows on the sentences. Then have them practice saying the sentences to a partner.

• Call on students to say a sentence for the class.

Communication

• Introduce the activity. Ask students if they have ever traveled in another country. Were there special papers to fill out? Explain that this is a form from an English-speaking country. Go over the information asked for on the form.

• Tell students that they will fill out the form using their partner's information (not their own!). Go over the questions they will ask: *What's your first name/nationality/principal destination?* and so forth. On the board, write, *How do you spell that?* and *Could you repeat that, please?* Finally, tell students they can give true answers or make up answers if they want.

• Walk around helping as needed.

☑ Goal 2

• Have students work with a partner to decide where and when they want to travel. Tell them to write a list of the things they need to do before and when they begin their trip. They can look back at the vocabulary in Lesson A for help.

• Call on students to present their travel plans to the class.

Expansion Activity

Have students work with a partner to prepare and practice a role-play in one of the situations they heard in the Listening section (a hotel reception desk, the immigration area of an airport, or an airline check-in counter). Have student pairs present their conversations to the class.

Give Travel Advice

Language Expansion

- Introduce the names of the documents shown in the pictures. Ask which ones the students use.

A • Have students work individually to complete the sentences with the names of documents.

- Check answers.

Answers: 1. international driver's license, 2. visa, 3. travel insurance, 4. passport, 5. airline ticket

- Tell the class, *I'm going to (Japan).* Ask, *What documents do I need?* Elicit, *You need an airline ticket/a visa*, etc. Talk about various countries.

B • Present the different forms of money in the pictures. Ask students which ones they use at home.

- Go over the expressions for giving an opinion. Explain that we say *I think* and *The best idea is* to give our opinions. We say *I don't agree* and *I agree* to react to another person's opinion.

- Go over the expressions for giving a reason. Explain that if stores *don't accept* a form of money, you can't use that form of money to buy things there. Explain that if banks *don't cash* traveler's checks, that means they won't change traveler's checks into money.

- Have students talk with a partner about the best kinds of money to take on a trip.

- Compare answers with the class. Talk about other forms of money that people use while traveling such as ATM cards (to get money from machines).

▲ travel insurance

▲ international driver's license

▲ visa

▲ passport

▲ airline ticket

Language Expansion: Travel documents and money

A. Complete the sentences. Use the names of the travel documents.

1. You need an _____ to drive a car in a foreign country.
2. In some countries you need a _____ to enter.
3. It's a good idea to buy _____. Medical bills are expensive.
4. Your _____ is your photo ID in any foreign country.
5. You can buy an _____ on the Internet. But you need to write down or print the confirmation number.

B. Talk to a partner. What is the best form of money to take on your trip? Why?

Give an opinion

> I think credit cards are good.

> The best idea is to take . . .

Give a reason

> People steal . . .

> . . . don't accept . . .

> People lose cash.

> . . don't cash checks.

▲ credit cards

▲ traveler's checks

▲ checks

▲ cash

32 Going Places

Word Bank: Exchanging money

exchange office	exchange rate
commission	currency
buy/sell rate	receipt
bills	coins

Grammar: Imperatives and *should* for advice

We use *should* and *shouldn't* to give advice. *Should* + base form of the verb is a tactful or "soft" way of giving advice. It means that the speaker thinks this would be a good idea.

Grammar: *Should* for advice

Should

Subject	*should*	Adverb of frequency	Verb	Complement
You	should	(always)	make	a copy of your passport.
You	shouldn't		wear	expensive jewelry.

*We use *should/shouldn't* to give advice.

Questions with *should*

Should	Subject	Verb	Complement
Should	I	take	a taxi from the airport?

*We use questions with *should* to ask for advice.

A. Ask for advice. Write the questions.

1. **Q:** Should I take the shuttle bus to the airport?
   A: Yes, you should. The shuttle bus is quick and cheap.
2. **Q:** _____
   A: No, you shouldn't. It is hot at the beach. You don't need a sweater.
3. **Q:** _____
   A: Yes, you should. Credit cards are accepted in a lot of shops.
4. **Q:** _____
   A: No, you shouldn't. It's dangerous to carry cash.

 B. Work with a partner. Take turns. Ask the questions in exercise **A** and give different advice. Use imperatives and *should.*

Conversation

 A. Listen to the conversation. What does Claudia want from the United States?

Track 1-14

Greg:	Hi, Claudia. You know the USA. Can you give me some advice? I'm going to New York in January.
Claudia:	Lucky you! How can I help?
Greg:	First. Should I buy travel insurance?
Claudia:	Yes, you should. Hospitals and doctors are very expensive in the U.S.
Greg:	OK. That's another $200. What about clothes? Should I take a coat?
Claudia:	Definitely. It's very cold in January. You should take a warm sweater as well and some gloves and a scarf.
Greg:	Mmm, that's another $100.
Claudia:	Oh, just one more thing! Don't forget to buy me a nice present.
Greg:	Oh no! That's another $500! Traveling is expensive.

B. Practice the conversation with a partner. Switch roles and practice it again.

 Goal 3 — **Give travel advice**

Take turns. Tell a partner where you want to go. Then give your partner travel advice. Use the conversation for ideas.

Grammar

- Introduce *should* for giving advice. Point out that *should* is used with the base form of the verb. Say, *I am from (Australia). I want to take a vacation in your country. Please give me some advice.* Elicit ideas such as *You should come here in summer. You shouldn't wear short skirts,* etc.

A
- Have students work individually to write the questions.
- Check answers.

Answers: 2. Should I bring a sweater to the beach? 3. Should I use a credit card? 4. Should I use cash?

B
- Match students with a partner and have them take turns asking and answering the questions, using their own ideas for advice.
- Call on student pairs to present a question and answer to the class.

Conversation

A
- Have students close their books. Write the question on the board: *What does Claudia want from the United States?*
- Play the recording. **(CD1 T14)**
- Check answers.

Answer: a nice present

B
- Play or read the conversation again for the class to repeat.
- Practice the conversation with the class in chorus.
- Have students practice the conversation with a partner and then switch roles and practice it again.

✓ Goal 3

- Have students work with a partner to give each other travel advice. They can make a new conversation like the one they just practiced.
- Call on students to present their conversations to the class.

Grammar Practice: *Should*

Have students work with a partner. Ask them to write a list of six problems, for example: 1. *I don't have any cash.* 2. *I'm cold.*

Match two pairs and have them take turns reading out a problem from their lists. The other pair needs to provide advice using *should.* Then do a class check. Elicit the most original advice from each of the groups.

Share Special Travel Tips with Others

Reading

- Introduce the topic of the reading. Ask students, *When you travel, do you take a lot of things? Or do you travel light? Why?*

- Have students read the article. Tell them to circle any words they don't understand.

- Go over the article with the class, answering any questions from the students about vocabulary.

Additional vocabulary:

medical = related to doctors and hospitals

bill = a paper that says you must pay an amount of money

minimum = the smallest amount you can have

delayed = late

snack = food you eat between meals

A • Tell students to reread the article and answer the questions.

- Check answers.

Answers: 1. Yes (because he knows a lot about travel), 2. Many countries won't let you enter with less than six months left on your passport. 3. So you can quickly see your bag on the airport carousel. 4. It helps to pass the time as you wait for your delayed flight. 5. Answers will vary.

Reading

📖 **A.** Answer the questions.

1. Do you think the author enjoys travelling? _____
   _____
   _____

2. Why should you check the expiration date of your passport? _____
   _____
   _____

3. Why should you tie a sock to your bags?
   _____
   _____
   _____

4. Why should you take a good book when you travel? _____
   _____
   _____

5. Write a list of snacks you would take when travelling by air. _____
   _____
   _____

Real Language

We use the expression *share some pointers* to say *give advice*.

Word Focus

expiration date = The *expiration date* of a document is the date it comes to an end or can no longer be used.

Smart Traveler

EXPERT OPINION

In his book Easy Travel, *Mike Connelly,* **shares some pointers** *on making travel easy:*

■ **DOCUMENTS** Make sure you have all your documents: passport, visas, tickets, traveler's checks, etc. You should always check the **expiration date** of your passport. Many countries won't let you enter with less than six months left on your passport. Don't forget to buy medical insurance. Medical bills

---

For Your Information: Travel tips

Here are more travel tips from experts.

- Always put your name and your itinerary inside each bag that you check in when flying. Name tags sometimes fall off of lost bags, and the airline checks inside the bag for information about the owner.

- Drink a lot of water on the plane. The air inside is very dry, and the water will make you feel much better. Don't drink coffee or tea, because they make your body even drier.

- On a long flight, don't watch the movie. Sleep as much as you can. If you arrive in the morning, try to stay awake all day and go to bed at your usual time. If you feel very tired, don't sleep for more than an hour during the day. This helps your body change to the new time.

- For your return flight, call the airline the day before you travel. Ask if the flight time has changed.

can be very expensive, especially in the United States and Europe. Finally, you should make copies of all your important documents and credit cards and keep them in another bag.

■ **PACKING** My advice is—always travel light! I hate to carry heavy bags. Just take the minimum. There is an old saying: *Breakfast in Berlin. Dinner in Delhi. Bags in Bangkok!* So, don't pack anything important in your check-in bag; put important things in your carry-on bag. You don't want to arrive home without your house keys. Another tip—don't use expensive suitcases. People don't steal dirty old bags. Finally, here's a good little tip—tie a sock or brightly colored string to your bags. Why? So you can quickly see your bag on the airport carousel.

■ **THE AIRPORT** My first piece of advice is that you should always carry a good book. It helps to pass the time as you wait for your delayed flight. Don't forget to take a sweater or a jacket on the plane. It can get very cold on a long night flight. And then there is airline food. Take a snack (cookies or fruit) with you. Sometimes the food is late, sometimes it doesn't arrive at all, and it's never very good.

B. Circle **T** for *true* and **F** for *false*.

1. You need a lot of documents to travel.   T   F
2. You need to take a lot of clothes in your bag.   T   F
3. Bags can be hard to identify at the airport.   T   F
4. Flights are never late.   T   F
5. Airplane food is always good.   T   F

Writing

Write some travel tips for your country. Think about the following topics:

- transportation
- how to carry money
- Can you drink the water?

Thailand is a safe country and the people are very friendly. But, like most places, you should be careful. Here are some tips:

- Taxis are cheap, but ask the price first.
- Many tourists use *tuk tuks*. However, they are dangerous. Be careful.
- Don't use the buses. They are slow and crowded.
- Don't carry a lot of money with you. Most shops accept credit cards.
- The water is not safe to drink, so you should buy water in bottles.
- Don't go out alone at night.

Have a nice stay!

✓ **Goal 4** | **Share special travel tips with others**

Read your travel tips to a partner. Then share them with the class.

B
- Tell students to reread the article and mark the statements *true* or *false*.
- Check answers.

Answers: 1. T, 2. F, 3. T, 4. F, 5. F

Writing

- Tell students to think about problems that foreign visitors have in their country. What information do they need? Go over the model writing sample about Thailand (a *tuk tuk* is a three-wheeled vehicle used as a taxi).
- Tell students to write at least five tips for visitors.

✓ **Goal 4**

- Match students with a partner and have them read their tips to each other and compare ideas.
- Call on students to read their papers to the class.

After Reading

Divide the class into groups of three or four students. Have each group choose a topic such as food, shopping, transportation, or health and create a poster for visitors with tips and illustrations. Have each group stand up in front of the class to present and explain their poster.

Before You Watch

A • Introduce the idea of working dogs. Have students look at the pictures and discuss these and other kinds of working dogs that students might know about (for example, search dogs who look for people who are lost, guard dogs who bark to alert their owners when strangers come near, etc.).

B • Go over the words and sentences with the class.

• Have students work individually to complete the summary.

• Check answers.

Answers: disease, illegal, bother

Before You Watch

A. Look at the photos. Do you have working dogs in your country? How do these dogs help us?

Florida, U.S.

▲ guide dog

▲ sheepdog

▲ detector dog

▲ police dog

B. Study the words and the sentences. Then read the video summary. Use the words to complete the text.

disease   to bother   illegal
Rats are dirty. Sometimes they carry **disease**. Hey kids! Please be quiet. I'm trying to work. You're **bothering** me. You can't park your car there. It's not allowed. It's **illegal**.

Video summary

Airline passengers sometimes carry food, for example fruit, that may bring _____ into a country. Detector dogs can find this food by smelling the passengers' bags. Brent Heldt is training a dog called Stockton to be a detector dog. Stockton has to find the _____ food, but also he must not _____ the passengers.

For Your Information: Beagles

The beagle is a small to medium dog that was originally used for hunting. Beagles weigh 18–35 pounds (8–16 kilograms) and have markings of brown, black, and white. Although the modern breed of beagles was developed in England in the 1830s, dogs similar to beagles were used for hunting in ancient Greece! Beagles are known for their excellent sense of smell and their ability to follow the trail of a scent. This makes them very well suited as detector dogs. They are also popular pets because they are small and have a calm personality. Probably the most famous beagle in the world is Snoopy, the dog in the well-known comic strip *Peanuts*.

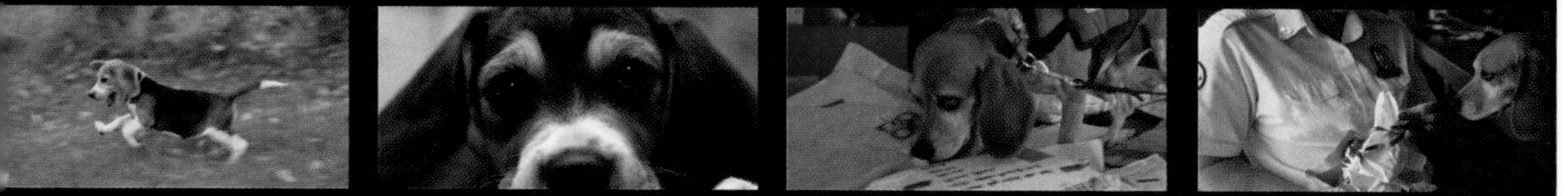

While You Watch

A. Watch the video. Circle the names of things you see.

uniform	**apples**	**suitcase**	**passport**
gun	**orange**	**mango**	**beef jerky**

B. Watch the video again. Circle **T** for *true* and **F** for *false*.

1. Brent and Stockton play before they start work. T F
2. Detector dogs look for meat. T F
3. Stockton does not find the meat. T F
4. Stockton eats the meat he finds. T F
5. Stockton is learning slowly. T F

After You Watch

In the video we saw that dogs can be very useful in airports. Work with a partner to write a list of possible problems with dogs in airports.

Communication

Role-play the following situations.

Situation 1
Student A is a dog handler.
Student B is a passenger. The dog is sniffing your bag. You don't like dogs. In your culture dogs are dirty. Complain to the dog handler.

Situation 2
Student A is a passenger. The dog finds some fruit in your bag. It is a gift for your mother.
Student B is the dog handler. Explain that the passenger shouldn't bring fruit into the county. Take the fruit.

While You Watch

A
- Tell students to watch the video the first time and circle the things they see. Play the video.
- Check answers.

Answers: uniform, apples, passport, orange, beef jerky, mango

B
- Tell students to watch the video again and respond *true* or *false*. Have the students read the statements. Play the video.
- Check answers.

Answers: 1. T, 2. T, 3. F, 4. F, 5. F

After You Watch

- Match students with a partner and have them work together to list possible problems.
- Compare answers with the class.

Possible answers: Some people are afraid of dogs. The dogs want to eat all the food. The dogs find the wrong food. The dogs make noise. The dogs make the airport dirty.

Communication

- Match students with a partner. Have them role-play the two situations.
- Call on students to present one of their role-plays to the class.

Teacher Tip: Encouraging use of English

A common challenge in monolingual classes is motivating students to use only English in group work. Here are some approaches to consider:

- Explain the rationale for using only English. Tell students, *We learn to speak English by speaking English.* If appropriate, tell students about your own language-learning experiences.
- Establish a clear policy. For example, you might tell students, *It's OK to ask questions in your native language, but for all other things we use only English.*
- Set an example for the students. Use only English for instructions and classroom management.

- Direct students' attention to the pictures. With the class, look at each picture in turn, and have students name as many things as they can in each one. Write lists on the board, explaining vocabulary as needed.

  Fruits and vegetables: apples, bananas, peaches, grapes, tomatoes, onions, cauliflower

  Staples: flour, sugar, oil, vinegar, beans, lentils, pasta, couscous

- Have students tell a partner about their favorite foods.

- Compare answers with the class, compiling a list on the board.

- Follow up with these questions, asking them orally or writing them on the board for students to answer in pairs:

  1. *Which foods in the pictures are very healthy?*

  2. *Which foods in the pictures do you eat every day/often/sometimes/never?*

- Go over the Unit Goals with the class, explaining and/or translating as necessary.

FOOD

1. Can you name any of the foods in the pictures?

2. What is your favorite food?

UNIT GOALS

Talk about food
Order a meal
Talk about diets
Discuss unusual and favorite foods

38

Unit Goals	Grammar	Vocabulary	Listening	Speaking and Pronunciation	Reading and Writing
• Talk about food • Order a meal • Talk about diets • Discuss unusual and favorite foods	Count and non-count nouns; *some* and *any* *We don't have* **any** *milk.* *How much* and *how many* with quantifiers: *lots of*, *a few*, *a little* **How many** *oranges do you need?* **A few.**	Food Diets	General and focused listening: in a restaurant	Role-play: purchasing food at a store Role-play: ordering from a menu Reduced forms: *do you have . . .* and *Would you like . . .*	"Bugs as Food" Writing a favorite recipe

UNIT 4

Unit Theme Overview

- Food is a complex and interesting topic, with cultural, social, health, and even moral aspects. Our food preferences are shaped not only by personal taste, but by custom, habit, and the physical environment we live in.

- This unit presents several different facets of food around the world. Students begin by looking at individual foods and describing the ingredients in favorite dishes, practicing the use of quantifiers and count/non-count nouns. Next, they talk about food in restaurants and ordering meals there. Another lesson brings in the theme of diet and health and why people eat certain kinds of food. Students also consider the cultural side of food and talk about foods that are considered delicious in some countries and disgusting in others.

Talk about Food

Vocabulary

- Go over the names of the foods in the picture. Ask, *Which of these foods do you like? Which foods do you eat often?*
- Have students work individually to choose the correct description for each group of foods.
- Check answers.

Answers: Dairy products: milk, butter, cheese; Protein: eggs, fish, shrimp, Meat (all meats are proteins): chicken; steak, (turkey) bacon, sausages; Fruit: oranges, bananas, apples, lemons; Vegetables: potatoes, peppers, tomatoes, lettuce, onions; Drinks: soda, tea, coffee, water, juice

Note: Bacon and sausages are prepared with either pork, chicken, turkey and sometimes beef.

Grammar

- Go over the information about count and non-count nouns. Explain that non-count nouns are things that we see as a whole and don't count (for example, *water, air, cheese*). Look at the foods and drinks in the illustration and give/ elicit examples of each (Count: eggs, bananas, peppers; Non-count: milk, butter, juice).
- Present the information about *some* and *any* .

Vocabulary

Talk to a partner. Choose a word or phrase from the box to describe each group of foods.

drinks	dairy products	vegetables	fruit	protein	meat

> Milk and Water are drinks.

cheese, butter, milk, juice, soda, tea, coffee, water, lemons, bananas, apples, oranges, chicken, eggs, fish, shrimp, turkey bacon, sausages, steak, onions, lettuce, peppers, tomatoes, potatoes

Grammar: *Some* and *any* with count and non-count nouns

Count and non-count nouns	
Singular	**Plural**
This is a lemon.	Those are lemons.
This is milk.	~~Those are milks.~~

*For nouns you can count, we add -s or -es to form the plural.
*Nouns you cannot count don't have a plural form.

Some and *any*			
	Count nouns		**Non-count nouns**
	Singular	**Plural**	
Statement	We need an apple.	There are **some** oranges on the table.	There is **some** cheese on the table.
Negative	We don't have a lemon.	There aren't **any** bananas at the store.	We don't have **any** milk.
Question	Do we have a red pepper?	Are there **any** eggs?	Do you have **any** butter?

*You can also use *some* for questions with *would* and *could*.
Would you like **some** *apples?*
Could I have **some** *milk?*

Word Bank: More foods

vegetables: carrots, cabbage, eggplant, beans, cucumbers, garlic, squash

fruit: grapes, mangoes, nectarines, melon, cherries, peaches, strawberries,

protein: turkey, pork, beef, mutton, tofu

Grammar: *Some/any*

Some is used in positive sentences, *any* is used in questions and negatives, and *some/any* are both used in questions that make offers. This rule has been simplified somewhat, but will always produce grammatical sentences. (Native speakers generally use *some* in offers when they anticipate a positive answer: *Do you want some ice cream?* They use *any* when they anticipate a negative answer: *Do you want any more ice cream, or should I put it away?*

A. Write the food words from the picture in the correct column.

Count nouns	Non-count nouns

B. Add other food words to the chart. Use your dictionary.

C. Complete the sentences with *a/an*, *the*, *some*, or *any*.

1. Do we have _____ tomatoes?
2. There aren't _____ eggs.
3. There is _____ milk in the fridge.
4. I think _____ cheese is on the table.
5. Pass me _____ apple, please.

Conversation

Track 1-15

A. Listen to the conversation. What do you need to make a Spanish omelet?

Lee: Let's make a Spanish omelet.
Hyejin: Great. What do we need?
Lee: OK, it says here you need some olive oil. Do we have any olive oil?
Hyejin: No, we don't, but it doesn't matter; we have some corn oil. That will do.
Lee: Next, we need some potatoes, a large onion, and a red pepper.
Hyejin: We don't have a red pepper.
Lee: Never mind. We can use a green pepper.
Hyejin: OK. And then we need some eggs. Four eggs.
Lee: OK, let's begin!

B. Practice the conversation with a partner. Switch roles and practice it again.

C. Choose a new recipe and repeat the conversation.

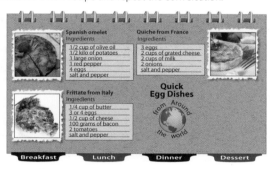

Lesson A   41

Goal 1   Talk about food

Tell a partner the name of a food dish you like. Talk about the ingredients you need to make it.

Real Language

We can use *never mind* or *it doesn't matter* to show something is not important.

Word Focus

Names of fractions:
½ = one half
1/3 = one third
¼ = one fourth
   or one quarter

A • Have students work individually to classify the items in the illustration. Check answers.

Answers: Count nouns: eggs, sausages, oranges, bananas, apples, lemons, potatoes, peppers, tomatoes, onions; Non-count nouns: milk, butter, cheese, fish, shrimp, chicken, steak, bacon, lettuce, soda, tea, coffee, water, juice

B • Have students work individually or with a partner to add words to the chart.

C • Have students work individually to complete the sentences.

   • Check answers.

Answers: 1. any, 2. any, 3. some, 4. the, 5. an

Conversation

A • Have students close their books. Write the question on the board: *What do you need to make a Spanish omelet?*

   • Play the recording. **(CD1 T15)**

   • Check answers.

Answers: oil, potatoes, an onion, a pepper, and (4) eggs

B • Play or read the conversation again for the class to repeat.

   • Practice the conversation with the class in chorus.

   • Have students practice the conversation with a partner and then switch roles and practice it again.

C • With the class, go over the recipes and their ingredients. Ask, *What ingredient is in all of the recipes?* (eggs)

   • Go over the words for fractions. Have students work with a partner to make a new conversation about one of the other recipes.

   • Call on student pairs to present their conversations to the class.

☑ Goal 1

   • Have students work with the same partner to talk about dishes they like and the ingredients in them.

Grammar Practice: Count/non-count nouns, *some*

Ask a student, *What's in your bag?* and start writing a list on the board: *two books, some paper, a dictionary* . . . Tell students to write a list of everything in their bag/purse/backpack without looking inside it. Give them a few minutes to write, and then match them with a partner. Have them give their list to their partner, who will read it out loud while they check what's actually inside. Who made the most accurate list?

Order a Meal

Listening

A • Tell students they are going to hear a conversation in the restaurant. Go over the terms *waiter* and *customer*. Students should listen to find the number of customers.

• Play the recording one or more times. **(CD1 T16).**

• Check answers.

Answer: two

B • Tell students to listen again to find what the customers ordered. Go over the items on the menu with the class. Explain that *filet mignon* (fee-LAY meen-YAWN) is a French name for a kind of steak.

• Play the recording one or more times. **(CD1 T16)**

• Check answers.

Answers: Man: red wine, filet mignon (steak); Woman: mineral water, chicken

Word Focus

waiter = A *waiter* is a person who works in a restaurant and serves food and drinks.
customer = A *customer* is a person who buys goods or services.

B   GOAL 2   ORDER A MEAL

Listening

Track 1-16
A. Listen to the **waiter** taking an order from **customers**. How many customers are there?

Track 1-16
B. Listen again and write the food and drink that each person ordered.

	Drink	Food
Man		
Woman		

Menu

Appetizers
Chicken n' Cheese
Deep-fried chicken served with fresh tomatoes and sliced Cheddar cheese

Vegetable Soup
Made from fresh vegetables

Main Dishes
Seashore Shrimp
Grilled shrimp served with broccoli and boiled rice

Butter-Baked Chicken
Roasted half-chicken in a mushroom sauce, served with steamed carrots

Filet Mignon
8 oz. grilled tenderloin steak, served with Iceberg salad and your favorite salad dressing

Drinks
Red wine, White wine, Beer, Soda, Coffee

42   Food

For Your Information: Restaurant expressions

The waiter might say:
Are you ready to order?
What would you like to drink?
Our special today is (fried chicken).
Is everything all right? (when coming back to the table to check if diners need anything during the meal)
Would you care for any dessert?

A customer might say:
How is (the fish) cooked?
What kind of (soup) do you have?
Could you please bring me (some butter)?
Excuse me, this dish is cold/too salty/not what I ordered.
Could we have the check, please?

C. Listen again. Who asked these questions?

Track 1-16
1. Are you ready to order? _waiter_____
2. Do you have any mineral water? _____
3. What would you recommend? _____
4. Does the filet mignon come with salad? _____
5. Anything else? _____

Pronunciation: Reduced forms *do you have . . .* and *would you like . . .*

A. Listen to the full form and the reduced form.

Track 1-17

B. Listen and check (✓) the correct column. Then listen again and repeat.

Track 1-18

Do you have any oranges?

Would you like some milk?

	Full form	Reduced form
1. Do you have a pen?		
2. Would you like some more bread?		
3. Do you have any paper?		
4. Would you like a cup of coffee?		
5. Do you have any change?		

Communication

Role-play the following situation.

Student A
You work in a food store. Serve the customer.

Student B
You want to make one of the dishes on page 41.
Ask for the food you need from the sales assistant.

✓ **Goal 2**   **Order a meal**

Work with a partner. Choose roles and role-play. Switch roles and role-play again.

Student A You are a customer in a restaurant. Order a meal from the menu on page 42.

Student B You are the waiter. Take the customer's order.

Lesson B   43

Expansion Activity

With the class, brainstorm the menu for a restaurant, including appetizers, main dishes, and drinks, and write it on the board. If desired, use this menu for the role-play activity for Goal 2.

C • Tell students to listen to the conversation one more time and write down the person who asked each question. Play the recording one or more times. **(CD1 T16)**

• Check answers.

Answers: 2. woman, 3. woman, 4. man, 5. waiter

Pronunciation

A • Remind students that when we speak quickly in English, some words and sounds are "reduced"—pronounced differently.

• Tell students to listen to the full and reduced forms of the two expressions. Play the audio. **(CD1 T17)**

B • Tell students to listen to the sentences and mark the pronunciation they hear. Play the audio one or more times. **(CD1 T18)**

• Check answers.

Answers: 1. reduced, 2. full, 3. full, 4. reduced, 5. reduced

Communication

• Write the following sentences on the board for students to refer to: *May I help you?/I'd like . . ./Anything else?*

• Match students with a partner and have them role-play the conversation in a market, then change roles and practice again with a different recipe.

• Call on student pairs to present a conversation to the class.

☑ **Goal 2**

• Match students with a partner. Have them role-play the situation in a restaurant.

• Call on student pairs to present their role-play to the class.

Talk about Diets

Language Expansion

- Introduce the idea of special diets. Why do people eat special diets? What kinds of special diets do students know about?

- With the class, read the menus for the two kinds of diets. Point out that one has foods with a lot of fiber, and the other has foods with a lot of protein. Clarify the meanings of *fiber* and *protein* if necessary. Explain the abbreviations and any other unfamiliar words: **tsp.** = teaspoon (small spoon); **Tbsp.** = tablespoon (large spoon); **oz.** = ounce (about 28 grams); **muffin** = a round, sweet bread; **multigrain** = made from many kinds of grain.

A • Have students work individually to classify the foods, referring to the menus to help them.

- Check answers.

Answers: High fiber: broccoli, cauliflower, baked beans, bagels, breakfast cereal; High protein: hamburger, tuna salad, nuts

B • With the class, brainstorm other foods to add to the chart.

Possible answers: High fiber: apples, oranges, lettuce, potatoes, red peppers, green peppers; High protein: milk, eggs, fish, shrimp, chicken, steak, bacon, sausages

---

C   GOAL 3   TALK ABOUT DIETS

Language Expansion: Diets

Many people eat a special diet. Sometimes they go on a diet to lose weight and sometimes so that they will feel healthier. Here are two diets.

	High-fiber diet	High-protein diet
Breakfast	1 bowl of high-fiber breakfast cereal or 2 slices of whole-grain bread or 1 bagel fruit	5 slices of bacon or 2 sausages 3 eggs a glass of milk
Snack	popcorn or dried fruit	1 hamburger (without the bread) or 2 hot dogs (without the bread)
Lunch or Dinner	vegetables dried pea, bean or lentil soup berries nuts	1 large steak or chicken cheese

A. Write the names of these foods in the correct column.

▲ broccoli   ▲ cauliflower   ▲ baked beans   ▲ bagels

▲ breakfast cereal   ▲ nuts   ▲ hamburger   ▲ tuna salad

High fiber	High protein

B. Add the names of other high-fiber and high-protein foods you know to the chart.

Word Bank: Nutrition words

carbohydrate
fat
vitamin (A, B, C, E)
mineral (calcium, iron)
calorie
serving

balanced diet
vegetarian (no meat or fish)
vegan (no meat, fish, eggs, milk, honey, or other foods from animals)

Grammar: *How much/many* and quantifiers

To use *how much/how many* and *lots of/a few/a little* correctly, students need to have a solid grasp of the count/non-count distinction. Many common errors result from confusing the two, such as ~~How much egg do we need?~~ and ~~How many milk do you drink?~~ For many non-count nouns, English has units that make them countable—for example, *milk/glasses of milk*, *lettuce/heads of lettuce*, *cheese/slices of cheese*.

Grammar: *How much* and *how many* with quantifiers: *lots of, a few, a little*

	Information question	Quantifiers	
		++++	+
Count	**How many** oranges do you need?	I need **lots of** oranges.	I need **a few** oranges.
Non-count	**How much** milk do we have?	We have **lots of** milk.	We have **a little** milk.

*We use *lots of* and *a few* to answers questions about quantity.
*We use *a little* to answer questions about small quantities we cannot count.

A. Match the questions and the answers.

1. How many lemons do you want? ___
2. How much chicken should I buy? ___
3. How many heads of lettuce do we need? ___
4. How much sugar do you want? ___
5. How much water do you want? ___

a. We need a lot. We don't have any meat at home.
b. I'm not very thirsty. Just a little, please.
c. We have a lot of lemons. We only need a few.
d. Just one. We have a lot of salad.
e. Just a little. I don't like sweet coffee.

B. Fill in the blanks with *How much, How many, lots of, a few, a little*.

1. **Q:** <u>How many</u> potatoes would you like? **A:** Just <u>a few</u>, thanks.
2. **Q:** _____ steak do we need? **A:** There are eight of us so we need _____ steak.
3. **Q:** _____ broccoli would you like? **A:** I'm not very hungry. Just _____.
4. **Q:** _____ apples do we need? **A:** We only need _____. We already have some at home.

Conversation

Track 1-19

A. Listen to the conversation. Can Pat eat popcorn?

Kim: You're looking good.
Pat: Thanks, Kim. I'm on a special diet. It's a high-fiber diet.
Kim: High fiber? You mean lots of bread and fruit?
Pat: That's right.
Kim: How much bread can you eat for breakfast?
Pat: I can eat two slices of whole grain bread for breakfast or one bowl of high-fiber cereal.
Kim: And what about snacks?
Pat: No problem. I can eat lots of popcorn and dried fruit.
Kim: Mmm, sounds like a delicious diet. Maybe I'll join you.

B. Practice the conversation with a partner. Switch roles and practice it again.

Goal 3 | **Talk about diets**

Repeat the conversation. Use the high-protein diet on page 44.

Grammar Practice: *How much/many* and quantifiers

Write these words on the board: *coffee, desserts, vegetables, water, milk, meat, eggs, fruit*.

Match students with a partner and have them ask their partner questions with *How much/how many* about each thing: *How much coffee do you drink?* Then call on students to tell the class if their partner has a healthy diet, and why: *She eats a lot of fruit.*

Grammar

- Go over the information in the chart. Ask, *How much coffee/milk/juice do you drink? How many eggs/vegetables/desserts do you eat?* Elicit answers with *a few/a little/lots*. Then have students ask you questions.

A • Have students work individually to match the columns.
- Check answers.

Answers: 1. c, 2. a, 3. d, 4. e, 5. b

B • Have students work individually to complete the sentences.
- Check answers.

Answers: 2. How much, a lot of, 3. How much, a little, 4. How many, a few

- Match students with a partner and have them read the conversations out loud. If desired, have them make a new conversation of their own, and present it to the class.

Conversation

A • Have students close their books. Write the question on the board: *Can Pat eat popcorn?*
- Play the recording. **(CD1 T19)**
- Check answers.

Answer: Yes

B • Play or read the conversation again for the class to repeat.
- Practice the conversation with the class in chorus.
- Have students practice the conversation with a partner and then switch roles and practice it again.

☑ Goal 3

- Match students with a partner and have them make a new conversation, using the information about the high-protein diet on the previous page.

Discuss Unusual and Favorite Foods

Reading

- Introduce the topic of the reading. Ask students, *What strange things do people eat in other countries?* Write answers on the board.

A
- Look at the photos with the class and talk about students' reactions.
- Point out the vocabulary that is defined in the picture dictionary illustration.
- Have students read the article. Tell them to circle any words they don't understand.
- Go over the article with the class, answering any questions from the students about vocabulary.

Additional words:

Yuck! = Children use this word when something tastes bad; **estimated** = we don't know exactly; **contain** = have inside; **hey** = people use this word to get other people to listen to them.

- Explain, if necessary, that the article talks about laws for selling food. For example, the United States government says that people can sell chocolate if it has less than 60 bits of bugs in it (per 100 grams).

B
- Have students work individually to answer the questions.
- Check answers.

Answers: 1. crickets, ant eggs, silk worms, 2. no, 3. 30, 4. chocolate-covered crickets, 5. answers will vary

---

▲ crickets, grasshoppers, and other insects on a stick for sale at a Donghaumen Night Market near Wangfujing Dongcheng, Beijing, China.

Reading

A. Look at the photos. Do people eat insects in your country?

B. Answer the questions.

1. What insects are on the menu in the restaurant? _____
2. In Thailand are insects luxury food? _____
3. How many bits of insects are allowed in peanut butter? _____
4. What does the author order? _____ _____
5. Do you like to eat insects? Give your reasons. _____ _____ _____ _____

Word Focus

luxury = A *luxury* is something we do not really need.
unintentionally = When something happens *unintentionally*, we don't mean for it to happen.

46 Food

New York City, USA

Bugs as Food

▲ worms at Thongkuean market, Chiang Mai, Thailand

I am sitting in an expensive New York restaurant and I read the menu. I can't believe my eyes! Chocolate-covered crickets. Yuck! I can also order Ant Egg Soup or Silkworm Fried Rice. And it's expensive—$25 for 5 crickets!

I don't like the idea of **eating** insects. However, in many countries insects are not **luxury** food. They are part of an everyday diet. In Thailand, open-air markets sell silkworms and grasshoppers. Movie theaters in South America sell roasted ants as snacks instead of popcorn.

I am probably eating insects without knowing it, anyway. "It's estimated that the average human eats half a kilogram of insects each year, **unintentionally**," says Lisa Monachelli, director of youth and family programs at New Canaan Nature Center in Connecticut. "For example, in the United States, chocolate can have up to 60 bits of bugs (like

---

For Your Information: Edible insects

Insects are used as food in some cultures of South America, Africa, Asia, and Australia, while in other cultures eating insects is uncommon or even taboo. Over 1,200 kinds of insects are eaten, most commonly grasshoppers, crickets, ants, tarantulas, and scorpions. In some situations, they are eaten for the nutrients they contain, and in others they are used as a condiment or snack. One problem with eating insects is that their bodies can contain a high concentration of pesticides. Today, foods containing insects (such as gourmet chocolates) can be ordered online, and there are even Web sites with recipes for cooking insects.

▲ roasted insects—Bangkok

legs and heads) per 100 grams. Tomato sauce can contain 30 fly eggs per 100 grams and peanut butter can have 30 insect bits per 100 grams."

Well, if I am eating insects anyway . . . I decide to order the chocolate covered crickets and hey, they taste good.

▲ boy eating insects

Writing

Write about your favorite food by answering the questions. Use the recipe below as a model.

- What is your favorite recipe?
- What are the ingredients?
- How do you make it?
- Do you eat it for breakfast, lunch, snack, or supper?

My favorite food is chicken pozole. It is a Mexican white-corn soup and it is delicious.

You need the following ingredients:
2 kilos chicken
½ kg canned hominy (white corn)
1 slice of onion
3 red chili peppers
1 head of garlic
1 teaspoon of cumin

Steps
1. Boil the chicken, slice of onion, and the head of garlic in 2 liters of water for 1 hour.
2. Cut the chicken into small pieces and return to the water.
2. Add the hominy, the ground red chili peppers, and the cumin. Cook for 15 minutes.
3. Serve with chopped lettuce, sliced radishes, chopped onion, cilantro, and lemon juice.

You can eat pozole at any time, but we usually eat it for supper.

▲ chicken pozole

▲ pozole ingredients

 Goal 4 | **Discuss unusual and favorite foods**

Tell a partner about your experiences eating unusual and favorite foods.

Writing

- Tell students they are going to write about their favorite dish. Go over the instructions and the model.
- Have students write their papers.
- Have students exchange papers with a partner. Ask students to mark corrections and suggestions for improvements on their partner's paper.
- If desired, have students rewrite their papers, to be collected for marking.

☑ Goal 4

- Match students with a partner and have them talk about their experiences.
- Ask the class, *Who heard something interesting?* Call on students to share what they heard.

After Reading

Have students work in small groups to prepare a poster about a traditional food in their city or country. The poster should include a description, pictures, and directions for making the food. Display the posters on the classroom walls.

Before You Watch

- Have students work with a partner to talk about the different kinds of fish, and discuss which ones are dangerous and why. Compare answers with the class.

Answers: 1. The great white shark, puffer fish, stone fish, and stingray can kill people. 2. The great white shark kills with its teeth. The others kill with poison.

While You Watch

A • Tell students they are going to watch a video about a dangerous fish. Have students watch and find which person said each sentence. Go over the sentences with the class. Play the video.

- Check answers.

Answers: 1. b, 2. c, 3. d, 4. a

B • Tell students to watch the video again and answer *true* or *false*. Have the students read the statements. Play the video.

- Check answers.

Answers: 1. F, 2. T, 3. F, 4. T, 5. T

C • Tell students to watch the video again and answer the questions. Have the students read the questions. Play the video.

- Check answers.

Answers: 1. Yes, he is. 2. Because people were dying from eating fugu. 3. in 1949, 4. The person can't breathe. 5. 30

E VIDEO JOURNAL *DANGEROUS DINNER*

Before You Watch

👥 Work with a partner. Discuss these questions.

1. Which of these fish can kill you?
2. How can they kill you?

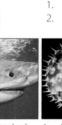

▲ great white shark   ▲ puffer fish   ▲ stone fish   ▲ sting ray   ▲ whale shark

While You Watch

A. Watch the video. Match the person with the comments.

1. Tom Cardonnam ___
2. Chef Hayashi ___
3. Hidenori Kadobayashi, Tokyo Health Department ___
4. Yuji Nagashima, Tokyo University of Fisheries ___

a. A tiger *fugu* has enough toxin to kill 30 people.
b. I can still breathe.
c. It'll be fine, don't worry.
d. About 70 percent of the poisonings happen in private homes.

B. Watch the video again. Circle **T** for *true* and **F** for *false*.

1. The puffer fish is not expensive.	T	F
2. Chef Hayashi has a license to prepare *fugu*.	T	F
3. About 30 people die every year because they eat *fugu*.	T	F
4. American General Douglas MacArthur introduced a test for *fugu* chefs.	T	F
5. Tom likes the *fugu*.	T	F

C. Answer the questions.

1. Is Tom worried about eating *fugu*?_____
2. Why did General Douglas MacArthur introduce a test for *fugu* chefs?
   _____
3. When did Chef Hayashi get his license? _____
4. How does *fugu* poison kill a person? _____
5. How many people can a tiger *fugu* kill? _____

48 Food

For Your Information: Puffer fish

Puffer fish are the second most poisonous animal in the world (only a species of frog is more toxic). There are more than 120 kinds of puffers, and they live in the sea and in marine estuaries. The skin and some internal organs contain the poison. Fishers have to wear gloves when handling puffer fish. These fish are called puffers because when danger approaches they are able to fill their bodies with more water so that they look much bigger. The poison in a puffer's body is produced from bacteria in its food, so puffers that are raised in an aquarium do not develop any toxins.

After You Watch

👥 Discuss these questions with a partner.

1. Why do you think people like to eat *fugu*?
2. Would you eat *fugu*?

Communication

👥 Read the menu. Take turns being a waiter and a customer at the Funky Food Restaurant.

Menu
Funky Food Restaurant

Ostrich Burger

Try our African Special.
Quarter pound $10
Half pound $15
Served with French fries and salad

Fugu

Prepared by our licensed chef
Small $50
Large $75

Frog Legs

Served in a cream sauce
6 legs $20
12 legs $35

▲ an ostrich

▲ a frog

After You Watch

- Match students with a partner and have them discuss the questions.
- Compare answers with the class.

Communication

- Match students with a partner. Go over the menu with them.
- Have them role-play the conversation and then change partners and switch roles to role-play again.
- Call on student pairs to present their role-plays to the class.

Teacher Tip: Errors in spoken English

Giving immediate corrections to students during group and pair work is not very effective. Students are too involved in the activity and won't retain the correct form.

Instead:

- Make notes on errors frequently heard during the activity, and give a mini-lesson after the activity contrasting the error and the correct form.
- Listen to different groups in rotation, write down important errors, and give the list to the group members to correct.
- Note sentences with errors during the activity, and write them on the board. Together, the class identifies the errors and corrects them.
- For all of these activities, it's best NOT to include the name of the student who made the error. Students generally recognize their own sentences even without names.

- Introduce the theme of the unit. Ask students how many sports they can name in English and write the names on the board.

- Direct students' attention to the pictures. With the class, look at each picture in turn and have students name things they see in each one.

- Have students work with partners to name the sports.

- Check answers.

Answers: (from left to right)
rock climbing, soccer, basketball, snowboarding

- Have students tell their partners about sports they play.

- Compare answers with the class, compiling a list on the board.

- Follow up with these questions, asking them orally or writing them on the board for students to answer in pairs:

  1. *Which sports do you watch?*
  2. *Which sports events do you go to?*

- Go over the Unit Goals with the class, explaining and/or translating as necessary.

SPORTS

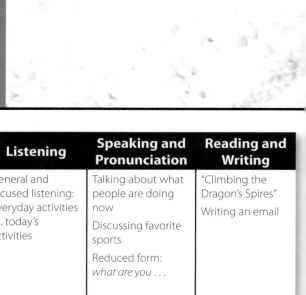

1. What are these sports?

2. What sports do you do? What sports would you like to do?

UNIT GOALS

Talk about activities happening now
Compare everyday and present-time activities
Talk about favorite sports
Discuss adventure holidays

50

Unit Goals	Grammar	Vocabulary	Listening	Speaking and Pronunciation	Reading and Writing
• Talk about activities happening now • Compare everyday and present-time activities • Talk about favorite sports • Discuss adventure holidays	Present continuous tense ***Are*** you ***studying*** right now? Stative verbs I ***like*** to be outdoors.	Doing sports Team sports Individual sports	General and focused listening: everyday activities vs. today's activities	Talking about what people are doing now Discussing favorite sports Reduced form: *what are you . . .*	"Climbing the Dragon's Spires" Writing an email

UNIT 5

Unit Theme Overview

• The world of sports includes everything from children kicking a soccer ball behind their house to the parade of top-notch athletes entering the stadium at the opening ceremony of the Olympic Games. Sports may be played individually or on teams, indoors or outdoors, by professionals or amateurs. This unit covers a broad variety of sports and invites students to consider the ones they enjoy most and why they enjoy them.

• Students begin by practicing use of the present continuous tense to talk about activities in progress and then learn to contrast these activities with routines and habits. They discuss their preferences in sports and learn to use stative verbs for feelings and mental states. They also read and write about unusual sports and discuss which ones they would like to try.

51

Talk about Activities Happening Now

Vocabulary

A • Have students work individually to read the conversations and label the photos.

• Check answers.

Answers: 1. taking a break, 2. swimming, 3. playing soccer, 4. rappelling, 5. lifting weights, 6. jogging, 7. climbing,

• (If necessary, explain that in rappelling, you go down, and in climbing, you go up.)

B • Have students work with a partner to read the descriptions and write the activities.

• Check answers.

Answers: 1. lifting weights, 2. swimming, 3. playing soccer, 4. jogging, 5. studying, 6. taking a break

A **GOAL 1** **TALK ABOUT ACTIVITIES HAPPENING NOW**

Vocabulary

A. Read the conversations. Use the words in **blue** to label the photos.

Anna is studying for a test. She is bored and tired, so she is calling some friends.

Anna: Bridget: Anna:	Hi! What's up? What are you doing? We're at the beach, Kenny's **swimming**, and the twins are **playing soccer**. How about you? What are you doing? I'm working! Grrrr!
Anna: Jill: Anna:	Hi Jill. What are you doing? I'm at the Extreme Sports Center with Alan and Pete. They're **climbing** and I'm **rappelling**. It's really cool. Why don't you come? I can't. I'm studying for the test.
Anna: Edith: Anna:	Hi Edith. What's happening? Hi. I'm at the gym. I'm **taking a break**. Mary and Jill are here too. Mary is **lifting weights** and Jill is **jogging**. What are you doing? I'm studying. Boring!!!

1. _____ 2. _____ 3. _____ 4. _____

5. _____ 6. _____ 7. _____

B. Take turns. Read the clues to a partner. Guess the activity. Write your answer.

1. You do this in the gym. _____
2. You do this in a swimming pool. _____
3. You play this with a ball. _____
4. It is like running. _____
5. You do this at home or in the library. _____
6. You do this when you are tired. _____

52   Sports

Word Bank: Adventure sports

scuba diving	hiking
kayaking	bungee jumping
whitewater rafting	skydiving
mountain biking (bicycling)	paragliding

Grammar: Present continuous tense

The present continuous tense is used for actions that are in progress at the time of speaking and actions that are not completed. It contrasts with the simple present tense, which is used to talk about routines and things that are always true. It is formed with *be* and the *-ing* form of the verb.

Grammar: Present continuous tense

Present continuous tense

Statement	I **am playing** soccer	right now.
Negative	They **are not taking** a break	at the moment. now.
Yes/no question	**Are** you **studying**	right now?
Wh- question	What **are** you **doing**	at the moment? now?

*We use the present continuous tense to talk about things that are happening at the moment.

A. Complete the email. Remember to use the present continuous tense.

⊗⊖⊕ Mail

📝 New   🖨 Print   🗑 Delete   ▭ Move   ✓ Spell Check

TO:
CC:
BC:
Subject: (no subject)

What's up? Ramon and I are at the Cybercafe. Ramon _____ computer games as usual of course. I _____ some research for my project. It's a bit boring, so I _____ some emails.

Salvador

Send ↵   Close

B. Ask a partner these questions.

What is Ramon doing?
What is Salvador doing?

Conversation

Track 1-20

A. Look at the picture and listen to the conversation. What are the twins doing?

Mom:	Hey, it's quiet today. Where are the kids?
Dad:	Well, Mario's playing basketball in the yard.
Mom:	What's Betty doing?
Dad:	She's swimming in the pool.
Mom:	And the twins? What are they doing?
Dad:	Uhh. I don't know.
Mom:	Hey, you two. What are you doing?
Twins:	We're playing soccer.

B. Practice the conversation with a partner. Switch roles and practice it again.

C. Make a new conversation using other sports.

 Goal 1   **Talk about activities happening now**

Talk to a partner. What are your family and friends doing now?

Grammar: Present continuous tense

- Present/review the present continuous tense. Tell the class, *Right now, I'm standing. I'm talking. What are you doing?* Elicit, *I'm studying/listening/writing,* and so on. Point to students and ask, *What is he/she doing? What are they doing?*
- Go over the information in the box.

A • Have students work individually to complete the email.
- Check answers.

Answers: is playing, am doing, am sending/writing

B • Have students work with a partner to ask and answer the questions.

Conversation

A • Have students close their books. Write the question on the board: *What are the twins doing?*
- Play the recording. **(CD1 T20)**
- Check answers.

Answer: They're playing soccer.

B • Play or read the conversation again for the class to repeat.
- Practice the conversation with the class in chorus.
- Have students practice the conversation with a partner and then switch roles and practice it again.

C • Have students work with the same partner to make a new conversation about the people, with different sports.
- Call on student pairs to present their conversations to the class.

☑ Goal 1

- Have students tell their partners about the activities their friends and family members are doing now, using the present continuous tense.
- Call on students to say a sentence for the class.

Grammar Practice: Present continuous tense

Mime an action and tell the class to guess what you're doing, using the present continuous tense: *You're playing tennis. You're watching a scary movie.* Tell the class when they have guessed correctly. Divide the class into pairs and have them plan a similar mime for the class to guess. When all pairs are ready, have one student from each pair come to the front of the class and present their mime for the class to guess. At the end of the activity, talk about any funny/difficult/surprising mimes.

Compare Everyday and Present-Time Activities

Listening

A • Tell students they are going to hear three telephone conversations. They should listen the first time to find what the people are talking about.

• Play the recording one or more times. **(CD1 T21)**

• Check answers.

Answer: c

B • Go over the activities in the pictures. Tell students to listen again to find what the people in the conversations usually do.

• Play the recording one or more times. **(CD1 T21)**

• Check answers.

Answers: 1. go to the movies, Fridays, 2. studies, evening, 3. goes to the ball game, Sundays

C • Tell students to listen again to the conversations and write what the people are doing today.

• Play the recording one or more times. **(CD1 T21)**

• Check answers.

Answers: 1. ice skating, 2. playing basketball, 3. fixing the roof

---

Listening

Track 1-21

A. Listen to the phone calls. The people are talking about _____.

a. what they usually do
b. what they are doing at the moment
c. both

▲ go ice skating   ▲ go to the movies   ▲ study

▲ play basketball   ▲ go to a ball game   ▲ fix the roof

Track 1-21

B. Listen again. What do these people usually do? When?

1. Allan and Karen always _____ on _____.
2. Dave always _____ in the _____.
3. Robin always _____ on _____.

Track 1-21

C. Listen again. What are they doing today?

1. Allan and Karen _____ .
2. Dave _____ .
3. Robin _____ .

Word Bank: Sports words

team	player
goal	uniform
point	scoreboard
match	referee
champion	league
score	coach

Pronunciation: Reduced form of *what are you . . .*

Track 1-22

A. Listen to the full form and the reduced form.

What are you doing?

What are you eating?

Track 1-23

B. Listen and check (✓) the correct column.

	Full form	Reduced form
1. What are you reading?		
2. What are you thinking?		
3. What are you playing?		
4. What are you cooking?		
5. What are you writing?		

Track 1-23

C. Listen again. Repeat the sentences.

Communication

One member of the group mimes a sport. The other members of the group try to guess the sport.

Are you playing basketball?

No, I'm not.

Are you rock climbing?

Yes, I am.

✓ **Goal 2** **Compare everyday and present-time activities**

Work with a partner. What are you doing now? What do you do at this time on a Sunday?

Pronunciation

A • Review the idea that when we speak quickly in English, some words and sounds are "reduced"—pronounced differently.

• Tell students to listen to the full and reduced forms of the expression. Play the recording. **(CD1 T22)**

B • Tell students to listen to the sentences and mark the pronunciation they hear. Play the recording one or more times. **(CD1 T23)**

• Check answers.

Answers: 1. full, 2. reduced, 3. reduced, 4. full, 5. reduced

C • Play the recording again for students to repeat the sentences. **(CD1 T23)** Then have them practice with partners, saying each sentence with the full form and then the reduced form.

• Call on students to read the sentences to the class in both forms.

Communication

• Divide the class into groups of five or six students. Explain the activity: One student mimes an activity, and the others try to guess what he or she is doing using the present continuous tense. Model for the class by miming and having them guess.

• Walk around the class helping groups with their guesses.

• Have one person from each group come up to the front of the class to mime an activity for the class to guess.

✓ Goal 2

• Match students with a partner and have them talk about their present and Sunday activities.

• Call on students to tell the class about their activities.

Expansion Activity

Collect magazine photos of people doing leisure activities, one for each group of four to five students. Put students in groups and give each group a picture. Tell students that the person in the picture is on vacation. Have a "secretary" in each group write down sentences about what the person is doing.

Then have groups imagine an interesting or unusual job for the person in the picture (for example, spy, movie star, race car driver). What does he or she usually do at work? The "secretary" writes down the group's answers on the other side of the paper. (Spy: *He travels to foreign countries. He looks for secrets.*)

Talk about Favorite Sports

Language Expansion

A • Introduce the idea of team sports (sports you play as part of a group that tries to win) and individual sports (sports where one person tries to win). Elicit examples from the class. Then talk about indoor and outdoor sports and elicit examples.

• Go over the names of sports in the box. Have students work individually to list the sports in the correct section of the chart.

• Check answers.

Answers: Indoor team: volleyball, ice hockey; Outdoor team: baseball, football; Indoor individual: diving, gymnastics; Outdoor individual: golf, skateboarding (note that there may be some differences in where these sports are played in different countries—for instance, ice hockey can be an outdoor sport in Canada, but not in Brazil)

B • Divide the class into groups of three to four students and have them think of another way to categorize sports—for example, expensive sports or dangerous sports. They should make a list of sports in that category.

• Have each group read its list to the class, without saying the name of the category. The class must then guess the category.

C • Go over the explanation in the Word Focus box.

• With the class (or in groups) have students list more names of sports in the appropriate categories.

Possible answers: play volleyball, basketball, ice hockey; **go** skiing, sailing, skateboarding

Language Expansion: Team sports and individual sports

A. Write the following sports in the correct box according to the categories.

| baseball   golf   gymnastics   football   volleyball   ice hockey   diving   skateboarding |

	INDOOR ⬇	OUTDOOR ⬇
TEAM ➡	1. _____ 2. _____	1. _____ 2. _____
INDIVIDUAL ➡	1. _____ 2. _____	1. _____ 2. _____

Word Focus

We use *play* for team games—for example *I **play** soccer.*
We use *go* for individual sports—for example *I **go** swimming.*

56   Sports

B. Work in groups. Think of other ways to categorize sports. Prepare a chart with your new groups of sports. Have the other groups guess the names of your categories.

C. Write the names of more sports.

play	soccer,
go	swimming,

Word Bank: More sports

tennis
skiing
bowling
ping-pong
 (table tennis)
track and field
 (running and
 jumping)

racquetball
wrestling
handball
archery
horse racing
horseback riding
boxing
cycling

Grammar: Stative verbs

Stative verbs are verbs for feelings, senses, emotions, and mental states. They do not describe *actions* that take place, but *states*. (Some books refer to them as *nonaction verbs*.) They are not used in the continuous tenses (present continuous, past continuous, etc.) except with certain special meanings: *Dr. Diaz is seeing a patient now.* (= meeting with) *She's having problems with her computer.* (= experiencing)

boat in a *floating village*. It isn't really a village because all the people live on boats. They move from one place to another. Nguyen catches **squid**, **shrimps**, and **crab**. He sells them to buy fresh water, vegetables, fuel, and clothes for his family.

So, what am I doing here? I am spending my vacation doing what I enjoy— rock climbing. Nguyen thinks I am crazy. But to me rock climbing is like dancing—dangerous dancing. I need some danger in my life.

B. Reread the article. Underline all the stative verbs.

C. Circle **T** for *true* or **F** for *false*.

1. Lynn is not a very good climber.   T   F
2. Nguyen Mien doesn't understand why Lynn is climbing the cliffs.   T   F
3. Nguyen Mien lives on his boat.   T   F
4. Lynn prefers dancing to rock climbing.   T   F
5. Nguyen Mien buys fresh water, vegetables, and fuel.   T   F

Writing

Read John's email. Then write a similar email about another sport.

✓ Goal 4	**Discuss adventure holidays**

Talk with a partner. What type of adventure holiday would you like to take? Why?

B • Tell students to reread the article and underline the stative verbs.
 • Check answers.

Answers: think, need

C • Tell students to read the article one more time to mark the statements *true* or *false*.
 • Check answers.

Answers: 1. F, 2. T, 3. T, 4. F, 5. T

Writing

 • Go over the email with the class.
 • Tell students to imagine a sport they would like to try and write their own emails.
 • Have students exchange papers with a partner. Ask students to mark corrections and suggestions for improvements on their partner's paper.
 • If desired, have students rewrite their papers, to be collected for marking.

✓ Goal 4

 • Talk about different kinds of adventure sports with the class, such as mountain climbing, scuba diving, and cycling. Write a list on the board.
 • Have students tell a partner about an adventure holiday that they would like to try.

After Reading

Have students work in small groups to put together a short oral report about another adventure sport. They should give information about who does the sport, what they do, and where they do it. Have groups present their reports to the class.

Video Journal

Before You Watch

A • Have students work with a partner to talk about the sports in the pictures and which ones they would like to try.

• Compare answers with the class.

B • Have students work individually to match the columns.

• Check answers.

Answers: 1. f, 2. e, 3. a, 4. b, 5. d, 6. c

E VIDEO JOURNAL *CHEESE-ROLLING RACES*

Before You Watch

👥 **A.** Which of these unusual sports would you like to try? Why?

▲ octopush

▲ sumo wrestling

▲ sepak takraw

▲ cheese rolling

B. Match the words with the definitions.

1. cheese ____
2. prize ____
3. crazy ____
4. injury ____
5. a race ____
6. spectator ____

a. unusual, mad
b. when you hurt yourself
c. a person who watches a race
d. a competition
e. something you get when you win a race
f. a food made from milk

For Your Information: Unusual sports

Sepak takraw is popular in Southeast Asia. Two teams of three players use their feet, knees, and heads to send a ball over a net.

Sumo wrestling is a sport from Japan. Two wrestlers stand inside a circle and try to force each other to step outside of the ring.

Octopush is an underwater form of hockey. Two teams try to push a puck across the bottom of a swimming pool into a goal.

Cheese rolling is a sport that was invented in one town in England. A big round cheese rolls down a hill, and people run down the hill after it.

While You Watch

A. Fill in the blanks. Use the words in the box. Watch the video and check your answers.

injuries	cold	spectators	winner

1. The first _____ of the day is Craig Brown, a pub worker.
2. One year, one of the cheeses rolled down the hill and went into the _____.
3. It's not just spectators who get injured: competitors do as well, especially when it's _____ or there hasn't been much rain.
4. Cheese-rolling spectator: "It's when the ground is really hard . . . that's when the _____ are going to happen."

B. Watch the video again. Circle **T** for *true* and **F** for *false*.

1. Cheese rolling is an indoor sport.   T   F
2. The prize is a wheel of cheese.   T   F
3. The spectators sometimes get injured.   T   F
4. The cheese-rolling race is not dangerous.   T   F
5. Only British people can enter the cheese-rolling race.   T   F

After You Watch

Discuss these questions with a partner.

1. Why do you think people join the cheese-rolling race?
2. Do they want the cheese?
3. Do they want to have fun?
4. Are they crazy?

Communication

Role-play the following situation.

Student A is a competitor in the cheese-rolling race.

Student B interviews him/her.

Where do you come from?

Do you come every year?

Why do you come?

While You Watch

A • Tell students to watch the video the first time and fill in the spaces. Play the video.
  • Play the video again for students to check their answers.
  • Check answers.

Answers: 1. winner, 2. spectators, 3. cold, 4. injuries

B • Tell students to watch the video again and mark the statements *true* or *false*. Have the students read the statements. Play the video.
  • Check answers.

Answers: 1. F, 2. T, 3. T, 4. F, 5. F

After You Watch

  • Match students with a partner and have them talk about the questions.
  • Compare answers with the class.

Communication

  • Match students with a partner and assign a role to each student. Have them role-play an interview for television.
  • Call on students to present their role-plays to the class.

Teacher Tip: Helping groups finish at the same time

A common situation in group work is that one group completes the task long before the others—or long after. Here are some approaches you can take with a group that finishes too quickly:

• Check to be sure they have understood the task and completed all parts correctly.
• Give them additional questions.
• Have the group prepare a written report of their ideas, answers, etc.

With a group that finishes too slowly:

• Tell them to omit parts of the task.
• Take over briefly as discussion leader to help them move along.
• Set a time limit. Tell them, *I'll ask for your answers in five minutes.*

- Introduce the theme of the unit. Call on students to give the name of a destination they have visited.

- Direct students' attention to the pictures. With the class, look at each picture in turn. Give/elicit the names of the places (left to right: the Taj Mahal, India; Disney World, United States; the Pyramids of Giza, Egypt; Machu Picchu, Peru).

- Have students work with a partner to talk about their opinions on travel.

- Compare answers with the class.

- Follow up with these questions, asking them orally or writing them on the board for students to answer in pairs:

  1. *Which place in the pictures do you want to go to?*

  2. *Why?*

- Go over the Unit Goals with the class, explaining and/or translating as necessary.

DESTINATIONS

1. Do you know the names of these places? Where are they?

2. Do you enjoy traveling? Why?

UNIT GOALS

Talk about past vacation trips
Exchange information about vacations
Use *was/were* to describe a personal experience
Talk about a discovery from the past

62

Unit Goals	Grammar	Vocabulary	Listening	Speaking and Pronunciation	Reading and Writing
• Talk about past vacation trips • Exchange information about vacations • Use *was/were* to describe a personal experience • Talk about a discovery from the past	Simple past tense I **didn't have** a reservation *yesterday*. Simple past tense: *to be* I **was** exhausted.	Travel activities Emphatic adjectives	Listening for general understanding: a vacation	Comparing vacations Describing personal experiences Sounds of *-ed* endings	"The City of Machu Picchu, the Cradle of the Inca Empire" Writing a postcard

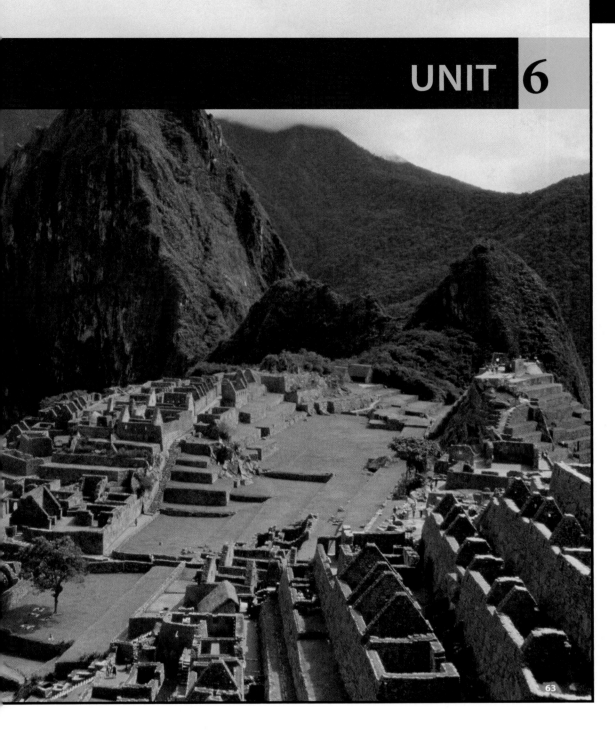

UNIT 6

Unit Theme Overview

- The World Tourism Organization compiles an annual ranking of the world's most popular tourist destinations. In 2007, the top country was France, with 82 million international visitors, followed by Spain (59 million), the United States (56 million), China (55 million), Italy (44 million), the United Kingdom (31 million), Germany (24 million), Ukraine (23 million), Turkey (22 million), and Mexico (21 million). That's a lot of travelers and a lot of fascinating cross-cultural experiences!

- In this unit, students practice the form, meaning, and uses of the simple past tense in the context of describing past travel experiences. They talk about their own vacation trips and those of others and learn about an explorer in the past who discovered what is today one of the world's great travel destinations—the amazing ruins of Machu Picchu in Peru.

Talk about Past Vacation Trips

Vocabulary

A • Ask the class, *What are these people doing?* (taking a vacation). Then have students work individually to number the phrases to correspond with the photos.

• Check answers.

Answers: 1. take photos, 2. pack/unpack suitcases, 3. take a bus tour, 4. check into the hotel, 5. visit places of interest, 6. rent a car, 7. buy souvenirs

• Explain that the prefix *un-* means *not* or *the opposite*. If you unpack a suitcase, you take out the things that you packed.

B • Have students work individually to categorize the activities.

• Check answers.

Answers: Before: pack suitcases; During: visit places of interest, take a bus tour, check into the hotel, rent a car, take photos, buy souvenirs

C • Match students with a partner. Have them take turns talking about their usual activities before and during a vacation.

• Compare answers with the class.

Grammar

• Introduce/review the simple past tense. Say, *Let's talk about yesterday. What did we do in class yesterday? We studied _____. We practiced _____. We learned _____.* Elicit more examples from the class with regular verbs like *talked, listened, checked*, and so forth.

• Go over the information in the chart. Point out that there are two kinds of verbs. The simple past tense of regular verbs is formed by adding *-ed*. Most verbs are regular. Some verbs are irregular. They don't use *-ed* to form the simple past tense. They are all different. Students have to memorize them. Go over the irregular verbs in the chart.

Vocabulary

A. Match the photos to an activity from the box.

visit places of interest ___	take photos___
take a bus tour ___	pack/unpack suitcases ___
check into the hotel ___	buy souvenirs ___
rent a car ___	

1.   2.   3.

4.   5.   6.   7.

B. Which of these do you do *before* and *during* your vacation?

Before _____
During _____

C. Take turns. Tell a partner what other things you do before or during a vacation.

Grammar: Simple past tense

Simple past tense	
Statement	He **rented** a car on his trip to Europe last November.
Negative	I **didn't have** a reservation yesterday.
Yes/no questions	**Did they go** to Asia last year?
Short answers	Yes, they **did**. No, they **didn't**.
Information questions	Where **did** you **go** for your vacation last year?

*We use the simple past tense to talk about completed actions or conditions.

*Some verbs are regular in the simple past tense. They have an *-ed* ending.		*Some verbs are irregular in the simple past tense. They have many different forms.	
learn — learned	travel — traveled	agree — agreed	tell — told
arrive — arrived	want — wanted	buy — bought	leave — left
play — played	need — needed	fly — flew	say — said
ask — asked	help — helped	know — knew	see — saw
		go — went	take — took

Word Bank: Vacation activities

Before:
make train/bus
  reservations
exchange money
buy a map
get vaccinations

During:
use a phrasebook
go to the tourist
  information
  office
take a walking tour
try local foods
go for a boat ride

Grammar: Simple past tense

The simple past tense is used to talk about actions that were completed in the past. Irregular verbs are those that don't follow the rule in forming the past tense and so must be learned individually. Practicing (with flash cards) is a good way to do this. Tell students that if they are unsure about a verb, dictionaries usually have a list of irregular verbs in the back.

A. Complete the sentences. Use the simple past tense form of the verb in parentheses.

1. Last year, we _____ (visit) Machu Picchu in Peru.
2. We _____ (not, like) the hotel.
3. We _____ (buy) some interesting souvenirs.
4. When _____ (you arrive) at the airport?
5. We _____ (go) to Paris and Rome last year.

B. Unscramble the words to write questions and answers.

1. **Q:** to Europe Did you go year? last

   _____

2. **A:** to we No, went America.

   _____

3. **Q:** did buy you those Where souvenirs?

   _____

4. **A:** them bought in We Egypt.

   _____

Real Language

You can use the following expressions to show interest.

Informal ──────────────────▶ Formal

Wow!   Sounds cool.   Really!   That's interesting.

Conversation

A. Listen to the conversation. How long did Maria stay in Cuzco?

Track 1-25

Christine:	Hey, I love that <u>poncho</u>, Maria. Where did you buy it?
Maria:	I bought it in <u>Peru.</u> We went to Peru for our vacation last year.
Christine:	Wow! Sounds cool. Did you go to <u>Lima</u>?
Maria:	No, we flew directly to <u>Cuzco</u>. We wanted to see the <u>Inca ruins at Machu Picchu.</u>
Christine:	How long did you stay there?
Maria:	We stayed for <u>five nights</u>.
Christine:	Lucky you!

B. Practice the conversation with a partner. Switch roles and practice it again.

C. Practice the conversation again and change the underlined words using the information in the chart.

Country	Italy	United States	Great Britain
Capital	Rome	Washington, DC	London
Other City	Venice	Orlando	Edinburgh
Place of special interest	Doge's Palace	Disneyland	The Castle

✓ Goal 1   Talk about past vacation trips

Take turns with a partner telling about a vacation you took.

Grammar Practice: Simple past tense

Prepare a list of students' names listed in random order on a piece of paper for your own use. Tell students to write three sentences in the past tense about things they did yesterday. Then play a memory game. Call on the first student on your list to say a sentence: *Yesterday I bought a new coat.* The second student repeats that sentence and then adds his/her own sentence: *Yesterday Lee bought a new coat, and I read the newspaper.* Each student continues in turn until one makes a mistake. Then that student starts over with a new sentence. Play until all students have had several turns. Ask, *Who remembered the most sentences?*

A • Have students work individually to complete the sentences.

• Check answers.

Answers: 1. visited, 2. didn't like, 3. bought, 4. did you arrive, 5. went

B • Have students work individually to unscramble the sentences. Check answers.

Answers: 1. Did you go to Europe last year? 2. No, we went to America. 3. Where did you buy those souvenirs? 4. We bought them in Egypt.

• Have students read the questions and answers out loud with a partner.

Conversation

• Go over the expressions in the Real Language box, explaining if necessary the concepts of formal (used with people you don't know well) and informal (used with family and friends).

A • Have students close their books. Write the question on the board: *How long did Maria stay in Cuzco?*

• Play the recording. **(CD1 T25)**

• Check answers.

Answer: five nights

B • Play or read the conversation again for the class to repeat.

• Practice the conversation with the class in chorus.

• Have students practice the conversation with a partner and then switch roles and practice it again.

C • Tell students to make three new conversations using the information in the chart. Go over the information with the class. Then have them practice the conversations.

• Call on student pairs to present a conversation to the class.

✓ Goal 1

• Have students work with the same partner to talk about a vacation or other trip they took. Remind them to use the simple past tense.

Exchange Information about Vacations

Listening

- Introduce the topic. Ask, *Do you tell your friends about your vacations? Do you like to hear about their vacations? Why, or why not?*

A • Tell students they are going to hear a conversation between two friends. Have them read the questions.

- Play the recording one or more times. **(CD1 T26)**

- Check answers.

Answers: 1. a, 2. b

B • Tell students to listen again to answer *true* or *false*. Go over the statements.

- Play the recording one or more times. **(CD1 T26)**

- Check answers.

Answers: 1. F, 2. F, 3. T, 4. F, 5. T

Pronunciation

A • Explain to students that the *-ed* ending on regular past-tense verbs has different pronunciation in different words. Tell students to listen to the recording and check the sound they hear. Play the recording one or more times. **(CD1 T27)**

- Check answers.

Answers: rented /id/, liked /t/

B • Tell students to listen to the recording and check the sound they hear. Play the recording one or more times. **(CD1 T28)**

- Check answers.

Answers: checked /t/, packed /t/, traveled /d/, stayed /d/

C • Tell students to listen again and repeat the sentences. Play the recording. **(CD1 T28)**

| **B** | **GOAL 2** | **EXCHANGE INFORMATION ABOUT VACATIONS** |

Listening

A. Listen to the conversation. Circle the correct answer.

Track 1-26
1. Glenn is telling his friend about _____.
   a. his vacation
   b. his hobby
   c. his work
2. His friend is _____.
   a. bored
   b. interested
   c. tired

B. Listen again. Circle **T** for *true* or **F** for *false*.

Track 1-26
		T	F
1.	Glenn went to Oklahoma.	T	F
2.	He visited five theme parks.	T	F
3.	He didn't like Sea World.	T	F
4.	He went to the Harry Potter exhibition.	T	F
5.	He visited Islands of Adventure.	T	F

Pronunciation: Sounds of *-ed* endings

A. Listen. Check the correct boxes. Then listen again and repeat.

Track 1-27
	/d/	/t/	/id/
arrived	✓		
packed		✓	
visited			✓
rented			
liked			

B. Listen to the sentences and check the pronunciation of the *-ed* ending.

Track 1-28
	/d/	/t/	/id/
We **checked** into the hotel.			
I **packed** my bags.			
He **traveled** to Europe.			
They **stayed** at an expensive hotel.			

C. Listen again and repeat the sentences.

Track 1-28

66 Destinations

For Your Information: Orlando

Orlando is a city in Florida in the United States and is a major tourist destination. It has an estimated 52 million tourists a year. They come to Walt Disney World, Sea World, Universal Studios Florida, a large number of golf courses, and one of the biggest shopping malls in the United States. The city also has several important art museums. The population is around 2 million.

Communication

 Read your travel blog. Take turns with a partner asking each other questions about your vacation.

> Where did you go next?
>
> What did you do?
>
> How long did you stay there?
>
> Did you enjoy it? Why?

STUDENT A

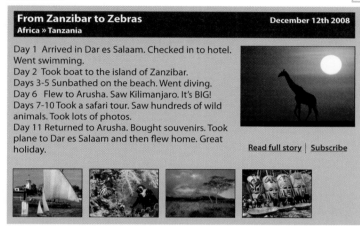

From Zanzibar to Zebras   December 12th 2008
Africa » Tanzania

Day 1 Arrived in Dar es Salaam. Checked in to hotel. Went swimming.
Day 2 Took boat to the island of Zanzibar.
Days 3-5 Sunbathed on the beach. Went diving.
Day 6 Flew to Arusha. Saw Kilimanjaro. It's BIG!
Days 7-10 Took a safari tour. Saw hundreds of wild animals. Took lots of photos.
Day 11 Returned to Arusha. Bought souvenirs. Took plane to Dar es Salaam and then flew home. Great holiday.

Read full story | Subscribe

STUDENT B

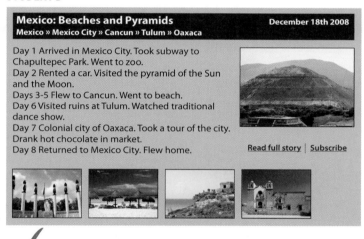

Mexico: Beaches and Pyramids   December 18th 2008
Mexico » Mexico City » Cancun » Tulum » Oaxaca

Day 1 Arrived in Mexico City. Took subway to Chapultepec Park. Went to zoo.
Day 2 Rented a car. Visited the pyramid of the Sun and the Moon.
Days 3-5 Flew to Cancun. Went to beach.
Day 6 Visited ruins at Tulum. Watched traditional dance show.
Day 7 Colonial city of Oaxaca. Took a tour of the city. Drank hot chocolate in market.
Day 8 Returned to Mexico City. Flew home.

Read full story | Subscribe

✓ **Goal 2** **Exchange information about vacations**

Join another pair of students. Tell them about your partner's vacation from the activity above.

Communication

- Introduce the idea of blogs—Web sites where people write about their experiences and ideas and post pictures for other people to see. Ask if students ever read/write blogs. What are some popular topics? (travel, politics, family life)

- Tell students they are going to read a travel blog about a vacation they took and talk to a partner about it.

- Assign a role to each student. Have them look over "their" blog. Answer any questions about vocabulary.

- Go over the questions at the top of the page.

- Have students take turns asking about each other's vacation. Walk around the class helping as needed.

✓ Goal 2

- Combine student pairs into groups of four and have each student tell the group what they heard from their partner in the previous activity.

- Finish with a whole-class discussion. Which trip would students like to take? Why?

Expansion Activity

Tell students to imagine they are foreign tourists on vacation in their country. Have them write a short email to a friend about what they did on one day of their trip. Have students read their emails to a partner. Then call on students to read their emails to the class.

Use *Was/Were* to Describe a Personal Experience

Language Expansion

- Introduce the idea of emphatic adjectives—"strong" adjectives. For example, *excellent* means *very, very good*. Go over the adjectives in the chart.

A • Have students work individually to describe each picture with adjectives.
- Check answers.

Answers: 1. awful/terrible/horrible, 2. exhausting, 3. filthy, 4. spotless, 5. enormous/huge

B • Have students work individually to complete the sentences.
- Check answers.

Answers: exhausting, magnificent, spotless, enormous

Grammar

- Go over the information in the box about the simple past tense of *to be* (*was* and *were*). Elicit more examples from the class. Ask, *How was your day yesterday?* (It was *good/bad/boring/fun*, etc.) How were your English classes last year? (*They were easy/ interesting/hard*, etc.)

Language Expansion: Emphatic adjectives

Adjectives	Emphatic adjectives
good/nice	excellent
	outstanding
	magnificent
	amazing
bad	awful
	terrible
	horrible
interesting	fascinating
tiring	exhausting
dirty	filthy
clean	spotless
big	enormous
	huge

A. Write an emphatic adjective below each picture.

_____ _____ _____ _____ _____

B. Use emphatic adjectives to complete the text.

We had an _____ vacation. We visited six European countries in six days. My favorite country was Italy. Rome is a _____ city. There is so much to see: museums, churches, ruins. We stayed in a _____ hotel. Everything about it was perfect. It had an _____ swimming pool and very friendly people.

Grammar: Simple past tense of *to be*

Simple past tense of *to be*	
Statement	I **was** exhausted.
Negative	The food **wasn't** great.
Information questions	Why **was** your vacation awful?
Yes/No Questions	**Were** they tired?
Short answers	No, they **weren't**.

Word Bank: Emphatic adjectives

hungry/starving	cold/freezing
surprised/	afraid/terrified
astonished	sad/miserable
hot/boiling	happy/delighted

Grammar: Simple past tense of *to be*

Was and *were* are used for states and situations in the past.

Yes/no questions are formed by inverting subject and verb:
He was happy. Was he happy?

Wh- questions are formed by adding the *Wh-* word
  to inverted subject and verb:
He was sad. Why/When was he sad?

A. Match the questions and the answers.

1. Were you tired? ___
2. Where were they? ___
3. Was the weather good? ___
4. Was he late? ___
5. Were the rooms clean? ___

a. No, he wasn't. He was on time.
b. They were in Peru.
c. No, they weren't. They were filthy.
d. Yes, I was. I was exhausted.
e. Yes, it was.

B. Complete the sentences with *was* or *were*.

1. We didn't enjoy our vacation. The weather _____ very bad.
2. How _____ the food?
3. _____ you tired when you got home?
4. I _____ really interested in the ruins. They were boring.
5. _____ the hotel clean?

Conversation

 A. Listen to the conversation. What was good about the vacation?

Track 1-29

Gill: How was your vacation?
Mike: It was terrible.
Gill: Why? What happened?
Mike: Well, first of all the weather was <u>bad</u>. It rained nonstop for two weeks.
Gill: Oh, no.
Mike: And the hotel was <u>dirty</u>. It was full of cockroaches.
Gill: Yuck! And how was the food?
Mike: Actually, the food was <u>good</u>.
Gill: Well, at least you enjoyed something.
Mike: Not really. I had a bad stomach and couldn't eat. Some vacation!

B. Practice the conversation with a partner. Switch roles and practice it again.

C. Practice again and change the underlined adjectives with emphatic adjectives.

 Goal 3 | **Use *was/were* to describe a personal experience**

Tell a partner about a good or bad experience you had.

> The weather was awful.

> The food was excellent.

A • Have students work individually to match the columns.
• Check answers.

Answers: 1. d, 2. b, 3. e, 4. a, 5. c
• Have students read the questions and answers with a partner.

B • Have students work individually to fill in *was* or *were*.
• Check answers.

Answers: 1. was, 2. was, 3. Were, 4. wasn't, 5. Was

Conversation

A • Have students close their books. Write the question on the board: *What was good about the vacation?*
• Play the recording. **(CD1 T29)**
• Check answers.

Answer: the food

B • Play or read the conversation again for the class to repeat.
• Practice the conversation with the class in chorus.
• Have students practice the conversation with a partner and then switch roles and practice it again.

C • Have student pairs practice again, substituting emphatic adjectives for the underlined words.

☑ **Goal 3**
• Match students with a partner and tell each student to think about a very good or very bad experience in the past.
• Have students take turns telling about their experiences.
• Call on students to tell you something interesting they heard from their partner.

Grammar Practice: Simple past tense of *to be*

Write these sentence stems on the board and have students copy them on paper:

1. _____ *was born in another city.*
2. _____ *was very busy yesterday.*
3. _____ *wasn't home last night.*
4. _____ *was absent from class last week.*

Add other sentence stems relevant to your class.

Have students stand up with paper and pencil and walk around the class asking questions with *Were you _____?* and filling in classmates' names. Have them sit down when they have filled in all the spaces. Finish with a whole-class discussion of interesting answers.

Talk about a Discovery from the Past

A • Introduce the topic of the reading. Direct students' attention to the picture. Ask if they think he is living now, or if he lived a long time ago. Talk about what he is doing in the picture.

• Point out the vocabulary that is defined in the picture dictionary illustration.

B • Have students read the article to check their ideas. Tell them to circle any words they don't understand.

• Go over the article with the class, answering any questions from the students about vocabulary.

Additional words:

ancient = very old, **modern** = new, **journey** = trip; **offer** = say you will do something; **gourd** = a plant used as a container; **shade** = not sunny; **agreeable** = nice.

• Have students read the article again to find the emphatic adjectives.

• Check answers.

Answers: Paragraph 1: amazing, Paragraph 2: exhausting, magnificent, Paragraph 3: amazing, Paragraph 4: outstanding, enormous

C • Have students read the article again to find the answers.

• Check answers.

Answers: 1. no, 2. 50 cents per day, 3. no, 4. in a little grass hut, 5. No one knows.

Reading

A. Look at the photo of Hiram Bingham. Is he on vacation? What is he doing?

▲ Hiram Bingham

B. Read the article. Underline the emphatic adjectives.

C. Answer the questions.

1. Did Hiram Bingham discover Inca ruins in Ollantaytambo? _____
   _____

2. How much did he pay Arteaga? _____
   _____

3. Was the climb to Machu Picchu easy?
   _____

4. Where did they eat? _____
   _____

5. How did the Incas cut the stones?
   _____

☐ The City of Machu Picchu, the Cradle of the Inca Empire

fortress
tropical forest
ladders
gorge
tree trunks

Most people travel for vacations, but some people travel to explore and discover new places. In 1911, Hiram Bingham, an American archaeologist, traveled to Peru where he discovered Machu Picchu, the lost city of the Incas. Read his report of the discovery.

In 1911, I went to Cuzco in Peru looking for ancient Inca ruins. We left Cuzco and traveled to the modern city of Urubamba and then continued down the Urubamba River until we came to the beautiful little town of Ollantaytambo with its amazing Inca **fortress.** At this point we entered the Urubamba **gorge** and the journey became more difficult. However, we continued down the river and six days after we left Cuzco, we arrived at a place called Mandorpampa. A

For Your Information: Machu Picchu

The city of Machu Picchu was built by the Incas around 1460, but was abandoned after only 100 years. Scientists are not sure why this happened, but they think it may have been because its inhabitants were wiped out by smallpox, brought by the Spanish. Because the city was hidden high in the mountains, it was never found and destroyed by the Spanish. The city is located on a high area between two mountains. The building technique used by the Incas (called dry stone because it is made without mortar) allows the stones to move slightly in an earthquake. As a result, the walls remained in good condition for centuries.

man came and introduced himself as Arteaga and I asked him about ruins. He told us of some ruins called Machu Picchu, 2,000 or more feet above the valley floor. I offered to pay him 50 cents per day to take us to the ruins and he agreed.

The next day, we crossed the river on a bridge made from four tree **trunks** and began an exhausting climb. At noon we arrived at a little grass hut. The **occupants** were very friendly and gave us some boiled potatoes and a gourd of cool water. The view was magnificent, the water was delicious, and the shade of the hut was agreeable, but there were no ruins. However, we continued upwards, sometimes climbing **ladders**, until at last we arrived in a **tropical forest** on top of the mountain.

Immediately we found some ancient Inca walls made of white stone. I knew at once that this was a truly amazing discovery.

I returned to Machu Picchu in 1912 and we began to clear the forest. The ruins started to appear and they were outstanding. The walls are made from enormous stones and they **fit** together perfectly. As we continued to clear the forest, we discovered more and more ruins, until at last the lost city of Machu Picchu stood before us.

▲ The walls of the main temple are made from enormous stones. The Incas had no metal tools, and no one knows how they cut the stones. We started to dig up the floor of the temple but we didn't find anything of interest.

Word Focus

occupants = The *occupants* of a house are the people that live there.
fit = If something *fits*, it is the right shape and size.

Writing

Read the postcard. Write a similar postcard about your last vacation or one of the vacations on page 67.

Hi everyone,

Greetings from Phuket. We're having a great time here. We arrived in Bangkok last Saturday and we went to The Golden Temple. It was fascinating. There was an enormous statue of the Buddha. The hotel was spotless and the food was excellent, but the traffic was terrible. It is much more relaxing here on the beach in Phuket.

Love
G&D

Goal 4 | **Talk about a discovery from the past**

Talk to a partner about another discovery from the past that you have read or heard about.

Writing

- Read the postcard with the class and go over the format of the message (greeting, message, closing, signature) and how to address it.
- Have students write their own postcard about a real or imaginary vacation.
- Have students exchange papers with a partner. Ask them to mark corrections and suggestions for improvements on their partner's paper.
- If desired, have students rewrite their papers, to be collected for marking.

 Goal 4

- Match students with a partner and have them talk about another explorer in a new place. If necessary, brainstorm examples on the board, such as Columbus sailing to the New World, Roald Amundsen walking to the South Pole, or Edmund Hillary and Tenzing Norgay climbing Mount Everest.

After Reading

Have students search online for tourist information about Machu Picchu. How do people go there today? What can they see? Have each student tell the class one interesting fact they learned.

Video Journal

Before You Watch

A • Have students look at the two pictures and tell a partner which beach they would prefer to visit and their reasons.

• Compare answers with the class.

• Review what students learned about Machu Picchu in the reading. Where is it? Who built it? Who found it again?

B • Have students work individually to complete the summary with the vocabulary in the box.

• Check answers.

Answers: quiet, tourists, business, environment

E VIDEO JOURNAL *MACHU PICCHU*

Before You Watch

A. Which of these beaches would you like to visit? Why?

Word Focus

Cuzco is also spelled Cusco.

B. Fill in the blanks. Use the words in the box to complete the video summary.

| tourists environment quiet business |

Video summary

When Hiram Bingham discovered Machu Picchu it was a _____ place. Now, many _____ go to Machu Picchu every day. Some people say it is good for _____, but other people say it is bad for the _____.

For Your Information: Tourism at Machu Picchu

Today Machu Picchu is one of the most important tourist destinations in South America and in the world. It is a UNESCO World Heritage site. Every year, over 400,000 people visit the site. There is a lot of concern over the damage that this tourism causes, with people walking on ancient paths and stone and leaving their trash behind. Air pollution is caused by the buses and other vehicles that bring the visitors. Experts say that steps must be taken to preserve this amazing city.

While You Watch

 A. Watch the video. Circle **T** for *true* and **F** for *false*.

1. Machu Picchu is a popular tourist destination.   T   F
2. Machu Picchu is sometimes known as the Lost Town of the Incas.   T   F
3. Conservationists think tourism is good for Machu Picchu.   T   F
4. Jose wants more people to come to Machu Picchu.   T   F

B. Watch again. Fill in the numbers and dates.

1. Machu Picchu is nearly _____ feet up in the Andes.
2. Machu Picchu is more than _____ years old.
3. Hiram Bingham found Machu Picchu in _____.

C. Answer the questions.

1. What is Julio's job? _____
2. What is Jose's job? _____
3. What jobs do the people of Aguas Calientes do? _____

After You Watch

Discuss these questions with a partner.

1. What are the big tourist attractions in your country?
2. Are there any problems with tourism in your country?
3. What are they?

Communication

A. Check (✓) the correct boxes.

	Advantage (+)	Disadvantage (−)
1. Tourism is good for business.	☐	☐
2. Tourists do not respect the local culture.	☐	☐
3. Tourists cause environmental damage.	☐	☐
4. Tourism helps people understand other cultures.	☐	☐

B. Discuss the question. Give examples.

Is tourism good or bad?

> Tourists buy presents and stay in hotels.

> That's good. It brings money to the country.

Teacher Tip: Roles in group work

It can be helpful to assign roles to students in each group. Some possibilities:

    Leader—asks questions and keeps the discussion on topic

    Secretary—takes notes on the group's ideas

    Reporter—tells the group's answers to the class

    Recorder—records the number of times each group member speaks and tells each member how often they spoke when the activity ends

Be sure to rotate these roles often.

While You Watch

A • Tell students to watch the video the first time and mark the statements *true* or *false*. Go over the statements. Play the video.

  • Check answers.

Answers: 1. T, 2. F, 3. F, 4. T

B • Tell students to watch the video again and fill in the numbers. Have the students read the statements. Play the video.

  • Check answers.

Answers: 1. 8,000, 2. 500, 3. 1911

C • Tell students to watch the video again and find the answers. Have the students read the questions. Play the video.

  • Check answers.

Answers: 1. tour guide, 2. hotel owner, 3. They sell art and handcrafts and depend on tourism.

After You Watch

• Have students discuss the questions with a partner. Then compare answers with the class, making lists on the board.

Communication

A • Introduce the ideas of advantage and disadvantage and have students work individually to mark the sentences.

  • Check answers.

Answers: 1. advantage, 2. disadvantage, 3. disadvantage, 4. advantage

B • Match students with partners and have them talk about the question and make notes of their examples.

  • Compare answers with the class.

  • Finish with a whole-class discussion about how people can be good tourists.

- Direct students' attention to the pictures. Talk about what the pictures have in common (they all show ways to communicate or send messages). With the class, look at each picture in turn and have students name things they see in each one (for example, a cell phone).

Answers: 1. They all are examples of communication. 2. signs, visually, orally, texts, etc.

- Have students work with a partner to talk about other ways that people communicate.

- Compare answers with the class, compiling a list on the board (for example, text message, email, radio, television).

- Follow up with these questions, asking them orally or writing them on the board for students to answer in pairs:

  1. *What ways do you use to communicate?*

  2. *What's your favorite way to communicate?*

- Go over the Unit Goals with the class, explaining and/or translating as necessary.

COMMUNICATION

1. Look at the pictures. What do they have in common?

2. What other ways do people communicate?

UNIT GOALS

Talk about personal communication
Give and write down contact details
Describe characteristics and qualities
Compare different types of communication

74

Unit Goals	Grammar	Vocabulary	Listening	Speaking and Pronunciation	Reading and Writing
• Talk about personal communication • Give and write down contact details • Describe characteristics and qualities • Compare different types of communication	Verbs with direct and indirect objects *I sent **Mike** an **email**.* Linking verbs *It **feels** soft.*	Communication Electronics The senses	Listening for specific information: a radio call-in program	Asking for contact information Describing sights, sounds, and other sensations Endings -*ty* and -*teen*	"The Secret Language of Dolphins" Writing a text message

UNIT 7

Unit Theme Overview

- Communication is the field of human activity that has changed and developed the most in recent years. Cell phones, the Internet, email, and text messages have all changed our daily lives. Some new technologies, such as answering machines, became popular then quickly became obsolete. At the same time, older ways of transmitting messages are still used and appreciated. Most people still enjoy receiving a letter in the mail or settling down to read the newspaper.

- This unit begins by considering common ways to communicate and gives students the vocabulary they need to discuss them. Students then learn to exchange contact information such as telephone numbers and email addresses. They then talk about verbs for feeling and sensing—ways that the body takes in information. Finally they look at the different ways that animals communicate and watch a video about new technology that humans can use to communicate about animals.

75

Talk about Personal Communication

Vocabulary

A • Go over the words in the box. Then have students work individually to use them to label the pictures.

• Check answers.

Answers: 1. email, 2. fax, 3. text message, 4. phone, 5. letter, 6. newspaper ad, 7. TV, 8. BlackBerry®

B • Ask students to classify the words from exercise A in the correct column of the chart. Point out that students might have different ideas.

• Check answers.

Answers: Fast/inexpensive: email, text message; Fast/expensive: BlackBerry®, TV, fax; Slow/expensive: newspaper ad

Grammar

• Review the object pronouns (*me, you, him, her, it, us, them*).

• Ask students, *Did you send someone an email yesterday? Who?* Elicit names. Write on the board:

I sent/my friend/an email.

I sent/Lara/an email.

I sent/her/an email.

• Elicit more examples from the class.

• Go over the information in the box. Point out that the indirect object (the person who receives the action) comes first in this type of sentence.

Vocabulary

A. Label the pictures. Use the words in the box.

email	fax	BlackBerry®
TV	text message	newspaper ad
letter	phone	

1. _____ 2._____ 3. _____ 4._____

5. _____ 6._____ 7. _____ 8._____

B. Write the words in exercise **A** in the correct column.

	Inexpensive	Expensive
fast		phone call
slow	letter	

Grammar: Verbs with direct and indirect objects

(Subject) + verb	Indirect object	Direct object
I sent	Mike	an email.
My parents bought	me	a BlackBerry®.
I wrote	Helen	a text message.
Find	me	his number, please.
I faxed	him	the diagram.
Give	me	a call.

Word Bank: Email vocabulary

sender	attachment
recipient	signature file
Cc (courtesy copy)	send
Bcc (blind courtesy copy)	reply
header	
body	

Grammar: Verbs with direct and indirect objects

In a sentence, a verb may have both a direct object (the object the action is done to) and an indirect object (the person for whom the object is done).

Two different patterns are possible. The direct object can also come first, with the indirect object preceded by *for* or *to*:

I sent an email to her.   I baked a cake for her.

Irregular past tense	
Present	**Past**
buy	bought
send	sent
write	wrote
find	found
get	got

A. Unscramble the words to write sentences.

1. sent a I fax Barbara. _____
2. sent My brother an me email. _____
3. address. me his Find email _____
4. new Jim a computer. I bought _____
5. a your mom Give call. _____

B. Read the situations and make requests. Use the verbs in parentheses.

Situation	**Request**
1. You lost your friend's phone number.	(send) _Please send me your phone number._
2. You want your friend to call you.	(give) _____
3. You want your parents to buy you a printer.	(buy) _____
4. You ask if you can pay someone by check.	(write) _____
5. You want your friend to fax you a chart.	(fax) _____

Conversation

Track 2-2

A. Listen to the conversation. How did Ken communicate with Chris?

Ken: Hey, Chris. I sent you <u>an email</u> yesterday and you didn't answer.

Chris: <u>Email</u>? What <u>email</u>? You didn't send me an <u>email</u>.

Ken: Come on! You got it. Then I sent you <u>a text message</u>.

Chris: <u>Text message</u>? What <u>text message</u>? You didn't send me a <u>text message,</u> either. Honest!

Ken: OK, well you've got no excuses now. Where's the $15 you owe me?

Chris: $15? What $15?

 B. Practice the conversation with a partner. Switch roles and practice it again.

 C. Practice the conversation again. Change the underlined words.

Real Language

We can use *Come on!* to show impatience.

✓ Goal 1 | Talk about personal communication

Write a list of all the types of personal communication that you use. Compare it with your partner's list.

Lesson A **77**

- Present the irregular past-tense verbs in the box.

A • Have students work individually to write sentences.
- Check answers.

Answers: 1. I sent Barbara a fax. 2. My brother sent me an email. 3. Find me his email address. 4. I bought Jim a new computer. 5. Give your mom a call.

B • Have students work individually to write an appropriate sentence for each situation.
- Check answers.

Answers: 2. Please give me a call. 3. Please buy me a printer. 4. Can I write you a check? 5. Please fax me the chart.

Conversation

A • Have students close their books. Write the question on the board: *How did Ken communicate with Chris?*
- Play the recording. **(CD2 T2)**
- Check answers.

Answer: by email and text message

B • Play or read the conversation again for the class to repeat.
- Practice the conversation with the class in chorus.
- Have students practice the conversation with a partner and then switch roles and practice it again.

✓ Goal 1

- Have students work individually to write a list of their ways of communicating with other people.
- Match students with a partner and have them compare and discuss their lists.
- With the class, discuss students' most popular ways of communicating. Why do they like them and use them?

Grammar Practice: Verbs with direct and indirect objects

Have students write sentences with direct and indirect objects about the last time they used these ways of communicating:

send an email *give a phone call*

write a letter *send a card*

For example, *I gave my brother a phone call.* Call on students to read sentences to the class.

Lesson A 77

Give and Write Down Contact Details

Listening

A • Tell students they are going to hear a radio program. Have them read the question.

   • Play the recording one or more times. **(CD2 T3)**

   • Check answers.

Answer: c

B • Tell students to listen again to find and write all the contact information in the chart. Go through the chart to point out what they must find.

   • Play the recording one or more times. **(CD2 T3)**

   • Check answers.

Answers: Telephone number: 34-36-29-18-34, Fax number: 34-30-14-76-22, Email address: kingstownradio@coolmail.com, Text message address: 333 317-3476, Mailing address: Kingstown Radio, 25 Main Street, Kingstown

Pronunciation: Endings -ty and -teen

A • Tell students to listen for the difference in pronunciation in the endings -ty and -teen and circle the word they hear. Play the recording one or more times. **(CD2 T4)**

   • Check answers.

Answers: thirty, fourteen, fifty, sixteen, seventeen, eighty, nineteen

B • Tell students to listen to the pairs of numbers and repeat them. Play the recording one or more times. **(CD2 T5)**

   • Have students read the numbers out loud as a class. Then have them practice reading the numbers to a partner. Walk around checking for good pronunciation.

   • Call on individual students to say a pair of numbers for the class.

| **B** | GOAL 2 | GIVE AND WRITE DOWN CONTACT DETAILS |

Listening

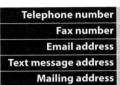

Track 2-3

A. Listen to the radio program. Circle the correct answer.

This is a __.
a. talk show
b. music show
c. phone-in program

Track 2-3

B. Listen again and complete the chart.

Telephone number	
Fax number	
Email address	
Text message address	
Mailing address	

Pronunciation: Endings -ty and -teen

🎧 Track 2-4

A. Listen and circle the word you hear.

1.	thirty	thirteen	5.	seventy	seventeen
2.	forty	fourteen	6.	eighty	eighteen
3.	fifty	fifteen	7.	ninety	nineteen
4.	sixty	sixteen			

🎧 Track 2-5

B. Listen and repeat the numbers.

thirty	sixteen
thirteen	seventy
forty	seventeen
fourteen	eighty
fifty	eighteen
fifteen	ninety
sixty	nineteen

78 Communication

For Your Information: Giving contact details

Email addresses: If there are no spaces in a multiword address, you can clarify by saying, *That's all one word*. The symbol _ is pronounced *underscore*, and – is pronounced *dash*. The symbol @ is *at*, and . is *dot*. Internet addresses are given similarly and may include a /, which is pronounced *slash*.

Phone numbers: These are sometimes preceded by an *area code* if you are calling from another city. Phone numbers are usually pronounced as single digits with a pause between each two or three digits. The number 0 is usually pronounced *oh*.

Example: (304) 922-0768 is *area code three-o- four (pause) nine-two-two (pause) oh-seven (pause) six-eight*.

Communication

A. Write your contact information in column 1 of the chart.

B. Ask three of your classmates for their contact information. Complete the chart.

	Me	Classmate 1	Classmate 2	Classmate 3
Name				
Home phone number				
Fax number				
Cell phone number				
Email address				
Mailing address				

Real Language

We say *sorry, I missed that* or *could you repeat that, please* when we want someone to repeat something.

✔ **Goal 2** **Give and write down contact details**

Give the contact details of a friend or family member to a partner.

Communication

A • Have students write down their contact information in the column for Me. Help as needed with any problems in the section for mailing address. Tell students that they can make up a number or address if they don't want to give their real information.

B • Model the activity. Ask a student, *What's your email address?* and write down the information. On the board, write the sentences, *What's your _____?* and *Sorry, I don't have one.*

• Have students stand up and walk around the class with their books, asking and giving information. Tell them to sit down when they've completed the chart.

• Ask, *Who has an unusual/ interesting email address? What is it?*

✔ Goal 2

• Have students work individually to write a list of a friend's or family member's contact information.

• Match students with a partner and have them share this information by asking and answering each other's questions. They should only refer to their lists if necessary.

Expansion Activity

Have students make an email and/or phone number list of all their classmates. Dictate a list of all students' names for them to write down on a sheet of paper, and then have them circulate around the classroom asking for and giving information.

Describe Characteristics and Qualities

Language Expansion

- Go over the names of the senses with the class. Give/elicit more examples of things we use sight, hearing, taste, smell, and touch for.

A • Match students with a partner and have them discuss which sense is used for each thing. Compare answers with the class.

Answers: Sweet: taste, Dirty: sight, Soft: touch, Salty: taste, Loud: hearing, Bad: smell, Green: sight, Wet: touch

B • Have students work with the same partner to list things they can see, hear, taste, smell, and touch.

- Compare answers with the class, making lists on the board.

Grammar: Linking verbs

- Go over the verbs in the box. Point out that they are used to talk about the thing that we are perceiving.

Language Expansion: The senses

The senses are the physical abilities of:

▲ sight   ▲ hearing   ▲ taste   ▲ smell   ▲ touch

With the senses we perceive (*see, notice, feel*) characteristics and qualities of people, animals, places, and things.

A. Discuss this question with a partner. What senses do you use to identify these characteristics?

▲ sweet   ▲ dirty   ▲ soft   ▲ salty

▲ loud   ▲ bad   ▲ green   ▲ wet

B. Work with a partner to make a list of other things you can perceive with your senses.

Grammar: Linking verbs

Linking verbs		
Subject +	**verb +**	**adjective**
The food	**smells**	delicious.
It	**feels**	soft.
You	**look**	cold.
It	**tastes**	salty.
He	**sounds**	tired.

*Verbs of the senses are *not* action verbs.
*They are usually followed by an adjective.
*They are not used in the simple progressive tense.

Word Bank: Sensations

taste: sour, bitter, spicy
hearing: quiet, musical
smell: sweet, pungent, smoky
touch: rough, smooth, hard, hot, cold
sight: light, dark

Grammar: Linking verbs of sensation

With these linking (or copular) verbs of sensation, the subject of the sentence is the thing that is producing the sensation. These are all stative verbs, which are not normally used in continuous tenses.

A. Complete the sentences with linking verbs.

1. That washing machine can't be OK. It _____ very old.
2. Did you wash the car? It still _____ dirty.
3. What are you cooking? It _____ delicious.
4. I don't like this part of the city. It _____ dangerous.
5. Hey, you changed your hair. It _____ much better.
6. I don't like these French fries. They _____ too salty.
7. I prefer this sweater. It _____ soft.
8. The mechanic says he fixed the rattle in the car, but it _____ worse.

 B. Take turns. Describe the pictures on page 80 by making statements with *looks, sounds, tastes, smells, feels,* and an adjective.

Conversation

Track 2-6

A. Listen to the conversation. What's wrong with the man's car?

Susan:	Your car sounds strange.
Bill:	I know. It started last week, but now it sounds worse.
Susan:	I think it's the brakes.
Bill:	It does feel funny when I use the brakes.
Susan:	You should take it to the mechanic.
Bill:	Maybe next week.
Susan:	Go soon. New brakes are expensive.

B. Practice the conversation with a partner. Switch roles and practice it again.

✓ **Goal 3** — **Describe characteristics and qualities**

Work with a partner. Use linking sense verbs to describe your classroom and your classmates.

Lesson C **81**

A • Have students work individually to complete the sentences with linking verbs from the box. Point out that more than one verb may be correct.
• Check answers.

Answers: 1. looks/sounds, 2. looks/feels, 3. smells/tastes, 4. looks, 5. looks, 6. taste, 7. feels/looks, 8. sounds

B • Match students with a partner and have them talk about the pictures on the previous page. Give an example: *The candy tastes sweet.*
• Call on students to talk about one of the pictures.

Conversation

A • Have students close their books. Write the question on the board: *What's wrong with the man's car?*
• Play the recording. **(CD2 T6)**
• Check answers.

Answer: The brakes sound strange.
• Explain that the brakes are the part of the car that makes it stop.

B • Play or read the conversation again for the class to repeat.
• Practice the conversation with the class in chorus.
• Have students practice the conversation with a partner and then switch roles and practice it again.
• Have students work with a partner to make a new conversation about another household problem.
• Call on student pairs to present their conversation to the class.

✓ Goal 3

• Match students with a partner and have them talk about people and things around them using the sense verbs they have learned. Call on students to tell the class one of the things they noticed.

Grammar Practice: Linking verbs of sensation

Have students write one sentence about something they like using each verb of sensation (*feel, smell, taste, look, sound*). Give an example: *These shoes feel comfortable.* Have them share their sentences with a group.

Compare Different Types of Communication

Reading

- Introduce the topic of the reading. Ask students how animals communicate (for example, by sounds and moving their bodies). Ask what, if anything, they know about dolphins.

A • Read the question. Have students read the article to find the answer. Point out the items in the Word Focus box and tell students to circle any words in the reading that they don't understand.

- Go over the article with the class, answering any questions from the students about vocabulary.

- Talk about how dolphins communicate: They use sounds.

B • Have students read the article again to find the answers.

- Check answers.

Answers: 1. hearing, 2. everything, food, sharks, 3. One sound can mean many different things. 4. no, 5. Answers will vary. Possible answers: dogs and cats communicate with sounds; snakes and bees communicate by moving their bodies

Reading

A. How do dolphins communicate? Read the article and find out.

Word Focus

aquarium = a place where people pay to look at fish
tank = a glass box
clap = when you *clap* something, you bring it together quickly and firmly
raise = lift

 B. Answer the questions.

1. What senses do dolphins use to communicate? _____

2. What do dolphins *talk* about? _____
   _____

3. Why is it difficult to understand dolphin communication? _____
   _____

4. Do scientists understand everything that dolphins *say*? _____
   _____

5. How do other animals communicate? Give some examples. _____
   _____
   _____

☐ The Secret Language of Dolphins

A mother dolphin talks to her baby . . . by telephone! The special call was made in an **aquarium** in Hawaii, where the mother and her two-year-old baby swam in separate **tanks**.

"It seemed clear that they knew who they were talking to," says Don White. But what did they say? Scientists are studying dolphins all over the world to understand their secret language. They don't understand everything yet, but they're listening . . . and learning.

For Your Information: Dolphins

Dolphins are sea mammals that live in shallow parts of the oceans near land. They range in size from 4–30 feet (1.2–9.5 meters). Dolphins eat smaller animals like fish and squid. Scientists believe that they are one of the most intelligent animals. Dolphins live together in groups of about 12 called pods. They swim together and help other members of their pod if they are sick or injured. They communicate with other dolphins by using sounds like whistles and clicks. Because of their friendly appearance and playful behavior, dolphins are very popular in movies and cartoons, and they are among the most popular exhibits at aquariums around the world.

Scientists think dolphins *talk* about everything, even such things as their age and how they are feeling. Scientists think that dolphins say things like "there are some good fish over here," or "watch out for that shark because he's hunting." "Sometimes one dolphin will speak and then another will seem to answer," says Sara Waller, who studies bottlenose dolphins off the California coast. Sometimes they all talk at the same time—like people at a party.

It is difficult to study *dolphin speak* in the sea because dolphins swim very quickly. Also, it seems that one sound can mean many different things. For example, when they are fighting, dolphins **clap** their mouths to say "go away!" But they make the same sound when they are playing. It's like humans. When you **raise** a hand, it might mean *hello*, *good-bye*, or *stop*.

Scientists still don't understand everything dolphins *say* but one day, who knows, maybe you'll get a phone call from a dolphin.

Writing

A. Writing text messages is slow so people use abbreviations. Can you read and understand these messages?

> HI. HRU?
> NOTHING. WANNA GO TO THE MOVIES TN?
> Y?
> OK LMK

> GREAT. WRUD?
> IDUNNO
> GOTTA FINISH MY PROJECT
> OK CU LATER

TEXTING GLOSSARY

2MOR	Tomorrow	NSISR	Not sure if spelled right
ASAP	As soon as possible	NVM	Never mind
B4N	Bye for now	OIC	Oh, I see
BCOS	Because	PLMK	Please let me know
BDAY	Birthday		
BOYF	Boyfriend	RU?	Are you?
CU	See you	THX	Thanks
DTS	Don't think so	WDYT?	What do you think?
FBM	Fine by me		
GTG	Got to go	WRUD	What are you doing?
HRU?	How are you?		
IDTS	I don't think so	WU?	What's up?
IDUNNO	I don't know	Y?	Why?
LMK	Let me know		
LTNS	Long time no see		

 B. Write a conversation with no abbreviations. Then write it as a text message. Give it to a partner to read.

 Goal 4 **Compare different types of communication**

Work with a partner. Compare human communication with animal communication. How are they the same? How are they different? Share your ideas with the class.

After Reading

Have students write a few sentences about their favorite way to communicate with their friends and why they like it.

Writing

A • Ask students if they send text messages. Who do they send them to? How often? If necessary, explain that when you send a text message, you must press many keys on a cell phone, so it takes a long time. Text messages must also be short. People use many abbreviations (short forms) in text messages.

• Have students read the messages. Go over the meanings. "Hi. How are you?" "Great. What are you doing?" "Nothing. Do you want to go to the movies tonight?" "I don't know." "Why?" "I've got to finish my project." "OK. Let me know." "OK. See you later."

• Have students read through the Texting Glossary. Emphasize that these expressions are ONLY for use in text messages. They are NOT used in normal English writing, and are NOT appropriate for use in homework.

B • Have students work individually to write a short conversation (six to eight sentences). Then have them rewrite their conversation as text messages.

• Have students exchange papers with a partner. Both students should try to read the text messages.

☑ Goal 4

• Review the idea of animal communication and list examples on the board.

• Match students with a partner and have them talk about similarities and differences between animal and human communication.

• Compare ideas with the class.

Video Journal

Before You Watch

A • Discuss the idea of symbols—pictures with special meanings.

• With the class, discuss the meanings of the symbols.

Answers: 1. for disabled people, 2. restaurant, 3. shopping, 4. AIDS awareness

• Call on students to draw other symbols they know on the board and have the class give the meaning of each symbol.

B • Have students work individually to match the words and meanings, using a dictionary as needed.

• Check answers.

Answers: 1. b, 2. c, 3. d, 4. a

While You Watch

A • Tell students to watch the video the first time and mark the statements true or false. Have them read the statements. Play the video.

• Check answers.

Answers: 1. T, 2. T, 3. F, 4. T, 5. T

E VIDEO JOURNAL *WILD ANIMAL TRACKERS*

Before You Watch

A. How can we communicate without using words? One way is to use small pictures or icons. What do these icons mean?

_____ _____ _____ _____

B. Match the words to the definitions.

1. conservationist ____   a. to follow wild animals
2. increase ____   b. a person who protects wild animals
3. decrease ____   c. to get (or make) bigger
4. to track ____   d. to get (or make) smaller

While You Watch

A. Watch the video. Circle **T** for *true* and **F** for *false*.

1. In the video, you see lions.   T   F
2. Louis Liebenberg is trying to collect information about the animals.   T   F
3. The Bushmen and the conservationists speak the same language.   T   F
4. The small computer that the Bushmen use is called the Cyber Tracker. T   F
5. Louis Liebenberg makes maps from the information.   T   F

84 Communication

For Your Information: Bushmen

The Bushmen are an ethnic group of indigenous people who live in many countries of southern Africa, from South Africa north to Mozambique and Angola. Traditionally they lived by hunting and gathering plants, though, starting in the 1950s, they changed to farming. In the past, they lived in small groups that traveled together in search of food. Their society was very egalitarian, with chiefs having very little power and men and women having equal status. Today, there are about 90,000 Bushmen.

B • Tell students to watch the video again and find the answers. Have the students read the statements. Play the video.

• Check answers.

Answers: 1. a, 2. c, 3. a

 B. Watch the video again and circle the correct answer.

1. The conservationists use Bushmen because ___.
   a. they are good trackers
   b. they can't read or write
   c. both of the above
2. The Bushmen collect information about ___.
   a. animals
   b. plants
   c. both of the above
3. The Cyber Tracker project started ___.
   a. 5 years ago
   b. 10 years ago
   c. 15 years ago

▲ A Bushman studies animal tracks in the mud.

After You Watch

 The Cyber Tracker is a very quick way of recording information about wild animals. Can you think of other uses for the Cyber Tracker? Discuss it with a partner.

Communication

In some languages people use small pictures (pictograms) instead of letters to write. For example, in Chinese:

人 = human   馬 = horse

A. Invent your own pictograms. Write a short message using your pictograms, not words.

 B. Exchange your pictogram messages with a partner. Read your partner's message. Do you understand it?

After You Watch

• Match students with a partner and have them talk about the question.

• Compare answers with the class. (For example, tourists could use the cyber tracker to read information about animals.)

Communication

• Introduce the idea of pictograms—pictures that represent words. If your students use pictograms in their first language, ask for volunteers to share examples on the board.

A • Ask each student to imagine and write a message of at least three words, using pictograms. Give help as needed.

B • Match students with a partner. Have them exchange messages and then try to read them.

• Call on students to write successful messages on the board for the whole class to read.

Video Journal **85**

Teacher Tip: Checking answers

There are many ways to check students' answers to activities, all with advantages and disadvantages.

Teacher reads the answers out loud, students check their work—the fastest way, but with the least student involvement

Teacher calls on students to give their answers—also fast, but may make students feel anxious

Students correct each other's work—gives students more responsibility, but they may not correct all mistakes

Volunteers each write the answer to one question on the board—gives the class an opportunity to work with common errors, but uses a lot of class time

Teacher corrects outside of class—an opportunity for detailed feedback, but requires a lot of work from the teacher

- Introduce the theme of the unit. Ask, *Do you watch movies about the future?* Elicit names of famous movies about the future.

- Direct students' attention to the pictures. With the class, look at each picture in turn and have students talk about what is happening in each one.

- Have students work with a partner to discuss the questions. Explain that if you are *looking forward to* something, you are happy about something in the future.

- Compare answers with the class.

- Follow up with these questions, asking them orally or writing them on the board for students to answer in pairs:

  1. *Do you like to talk and think about the future?*

  2. *Why, or why not?*

- Go over the Unit Goals with the class, explaining and/or translating as necessary.

THE FUTURE

1. Which of these events are in your future?
   a. buying a new car
   b. graduating from school
   c. getting married
   d. taking a trip

2. Are you looking forward to these events? Why?

UNIT GOALS

Talk about plans
Discuss long- and short-term plans
Make weather predictions
Discuss the future

86

	Unit Goals	Grammar	Vocabulary	Listening	Speaking and Pronunciation	Reading and Writing
	• Talk about plans • Discuss long- and short-term plans • Make weather predictions • Discuss the future	*Be going to* We'**re going to** buy a new car *tomorrow.* *Will* for predictions *I think it **will** rain this afternoon.*	Plans Weather Conditions	Listening for general understanding: a talk show	Talking about weekend plans Discussing the weather Reduced form of *going to*	"Future Energy" Writing statements about the future

UNIT 8

Unit Theme Overview

- People in every country are fascinated with the future. They flock to science fiction movies to see visions of what our lives could be like a hundred years from now. They read analyses of what the stock market will do or who will win the soccer World Cup next year. They pick up the newspaper or visit a Web site to find out what the weather will be like tomorrow or three days from now. There is even a branch of social science called *futurology* dedicated to understanding future trends, predicting what is likely to continue, and what will be new. Futurologists look at possible, probable, and preferable scenes in the future. They also use computer simulations to look at the possible results of current decisions.

- Learning to talk about the future in English is complex, because, unlike some other languages, English uses a number of different structures to talk about future time. In this unit, students are introduced to two of them: *going to* for plans and predictions and *will* for predictions. They consider many different aspects of the future, from their own personal short- and long-term plans, to tomorrow's weather, to new technology in the future and how it will affect us.

Talk about Plans

Vocabulary

A • Tell students they are going to learn expressions for future plans. Go over the expressions in the box.

• Have students work individually to write the correct phrase for each picture.

• Check answers.

Answers: Top, left to right: 6. clean the house, 4. buy a new car, 7. buy my own house, 5. have children **Bottom, left to right:** 1. study for the next test, 3. do the laundry, 2. get a new job, 8. speak English fluently

• Ask, *Which of these plans are in your future?*

B • Discuss the meanings of short-term (close in the future—for example, in the next week or month) and long-term (far away in the future—for example, next year). Have students work individually to categorize the plans.

• Check answers.

Answers: Short-term plans: clean the house, study for the next test, do the laundry; Long-term plans: buy a new car, buy my own house, have children, get a new job, speak English fluently

C • Have students work individually to rank the long-term plans in the chart from most important to least important.

• Then match them with a partner and have them discuss their answers.

• Compare answers with the class.

Grammar

• Introduce the structure. Tell students (for example), *I have lots of plans for the weekend. On Friday night, I'm going to have dinner at a restaurant. On Saturday morning, I'm going to clean my house. On Saturday afternoon, I'm going to go shopping.* Ask questions like, *What are you going to do on Friday night/Saturday?* Elicit answers with *going to.*

• Go over the information in the box.

Vocabulary

A. Number the pictures to match phrases from the box.

1. study for the next test	4. buy a new car	7. buy my own house
2. get a new job	5. have children	8. speak English fluently
3. do the laundry	6. clean the house	

B. Write the plans from exercise **A** in the correct column.

Short-term plans	Long-term plans

I don't want to have children now. I'm too young.

I need to buy a new car. My car is really old.

C. Number the long-term plans in order of importance for you (1 for the most important plan). Compare your list with a partner's list. Give reasons.

Grammar: *Be going to*

Be going to	
Statement	We**'re going to** buy a new car tomorrow.
Negative	He**'s not going to** get a new job next year.
Yes/no question	**Are** you **going to** do the laundry this weekend?
Wh- question	When **are** you **going to** pay the phone bill?

*We use *be going to* to talk about our plans for the future.

Word Bank: Future plans

get engaged
get married
apply to a college/
    university/graduate
    school
study abroad
start a business
change careers

take up skiing/playing
    the guitar/writing
    poems
learn to drive/cook/
    swim
take tennis/Spanish/
    computer lessons

Grammar: *Be going to*

English uses a variety of different ways to talk about future time. One of them is *be going to*, which is used to talk about plans and intentions. It is also used informally for making predictions, which will be covered in Lesson C of this unit. One common error to watch out for is omitting the *be* verb We going to watch videos.

A. Match the questions and the answers.

1. Where are you going to have lunch today? ____   a. Yes, I am. He loves dancing.
2. Are you going to invite Alan to the party? ____   b. Maybe. I would take an umbrella.
3. What are you going to do on Saturday? ____   c. At Luigi's.
4. When is Nicola going to arrive? ____   d. We're going to go ice skating.
5. Is it going to rain this evening? ____   e. Her plane arrives at five o'clock.

B. Unscramble the words to write sentences. Number the sentences to make
a conversation.

__. are   going   What   to   see?   you

__. to   the   movies.   to   going   go   I'm

__. going   the   new   We're   James   Bond   movie.   to   see

__. you   going   this   evening?   to   do   What   are

Real Language

We can say *mmm* or
I'm not sure to show
uncertainty.

Conversation

Track 2-7

A. Listen to the conversation. Is Kiri going to go to the beach?

Vera: Hi Kiri. What are you going to do this weekend?
Kiri: Well, I'm going to <u>study for the test</u> and <u>do the laundry</u>. Why do you ask?
Vera: We're going to <u>go to the beach</u>. Do you want to come?
Kiri: Mmm, I'm not sure. I'd love to but, . . . you know . . . work.
Vera: Danny <u>is going to be</u> there.
Kiri: Oh, I see. Well, maybe I can <u>study for the test</u> tonight. And I can <u>do the laundry</u> when we come back.
Vera: So, you're going to come?
Kiri: Sure!

B. Practice the conversation with a partner. Switch roles and practice it again.

C. Change the underlined words and practice it again.

 Goal 1   **Talk about plans**

Tell a partner your plans for this weekend.

Lesson A   **89**

A • Have students work individually to match the columns.
• Check answers.

Answers: 1. c, 2. a, 3. d, 4. e, 5. b

B • Have students work individually to write the sentences.
• Check answers.

Answers: 1. What are you going to see? 2. I'm going to go to the movies. 3. We're going to see the new James Bond movie. 4. What are you going to do this evening?

• Then have students write numbers to put the sentences in order.
• Check answers.

Answers: 4, 2, 1, 3

• Ask students about their plans for this evening.

Conversation

A • Have students close their books. Write the question on the board: *Is Kiri going to go to the beach?*
• Play the recording. **(CD2 T7)**
• Check answers.

Answer: yes

B • Play or read the conversation again for the class to repeat.
• Practice the conversation with the class in chorus.
• Have students practice the conversation with a partner and then switch roles and practice it again.

C • Have student pairs think of new information to substitute for the underlined words. Then have them make a new conversation.
• Call on student pairs to present their conversations to the class.

☑ Goal 1

• Match students with a partner and have them share their weekend plans.
• Call on students to tell the class about their partner's plans.

Grammar Practice: *Be going to*

Have students take a piece of paper and make seven columns with the days of the week at the top. This is their "calendar" for next week. Then have them write an activity (real or imaginary) for five of the seven days (such as *see a movie, study English,* etc.). Have students work with a partner to plan an activity (such as *have a cup of coffee*) they want to do together. They should not look at their partner's calendar. Model sentences like, *I'm going to do the laundry on Monday night* and *What are you going to do on Tuesday night?* When all student pairs have finished, call on students to talk about their plans.

Discuss Long- and Short-Term Plans

Listening

A • Tell students they are going to hear an interview with a famous singer. Have them read the question.

• Play the recording one or more times. **(CD2 T8)**

• Check answers.

Answer: short-term plans

B • Tell students to listen again to the conversation and mark the statements *true* or *false*. Read through the statements with the class.

• Play the recording one or more times. **(CD2 T8)**

• Check answers.

Answers: 1. F, 2. F, 3. F, 4. T, 5. T

• Ask, *What do you think? Is his life going to change with a baby? Why, or why not?*

Pronunciation

A • Remind students that many words and sounds in English are reduced when we are speaking quickly. Tell students to listen to the reduced form of *going to*. Play the recording. **(CD2 T9)**

• Ask, *What does the reduced form of* going to *sound like?* (gonna) Point out that *gonna* is used only in speaking, NEVER in writing.

B • Tell students to listen and mark the pronunciation they hear, full or reduced. Play the recording one or more times. **(CD2 T10)**

• Check answers.

Answers: 1. reduced, 2. full, 3. full, 4. reduced, 5. reduced

C • Tell students to listen to the recording again and repeat the sentences. **(CD2 T10)**

• Have students practice reading the sentences to a partner, giving both pronunciations. Walk around the class listening for correct pronunciation.

B GOAL 2 DISCUSS LONG- AND SHORT-TERM PLANS

Listening

🎧 **A.** Listen to the interview with a pop singer. Is he talking about his short-term plans or long-term plans?
Track 2-8

🎧 **B.** Listen again and circle **T** for *true* and **F** for *false*.
Track 2-8

1. Pete is going to record his new album in June.	T	F
2. Pete is going to do a world tour this year.	T	F
3. Babs is going to have a baby in May.	T	F
4. The baby isn't going to change Pete's life.	T	F
5. Pete is going to start making a film at the end of the year.	T	F

Pronunciation: Reduced form of *going to*

🎧 **A.** Listen to the sentences.
Track 2-9
1. I'm going to buy a new computer.
2. Are you going to come?

🎧 **B.** Listen to the sentences and check (✓) the box.
Track 2-10

	Full form	Reduced form
1. When are you going to finish?	☐	☐
2. They're not going to like it.	☐	☐
3. We're going to leave at three thirty.	☐	☐
4. I'm going to take a shower.	☐	☐
5. Are you going to take a taxi?	☐	☐

🎧 **C.** Listen again and repeat the sentences.
Track 2-10

90 The Future

For Your Information: Life changes from having children

According to experts, having a baby, especially a first baby, changes many aspects of one's life. It can cause pressure in the relationship with one's partner and requires changes and adjustment in both parents' career goals. It can have both positive and negative effects on friendships, as well as affecting relationships with your own parents and your in-laws. It even brings changes in people's identity and sense of who they are.

Communication

A. What are your short-term and long-term plans? Check (✓) the correct column.

Short-term plans

Are you going to . . .	Yes, I am.	I'm not sure.	No, I'm not.
eat out tonight?			
go to a party this weekend?			
play or watch a sport this evening?			
rest this weekend?			

Long-term plans

Are you going to . . .	Yes, I am.	I'm not sure.	No, I'm not.
start your own business?			
learn another language?			
move to another country?			
buy a new car?			

B. Take turns asking and answering the questions in exercise **A** Then ask a *wh-* question.

> Are you going to eat out tonight?
>
> Yes, I am.
>
> Where are you going to go?
>
> I'm not sure. Maybe to an Italian restaurant.

✓ **Goal 2**   **Discuss long- and short-term plans**

Tell a partner your plans for tonight and your plans for the next five years.

Communication

A • Have students work individually to mark their short-term and long-term plans.

B • Match students with a partner and explain the activity: They should ask the questions in exercise **A**, and after each question they should ask for more information. Go over the example. On the board write the question words *who/where/when/why/what,* to prompt them in asking *wh-* questions.

• Have students discuss the questions with a partner. Walk around the class, helping as needed.

• Call on students to tell the class about one plan their partner has.

✓ **Goal 2**

• Have students work with a partner to talk about two future plans, for the short term and the long term.

• Call on students to tell the class about one of their plans.

Expansion Activity

Have students choose one of their long-term plans and write several sentences about it, answering questions that begin with *who/where/when/why/what*. Divide the class into groups of three to four and have students share their work with their group.

Make Weather Predictions

Language Expansion

- Go over the adjectives for weather conditions in the box. Ask students, *How is the weather today?* Elicit, *It's (hot and sunny).* Ask, *How's the weather in January/April/August/October?*

- Go over the vocabulary for clothing. Ask, *Which things do you need today/for rain/for cold weather/at the beach?*

A • Have students work individually to fill in the spaces.
- Check answers.

Answers: 1. umbrella, raincoat, 2. cool/cold, 3. sunglasses, 4. sunny/bright, hot

B • Ask the class, *How is the weather going to be (tonight)?* Elicit, *It's going to be (rainy). You need (your umbrella).*

- Match students with a partner and have them give predictions for the weather at different times with *going to* and recommendations with *need*. If desired, you can write times on the board: *tomorrow/the weekend/next month*.

- Compare answers with the class.

Grammar

- Explain that another way to make predictions in English is with *will*. Go over the information in the box.

◄ umbrella

◄ sunglasses

◄ rubber boots

◄ raincoat

◄ swimsuit

◄ scarf

◄ sweater

◄ sun hat

92   **The Future**

Language Expansion: Weather conditions

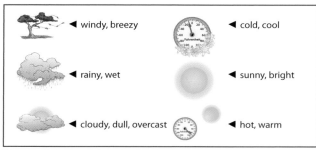

◄ windy, breezy   ◄ cold, cool

◄ rainy, wet   ◄ sunny, bright

◄ cloudy, dull, overcast   ◄ hot, warm

We use adjectives to describe the weather.
Today is **sunny** *and* **warm**.

A. Complete the sentences. Use words from the box and the pictures.

1. It's not going to rain tomorrow. You don't need to take your _____ and your _____.
2. You should put on your sweater. It's going to be_____ outside.
3. The weather forecast says it's going to be cloudy today. You don't need to take your _____.
4. It's going to be _____ and _____ tomorrow, so don't forget your sun hat.

B. Take turns. Make predictions about the weather. Tell a partner how to dress for it.

Grammar: *Will* for predictions

Will	
Statements	I think it **will** rain this afternoon. It **will** be windy tomorrow.
Negatives	Don't take your sweater. I'm sure it **won't** be cold.
Yes/no questions	**Will** it be windy?

*We use *be going to* and *will* to make predictions.
*We only use *will* when we decide on an immediate plan.
*I'***ll** *answer the phone.*

Word Bank:
More weather adjectives

humid
foggy
chilly/freezing
muggy
stormy
snowy

Grammar: *Will* for predictions

Another structure English uses to talk about future time is *will*. In this lesson, *will* is introduced as an alternative to *going to* for making predictions. *Will* is slightly more formal than *going to* for predictions. *Will* is also used to talk about decisions made at the time of speaking: *The phone is ringing. I'll answer it.* In everyday speech, *will* is generally used in its contracted form. Using the full form makes speakers sound overly formal.

A. Rewrite the sentences using *be going to* or *will*.

Be going to

1. I think it's going to rain tomorrow.

2. _____

3. Are temperatures going to rise in the next 100 years?

4. _____

5. Is it going to be overcast tomorrow?

Will

I think it will rain tomorrow.

I'm sure it won't be sunny this afternoon.

_____

What will the weather be like on the weekend?

_____

B. Write statements that are true for you. Use *be going to* or *will*.

Conversation

 A. Listen to the conversation.

Track 2-11

Andrew:	Do we have everything ready for the beach?
Barbara:	Sure. Everything's ready.
Andrew:	Do you think it's going to rain?
Barbara:	No, they say it's going to be hot.
Andrew:	Are you going to take your umbrella?
Barbara:	No, I said it's going to be hot. It's not going to rain.
Andrew:	No, I mean your beach umbrella for the sun.
Barbara:	Oh, I see. Yes, that's a good idea.

 B. Practice the conversation with a partner. Switch roles and practice it again.

 C. Circle the predictions. Change the predictions to *will* and practice it again.

 Goal 3 **Make weather predictions**

Talk to a partner. What is the weather like now? What is it going to be like tomorrow?

Lesson C **93**

A • Have students work individually to rewrite the sentences.
  • Check answers.

Answers: 2. I'm sure it isn't going to be sunny this afternoon. 3. Will temperatures rise in the next 100 years? 4. What is the weather going to be like on the weekend? 5. Will it be overcast tomorrow?

B • Have each student write three sentences about the weather with *going to* or *will*.
  • Call on students to read a sentence to the class.

Conversation

A • Have students close their books. Play the recording for students to listen to. **(CD2 T11)**

B • Play or read the conversation again for the class to repeat.
  • Practice the conversation with the class in chorus.
  • Have students practice the conversation with a partner and then switch roles and practice it again.

C • Have students work with their partner to find the predictions and change them to *will*.
  • Check answers.

Answers: Do you think it will rain? No, they say it will be hot. Will you take your umbrella? No, I said it will be hot. It won't rain.
  • Have students practice the new conversation with a partner.

✓ Goal 3

  • Have students discuss the questions with a partner. Compare answers with the class.

Grammar Practice: *Will* for predictions

Divide the class into groups of three to four. Assign each group one of these topics: food, clothes, schools, houses, TV (more than one group can do the same topic). Tell each group to think about life 20 years from now and write as many predictions about their topic as they can with *will*. Set a time limit (for example, five minutes). Then ask one member of each group to read the group's predictions to the class.

Discuss the Future

- Introduce the topic of the reading. Ask students, *What are some kinds of energy that we use?* Elicit/give words like *oil, gas, electricity*, and so forth.

A • Match students with a partner and have them discuss the questions. Tell them that they will find the answers in the article.

- Have students read the article to check their guesses. Tell them to circle any words they don't understand.

- Check answers.

Answers: 1. coal, oil, and natural gas; 2. things like solar power and wind power

- Go over the article with the class, answering any questions from the students about vocabulary.

B • Have students underline the sentences from the reading that have *will* and rewrite them using *be going to*.

- Check answers.

Answers: I am not going to worry about electric bills . . . I am not going to feel guilty about pollution. How are we going to get the energy? We are going to find alternatives. We are going to need renewable energy. The cost of solar energy is going to fall. In the future most houses are going to have solar panels. Are our grandchildren going to get their energy from the sun?

C • Have students work individually to answer the questions.

- Check answers.

Answers: 1. So he won't worry about electric bills. 2. 66, 3. It's expensive, it needs a lot of space, and it doesn't work at night. 4. Turbines are ugly and the wind doesn't blow all the time. 5. He isn't sure.

D   **GOAL 4**   **DISCUSS THE FUTURE**

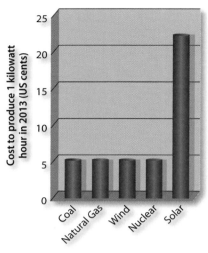

Cost to produce 1 kilowatt hour in 2013 (US cents) — Coal, Natural Gas, Wind, Nuclear, Solar

Reading

A. Discuss these questions with a partner. Read the article to check your answers.

1. What are fossil fuels?
2. What is alternative energy?

B. Underline the sentences in the article that contain *will*. Rewrite them using *be going to*.

C. Answer the questions.

1. Why did the author put solar panels on his roof? _____
2. In 2100, the world's energy will be equal to how many light bulbs per person?
   _____
3. What are three problems with solar power? _____
   _____
4. What are two problems with wind energy? _____
5. Does Michael Pacheco think there will be enough energy in the future?
   _____

Future Energy
WHERE WILL WE GET OUR ENERGY?

It's a bright sunny day. I put the last solar panel on my roof, I switch it on, and I have electricity. I'm free! Now, I won't have to worry about electric bills or oil prices, and I won't feel guilty about pollution. But what's this? A cloud passes in front of the sun and my lights go out! I'm going to have to start my generator and burn some more gasoline. This isn't going to be easy after all.

We are going to have a big energy problem in the future. Today, the world uses 320 billion kilowatt-hours of energy a day. That's equal to about 22 light bulbs burning nonstop for every person on the planet. By 2100 we will use three times as much energy. How will we get the energy? At the moment, we get most of our energy from fossil fuels: coal, oil, and natural gas. But fossil fuels are dirty and they will not last forever. In the long term, we will have to find **alternatives**. We will need **renewable** energy.

SOLAR POWER

On a cloudy day near the city of Leipzig in the former East Germany, I walked across a field with 33,500 solar panels. It produces enough energy for 1800 homes.

For Your Information: Renewable energy facts

- Enough sunlight falls on the earth's surface in one hour to meet the world's energy demands for a whole year.
- More than 10,000 homes in the United States use solar electricity.
- Albert Einstein won the Nobel Prize in 1921 for his work producing electricity from sunlight.
- One wind turbine produces enough electricity for 300 homes.
- People in China used wind power to grind grain in 200 BC.
- To produce wind power, the wind must blow at least 14 mph (20 kph).

One problem with solar power is that it is expensive, but the cost of solar will fall as technology improves. "Thirty years ago it was **cost-effective** on satellites," says Daniel Shugar, president of PowerLight Corporation. "Today it can be cost-effective for powering houses and businesses." He tells us that in the future most houses will have solar panels.

There are other problems with solar power. It needs a lot of space and, of course, it doesn't work at night.

WIND POWER

One afternoon I stood in a field in Denmark under a dark, cloudy sky. My solar panels produce very little energy in this weather. But above me a wind turbine was producing clean, renewable electricity. At the moment, wind power is the best of all the alternative energy sources. But again, there are problems. First, they are **ugly**; people don't like to see wind turbines in fields. And of course the wind doesn't blow all the time.

So, will our grandchildren get their energy from the sun, wind, or some other source? "We're going to need everything we can get from solar, everything we can get from wind," says Michael Pacheco, director of the National Bioenergy Center, part of the National Renewable Energy Laboratory (NREL) in Golden, Colorado. "And still the question is—can we get enough?"

Word Focus

alternative = something different *I don't like this idea. Is there an alternative?*
renewable = something you can use again and again
cost-effective = something that is cost-effective saves a lot of money
ugly = not beautiful

Writing

 A. Work with a partner. Write statements about the future using the information in the box. Make your statements positive or negative.

people/live under the sea	researchers/find alternative fuels
people/enough food to eat	people/travel to Mars
scientists/find a cure for AIDS	wars/end

B. Use your ideas from exercise **A** to write a paragraph about the future.

In the next twenty-five years . . .

✔ Goal 4 — Discuss the future

Join two or three other students and discuss your ideas about the future.

- Talk about other kinds of renewable energy the students may be familiar with—for example, water power, wood, and other natural fuels, and geothermal power (power from the earth's heat). Ask, *Which ones do we use here? What do people use them for?* Ask students to make predictions about energy in the future with *will*.

Writing

A • Have students talk with a partner to discuss their predictions about the future, using *will* or *won't*.

B • Have students write a group of sentences about their opinions from exercise **A** using the phrase given to begin their paper.

- Have students exchange papers with a partner. Ask students to mark corrections and suggestions for improvements on their partner's paper.

- If desired, have students rewrite their papers, to be collected for marking.

✔ Goal 4

- Divide the class into groups of three to four students and have them share their ideas from their papers. Appoint a secretary in each group to write down the most interesting ideas.

- Call on the secretaries to present two to three ideas to the class.

After Reading

Have students work in pairs to search online for information about a place where people are now using one of these forms of renewable energy: solar, wind, biomass, geothermal, or water. Have them tell the class about the place and what people are doing with that form of energy.

Video Journal

Before You Watch

- Have students answer the questions with a partner. Then compare answers with the class.

Answers: 1. gas, electricity, and wood; 2. Answers will vary.

While You Watch

A • Tell students to watch the video the first time and find which person said each statement. Play the video.

- Check answers.

Answers: 1. b, 2. c, 3. a

B • Tell students to watch the video again and mark the answers. Point out that more than one answer may be correct. Have the students read the statements. Play the video.

- Check answers.

Answers: 1. environmental, 2. health, 3. environmental, health, 4. health, 5. environmental

E   VIDEO JOURNAL   *SOLAR COOKING*

Before You Watch

👥 Discuss these questions with a partner.

1. What fuels can you use to cook food?
2. What fuel do you use to cook food?

▲ gas   ▲ electricity   ▲ firewood   ▲ solar energy   ▲ wind

While You Watch

 A. Watch the video and match the people and their comments.

1. Eleanor Shimeall ____   a. And the smoke from that fire—it burns their eyes and chokes their lungs.

2. Dr. Bob Metcalf ____   b. I'm going to check on this chicken and rice and see how it's cooking. Ah, it's doing a good job.

3. African woman ____   c. We're all amazed that a cardboard box can cook.

 B. Watch the video again. Check (✓) the correct box.

| | Benefits of solar ovens | |
	Health	Environmental
1. You don't have to cut down trees.	☐	☐
2. African women don't have to walk a long way to collect firewood.	☐	☐
3. There is no smoke.	☐	☐
4. Solar ovens can be used to make water clean.	☐	☐
5. Solar ovens don't cause pollution.	☐	☐

For Your Information: Solar cooking

There are many different types of solar cookers—more than 65 different designs are available today, and people are inventing their own variations every day. All of them work in similar ways. Some kind of reflective material concentrates sunlight in a small cooking area, where a black surface turns the light into heat. A clear material lets light enter but keeps the heat inside so it can cook the food. Solar cooker projects are being carried out around the world. For example in Lesotho in southern Africa, women have started bakeries that use solar ovens. In Sudan, refugees in camps make their own solar cookers from local materials. And in India, entire villages have started cooking all their food in solar ovens.

C • Tell students to watch the video a third time and find the information. Play the video.

• Check answers.

Answers: 1. meat, fish, grains, and vegetables, 2. stop deforestation and make women's lives easier, 3. 65 degrees Celsius/149 degrees Fahrenheit

After You Watch

• Match students with a partner and have them try to work out a way to make a solar oven. Point out that a solar oven should be cheap and easy to make so that many people can have one.

• If this is difficult for your students, do this activity as a whole class. Prompt them as needed: *What kinds of things get hot in the sun? (dark things) What will let the sun in but keep the heat from getting out? (clear material like glass or plastic)*

• Make drawings on the board to show how the students' inventions will work.

Communication

• Match students with a partner and go over the situation. Assign roles to the students and have them role-play the conversation.

• Call on student pairs to present their role-plays to the class.

C. Watch again and answer the questions.

1. What can you cook in a solar oven? _____
2. What are the goals of Solar Cookers International? _____
3. To what temperature must you heat water to make it safe to drink?

_____

After You Watch

Work with a partner. Could you make a solar oven? Make a list of material you need to make a solar oven. Write instructions on how to make a solar oven. Use drawings if necessary.

▲ solar cooking

Communication

Role-play the following situation.

Student A
You are running a workshop in Africa. You have to explain the benefits of using solar ovens. Some of the participants have doubts.

Student B
You are a participant in the workshop. Your mother cooked with wood and you cook with wood. You have doubts about changing to something new. Express your doubts. Ask questions.

Teacher Tip: Giving students more responsibility

Giving students responsibility for everyday classroom tasks can not only lighten the teacher's workload but can help students feel more involved. Here are some tasks that your students may be able to perform:

• handing back homework
• distributing papers
• calling the class to order at the beginning
• setting up audio equipment
• erasing/washing the board

- Introduce the theme of the unit. Ask students, *What are you wearing today? Where did you buy it?*

- Direct students' attention to the pictures. With the class, look at each picture in turn, and have students name things they see in each one (for example, a kimono).

- Have students work with a partner to discuss the questions.

Answers: Answers will vary.

- Compare answers with the class.

- Follow up with these questions, asking them orally or writing them on the board for students to answer in pairs:

  1. *Do you like shopping for clothes? Why, or why not?*

  2. *Where do you go shopping for clothes?*

- Go over the Unit Goals with the class, explaining and/or translating as necessary.

SHOPPING FOR

1. Where are these people from?

2. Which clothes do you like? Why?

UNIT GOALS

Make comparisons
Explain preferences
Talk about clothing materials
Understand and describe a process

98

	Unit Goals	Grammar	Vocabulary	Listening	Speaking and Pronunciation	Reading and Writing
	• Make comparisons • Explain preferences • Talk about clothing materials • Understand and describe a process	Comparatives *This dress is **prettier than** that one.* Superlatives *The cotton pajamas are **the cheapest**.*	Clothing Descriptive adjectives Clothing materials	Listening for specific information: shoe shopping	Talking about clothes Shopping—at the store and online Rising and falling intonation	"Silk—the Queen of Textiles" Writing about favorite clothes

CLOTHES

99

Unit Theme Overview

- Along with so many other things, fashion and the way we shop for clothes have changed in recent years. With the Internet, new styles and fads move around the world faster than ever; the globalization of manufacturing has reduced prices for clothing and made it possible for people to afford a greater variety of clothing than previously. And online shopping makes it possible for people in even small or remote places to purchase the latest fashions and seek out clothing that matches their tastes exactly.

- In this unit, students acquire basic vocabulary for clothing and learn to talk about their tastes and preferences by making comparisons. They practice superlatives and use them while practicing the language they need for shopping in stores. Finally, they will learn the history and culture behind the most exotic and treasured of clothing materials—silk.

Make Comparisons

Vocabulary

- Go over the vocabulary for types of clothing presented in the illustrations. Ask if students are wearing any of the items (such as a sweater, flats, or loafers). Point out that some of these items are used by men as well as women: coat, sweater, hat, gloves, scarf, boots, pajamas, slippers, and loafers. The other items are worn by women.

A
- Have students work individually to find the word in each row that is different.
- Match students with partners and have them compare answers and explain their reasons.
- Check answers with the class.

Answers: 1. dress (we wear the others at home), 2. swimsuit (the others are for cold weather), 3. hat (the others are for your feet), 4. pumps (the others are for your body, not your feet), 5. handbag (the others are shoes), 6. coat (the others are shoes)

B
- Have students work individually to find the adjectives in the sentences.
- Check answers.

Answers: thick, handmade, poor quality, thin, expensive, formal, cheap, casual, soft, warm, poor quality, thin, modern, cool, old-fashioned

- Go over the meanings of the adjectives with the class.

C
- Have students work individually to complete the sentences with the adjectives.
- Check answers.

Answers: 1. warm, 2. old-fashioned, 3. Handmade, 4. formal, 5. thick

D
- Have students work individually to find the opposite of each adjective.
- Check answers.

Answers: 1. e, 2. c, 3. b, 4. g, 5. f, 6. h, 7. a, 8. d

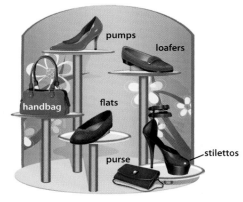

100   **Shopping for Clothes**

Word Bank: More clothing

pants	skirt
blouse	shirt
shorts	sweatshirt
tank top	jacket
(neck)tie	socks
underwear	sneakers
belt	sandals

Vocabulary

A. Circle the word in each row that does not belong. Tell a partner why.

1. dress	pajamas	robe	nightgown
2. sweater	gloves	swimsuit	coat
3. shoes	socks	hat	loafers
4. jeans	T-shirt	suit	pumps
5. handbag	stilettos	pumps	loafers
6. stilettos	boots	slippers	coat

B. Underline the adjectives that describe clothes.

1. Fatima is wearing a thick, handmade sweater and she's warm.
2. Charles is wearing a poor quality, thin coat and he's cold.
3. John wore an expensive, formal business suit to the interview.
4. Andrew wore a cheap, casual jacket. Guess who got the job!
5. Aisha bought her daughter a soft, warm pair of pajamas.
6. Betty bought her child some poor quality, thin pajamas. Which child woke up at 3:00 a.m.?
7. Fiona went to the beach wearing a modern pair of cut-off jeans and a cool sleeveless top.
8. Elena went wearing old-fashioned khaki pants and a sweatshirt. Guess who was hot!

C. Complete the sentences with the words that you underlined in exercise **B**.

1. It's going to be cold tomorrow. You should take a _____ jacket.
2. You can't wear those _____ jeans. You need to buy some modern ones.
3. _____ clothes are always more expensive than machine-made clothes.
4. Looks are important, so I always wear a _____ suit when I meet clients.
5. This sweater is too light. Where is my _____ one?

D. Match the opposites.

1. formal ___	a. cool
2. old-fashioned ___	b. expensive
3. cheap ___	c. fashionable, modern
4. rough, hard ___	d. heavy
5. handmade ___	e. casual, informal
6. thick ___	f. machine made
7. warm ___	g. soft
8. light ___	h. thin

Grammar: Comparatives

Comparative forms of adjectives

Adjectives with one syllable Add *-er*.	cheap	Machine-made sweaters are **cheaper than** handmade sweaters.
Adjectives that end in *-y* Change the *-y* to *i* and add *-er*.	pretty	This dress is **prettier than** that one.
Adjectives with two or more syllables Use *more* or *less* before the adjective.	beautiful	Eleanor is **more beautiful than** Eva.
	expensive	These suits are **less expensive than** those.
Irregular comparatives	good	Shopping in a store is **better than** shopping online.
	bad	My grades are **worse than** yours.

*The comparative form is followed by *than*.
*Use *much* to make a comparison stronger.
  This coat is **much better than** the other one.

Complete the sentences. Use the comparative form of the word in parentheses.

1. I prefer the green handbag, but it is _____ (expensive) than the blue purse.
2. These scarves are _____ (nice) than those.
3. These shoes are _____ (formal) than those.
4. The wool gloves are _____ (soft) than the leather ones.
5. I think the blue slippers are _____ (pretty) than the black ones.

Conversation

Track 2-12

A. Listen to the conversation. Danny and Elena are shopping. What is Elena looking for?

Danny: Look at these black shoes. They look nice.
Elena: I don't know. I need something more formal. They're for work.
Danny: What about these blue ones?
Elena: Mmm, I'm not sure. They're a little expensive.
Danny: Look! Here are some cheaper ones.
Elena: Yes, they're very nice. Oh, they're a size 8. Do they have them in a smaller size?
Danny: Yes, here we are.
Elena: Perfect.

Real Language

We can say *I don't know* or *I'm not sure* to show uncertainty.

B. Practice the conversation. Switch roles and practice it again.

 Goal 1 — **Make comparisons**

Compare your clothes with a partner's clothes.

I like your jeans. They're nicer than mine.

Grammar

A • Introduce the structure. Draw two people on the board, John (tall, heavy, age: 25, holding a paper with *Test score: 72%* on it) and Fred (short, thin, age: 21, holding a paper with *Test score: 100%* on it). Ask students, *Who is taller?* Elicit, *John is.* Ask, *Who is younger/thinner/heavier/older/more intelligent?*

• Go over the information in the box. Give/elicit more examples of each type of adjective.

• Have students work individually to fill in the comparative adjectives.

• Check answers.

Answers: 1. more expensive, 2. nicer, 3. more formal, 4. softer, 5. prettier

Conversation

A • Have students close their books. Write the question on the board: *What is Elena looking for?*

• Play the recording. **(CD2 T12)**

• Check answers.

Answer: shoes

B • Play or read the conversation again for the class to repeat.

• Practice the conversation with the class in chorus.

• Have students practice the conversation with a partner and then switch roles and practice it again.

☑ Goal 1

• Have students work with partners to talk about their clothes and compare them.

Grammar: Comparative adjectives

English forms the comparative of adjectives in two different ways: with *-er* (for short adjectives) and with *more* (for long adjectives). Students occasionally use a combination of both, erroneously: ~~He is more taller than I am.~~ They may also need to be reminded of spelling changes: *big → bigger*; *happy → happier*.

Grammar Practice: Comparative adjectives

Bring magazines to class. Divide students into groups of three. Have groups compare the different articles of clothing worn by people in the magazines using comparative adjectives: *That green sweater is more fashionable than the blue one.*

Explain Preferences

Listening

- Introduce the topic by asking, *Where do you go to buy shoes? Do you like shopping for shoes? Why, or why not?*

A • Tell students they are going to hear a conversation in a shoe store. Have them read the question. Play the recording one or more times. **(CD2 T13)**

- Check answers.

Answer: blue shoes

B • Tell students to listen again to find the information. Go over the questions.

- Play the recording one or more times. **(CD2 T13)**
- Check answers.

Answers: 1. two, 2. $80, 3. $75, 4. seven or seven and a half, 5. blue

C • Have students work individually to match the columns. Play the recording for students to check. **(CD2 T13)** Then go over the answers with the class.

Answers: 1. c, 2. d, 3. a, 4. b

Pronunciation

- Remind students that when we say a sentence, our voice goes up and down (intonation).

A • Point out the arrows in the first sentence that show rising and falling intonation.

- Tell students to listen to the recording and mark arrows on the other sentences. Play the recording several times. **(CD2 T14)**
- Check answers.

Answers: 2. ↘prettier ↗Karen's ↘Mia's, 3. ↘easier ↗online ↘shopping, 4. ↘warmer ↗sweater ↘jacket, 5. ↘handsome ↗Ian ↘Mario

B • Play the recording again for students to repeat. **(CD2 T14)**

- Then have them read the sentences to a partner.

B GOAL 2 EXPLAIN PREFERENCES

Listening

Track 2-13

A. Listen. What is the woman buying?

Track 2-13

B. Listen again and answer the questions.

1. How many pairs of shoes does the woman try on? _____
2. How much did the white shoes cost? _____
3. How much did the black shoes cost? _____
4. What size shoes does the woman wear? _____
5. What color were the shoes that the woman bought? _____

C. Match the questions and the answers.

1. Can I try them on? ____
2. Cash or charge? ____
3. How much are they? ____
4. What size are you? ____

a. They're $65.
b. I'm a 12.
c. Yes, the dressing rooms are over there.
d. I'll put it on my card.

Pronunciation: Rising and falling intonation

Track 2-14

A. Listen to the sentences. Write the arrows to show rising or falling intonation.

1. Which swim suit is cheaper? The blue one or the red one?
2. Whose dress is prettier? Karen's or Mia's?
3. Which is easier? Shopping online or store shopping?
4. Which do you think is warmer? The sweater or the jacket?
5. Who is more handsome? Ian or Mario?

Track 2-14

B. Listen again. Repeat the sentences.

102 Shopping for Clothes

For Your Information: Shoe sizes

Different countries use different systems of shoe sizes. Here are some common equivalents.

Women:			Men:		
Metric	US	UK	Metric	US	UK
36	5–5.5	2–2.5	41	7–7.5	6–6.5
37	6–6.5	3–3.5	42	8–8.5	7.5–8
38	7–7.5	4–4.5	43	9–9.5	8.5–9
39	8–8.5	5–5.5	44	10–10.5	9.5–10
40	9–9.5	6–6.5	45	11–11.5	10.5–11

Communication

👥 Discuss the questions with a partner. Make a list of your ideas.

1. What are the advantages and disadvantages of shopping online?
2. What are the advantages and disadvantages of shopping in a store?

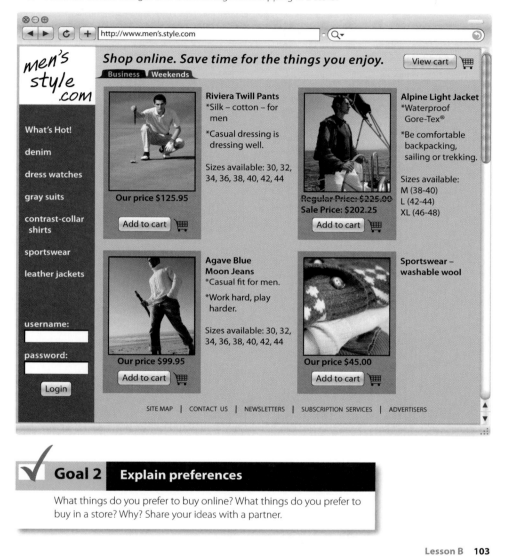

✓ Goal 2 | Explain preferences

What things do you prefer to buy online? What things do you prefer to buy in a store? Why? Share your ideas with a partner.

Communication

- Go over the concept of advantages (good points) and disadvantages (bad points).
- Match students with partners and have them discuss the questions, taking notes about their ideas.
- Compare ideas with the class, making lists on the board.

☑ Goal 2

- Have students discuss the questions with the same partners.
- Call on students to explain their preferences to the class.

Expansion Activity

Have students work with partners to read the Web site on the page and choose a gift for a friend or family member. Call on students to explain what they chose, and why.

Talk about Clothing Material

Language Expansion

A • Go over the materials and clothing in the pictures. Ask for/point out more examples of clothes that students are wearing which are made out of the different materials.

• Match students with partners and have them talk about the clothes in the pictures, describing them and giving their opinions.

B • Go over the symbols and terms in the clothing care instructions. Explain that *bleach* is a kind of liquid that we use to make clothes white, and a *tumble dryer* is a machine that makes clothes dry. To *dry clean* clothes, you take them to a special store.

• Have students work individually to mark the statements true or false.

• Check answers.

Answers: 1. T, 2. F, 3. T, 4. T, 5. T

Grammar

• Review comparative adjectives. Remind students that they are used when we talk about how two things are different.

• Introduce the structure. Ask a number of students, *How tall are you?* (If necessary, teach them, *I'm five foot eight or one meter seventy*, etc.) Say, *(Name) is the tallest student in our class.* Ask students, *Who has long hair?* Say, *(Name) has the longest hair.* Continue with other examples as appropriate —oldest/youngest student, and so on.

• Go over the information in the chart. Give/elicit more examples for each pattern.

> I really like that leather jacket.

Language Expansion: Clothing materials

A. Take turns describing the clothes in the pictures to a partner.

100% Cotton Made in USA	100% Wool Made in Scotland	Man-made fiber Made in Taiwan	100% Leather Made in Argentina	Pure Silk Made in China
Machine Wash, WARM	Hand Wash	Machine Wash, HOT Permanent Press	Do Not Wash	Dry Clean
Bleach as Needed	Do Not Bleach	Bleach as Needed		Do Not Bleach
Tumble Dry, HIGH	Dry Flat	Tumble Dry, MEDIUM		Tumble Dry, MEDIUM
Iron, Steam, or Dry, with HIGH HEAT	Do Not Iron	Iron, Steam, or Dry, withLOW HEAT		Iron, Steam or Dry, with LOW HEAT

B. Read the different care instructions above. Circle **T** for *true* and **F** for *false*.

1. You can use bleach with cotton.   T   F
2. You can dry wool in a tumble drier.   T   F
3. You have to dry clean silk.   T   F
4. You can iron cotton.   T   F
5. You mustn't wash leather.   T   F

Grammar: Superlatives

Superlative forms of adjectives		
Adjectives with one syllable Add *-est*.	cheap	The cotton pajamas are **the cheapest**.
Adjectives that end in -y Change the *-y* to *i* and add *-est*.	pretty	Helen is **the prettiest** girl in the class.
Adjectives with two or more syllables Use *most* or *least* before the adjective.	beautiful	These are **the most beautiful** shoes in the store.
	expensive	This suit is **the least expensive** one they have.
Irregular superlatives	good	Turner's is **the best** shoe store in town.
	bad	My English isn't good, but I don't have **the worst** grades in class.

*The superlative form is preceded by *the*.

Word Bank: More clothing materials

rayon	denim
polyester	suede
nylon	corduroy
vinyl	canvas

Grammar: Superlative adjectives

Superlative adjectives are used to compare one item with a whole group to which it belongs. Often the group is stated in the sentence:

Yoshi is the tallest student in the class.

Superlative adjectives are normally used with *the*. Common errors with superlatives include spelling mistakes and incorrect use of *most* and *-est*.

A. Complete the sentences. Use the superlative form of the adjective in parentheses.

1. These are _____ (expensive) shoes in the store.
2. Which is _____ (warm) jacket? The red one, the brown one, or the blue one?
3. Granger's Discount Store has _____ (good) prices.
4. These are _____ (formal) shoes that we have.

B. Write sentences using the pairs of adjectives in the box.

| cheap/expensive   light/heavy   warm/cool   rough/smooth |

1. _Wool is usually more expensive than cotton, but silk is the most expensive material._
2. _Wool is cheaper than silk, but usually cotton is the cheapest._
3. _____
4. _____
5. _____
6. _____

Conversation

Track 2-15

A. Listen to the conversation. Why doesn't Steve like the leather jacket?

Steve:	Excuse me, could you help me? I'm looking for a jacket.
Shop attendant:	Certainly, sir. I have some over here.
Steve:	Mmm, very nice. Which is the warmest?
Shop attendant:	Well, these GORE-TEX® jackets are the warmest. They're waterproof and not too expensive
Steve:	No, I don't really like man-made material.
Shop attendant:	Well, we have some nice leather jackets.
Steve:	No, I don't really like leather. It's very heavy, and I suppose they are the most expensive.
Shop attendant:	Yes, I'm afraid so. The cheapest is $250.

B. Practice the conversation. Switch roles and practice it again.

C. Work with a partner to make a new conversation. This time try on something different.

✔ **Goal 3**   **Talk about clothing materials**

Talk with a partner. Which is your favorite material? Why?

Lesson C   **105**

Understand and Describe a Process

Reading

- Introduce the topic of the reading. Ask students, *What kinds of clothes are made of silk?* (dresses, blouses, scarves, neckties) *Do you have anything made of silk? What is it?*

A • Match students with partners and have them discuss the questions.

- Point out the vocabulary that is defined in the Word Focus box.

B • Have students read the article. Tell them to circle any words they don't understand.

Additional words:

sophisticated = not simple; **textile** = cloth; **ancient** = a long time ago; **indeed** = really; **discover** = find out about; **mysterious** = not easy to understand; **producer** = maker; **prepare** = make; **fibers** = lines of material in cloth

---

- Go over the article with the class, answering any questions from the students about vocabulary.
- Tell students to read the article again and find the answers.
- Check answers.

Answers: 1. silk, 2. China, 3. In ancient times, weaving was done from the heart. 4. to make them softer, 5. Answers will vary.

▲ Hubert de Givenchy, a French fashion designer, loves working with silk. "It is living. It moves," he says. "It immediately suggests the design of the dress."

Reading

A. Discuss these questions with a partner.

1. What do you know about silk?
2. How is silk made?

B. Answer the questions.

1. Which is the most expensive—cotton, wool, or silk? _____
2. Which country is the biggest producer of silk? _____
3. Why does Shen Congwen think that old silks are more beautiful than modern silks? _____
4. Why do the workers put the cocoons into hot water? _____
5. Do you agree that "A woman is more gentle when she wears a silk kimono"? Give your reasons. _____
   _____

106 **Shopping for Clothes**

Silk—the Queen of Textiles

Cotton is cool; wool is warm. They're practical. But silk? Silk is soft, it is smooth, it is sophisticated—the queen of textiles. It is also possibly the most expensive material in the world, and indeed in ancient Rome it was more expensive than gold. But it is strong as well—a thread of silk is stronger than **steel**.

I wanted to discover more about this **mysterious** material, so I decided to go to China. China is where the secret of silk was discovered more than 4,000 years ago, and today it is still the biggest producer of silk in the world.

The first person I visited was Shen Congwen, advisor on ancient textiles to the Palace Museum in Beijing. He showed me some silk that workers found in a **tomb** in Jianglin, in Hubei Province. It was more than 2,000 years old but still beautiful. He told me that he thinks these old silks are more beautiful than modern silks. "In ancient times, weaving was done from the heart. In modern times, weaving is done for **commerce**."

So, how do you make silk? The first problem is that the silkworm only eats leaves from one tree—the mulberry tree. "It

---

For Your Information: Silk

After the secret of making silk was discovered in China, silk production spread to Korea and India, then across Asia to Europe. Today, over 30 countries produce silk. The biggest producers of silk are China (54 percent of world production), India (14 percent), and Japan (11 percent). Silk is used in many types of clothing, but it is also used in parachutes and bicycle tires.

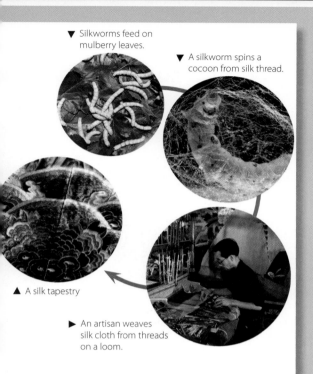

▼ Silkworms feed on mulberry leaves.

▼ A silkworm spins a cocoon from silk thread.

▲ A silk tapestry

▶ An artisan weaves silk cloth from threads on a loom.

is easier to prepare food for a human than a silkworm," says Toshio Ito, a Japanese silkworm physiologist. Silkworms only live for about 28 days, but in that time they increase in weight 10,000 times. At the end of their short lives, they **spin** a **cocoon**. In China, I watched workers collect the cocoons and kill the silkworms with steam or hot air. They then put the cocoons into hot water to make them softer. Next, they pulled the fibers from the cocoon and spun them to make silk thread. Finally, they wove the thread into cloth on machines called **looms**.

But why is silk so expensive? Well, it takes 110 cocoons to make a man's tie, 630 cocoons to make a blouse and 3,000 cocoons to make a heavy silk kimono. That's a lot of mulberry leaves and many hours of hard work. But many people believe its beauty is worth it. As Kokoh Moriguchi, a textile artist told me, "A woman is more gentle when she wears a silk kimono."

Writing

Write a paragraph about your favorite piece of clothing. Answer the questions.

- What is it made from?
- Where did you get it?
- When did you get it?
- How much did it cost?
- Why do you like it?

> My favorite piece of clothing is a silk scarf. It was a present from my grandmother. She gave it to me when I was 10 years old. I don't know how much it cost but silk is very expensive. It is a beautiful deep red and it is very, very soft. I love it.

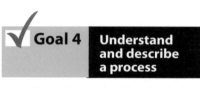

✓ **Goal 4** | **Understand and describe a process**

Work with a partner. Describe the process for making silk.

Lesson D   107

Writing

- Ask students to think about their favorite piece of clothing and why they like it. Tell them they are going to write about this item. Go over the writing model and have them write a similar composition about the item they have chosen

- Have students exchange papers with a partner. Ask students to mark corrections and suggestions for improvements on their partners' papers.

- If desired, have students rewrite their papers, to be collected for marking.

☑ **Goal 4**

- Have students close their books and work with partners to describe as much of the silk-making process as they can remember.

- Work with the class to describe the process together. Ask, *What happens first? Next?* and so forth.

After Reading

Have students search online for an item of silk clothing that they like (for instance, a necktie, shirt, or blouse). Remind them NOT to enter any credit card information and to be careful NOT to buy anything. Ask them to print a copy of the Web page and write a few sentences about why they chose that item.

Video Journal

Before You Watch

A • Students should have all the information they need from the article in the previous lesson. If they need more help, brainstorm as a class a list of adjectives to describe all the materials.

B • Have students work individually to find the opposite of each word.

• Check answers.

Answers: 1. c, 2. a, 3. d, 4. b, 5. e

C • Tell students to think about the topic of the video and then choose the words they think will be in the video.

Answers: ancient, noisy, slowly, beautiful

While You Watch

A • Tell students to watch the video the first time and mark the statements *true* or *false*. Go over the statements. Play the video.

• Check answers.

Answers: 1. F, 2. T, 3. T

B • Tell students to watch the video again and find the answers. Have the students read the statements. Play the video.

• Check answers.

Answers: 1. a, 2. b, 3. c, 4. b, 5. c

 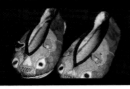 

E VIDEO JOURNAL   *TRADITIONAL SILK MAKING*

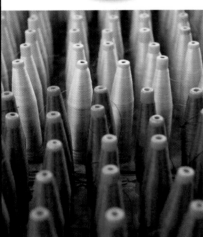

Before You Watch

A. Talk to a partner. Discuss how silk thread is different from wool, cotton, and synthetic threads.

B. Match the opposites.

1. noisy ____   a. different
2. same ____   b. quickly
3. modern ____   c. quiet
4. slowly ____   d. ancient
5. beautiful ____   e. ugly

C. Circle the words in exercise **B** that you think you will hear in the video. Watch the video and check your answers.

While You Watch

A. Watch the video and circle **T** for *true* and **F** for *false*

1. Florence is a modern city.   T   F
2. The factory manager is a man.   T   F
3. There are lots of women working in the factory.   T   F

B. Watch again. Circle the correct answer.

1. The Industrial Revolution, _____, and floods forced change.
   a. world wars
   b. the cold war
   c. world laws
2. The mechanical looms were made _____.
   a. in 1780
   b. in the 19th century
   c. 500 years ago
3. Other manufacturers threw away their old hand looms _____.
   a. after World War I
   b. 500 years ago
   c. after World War II

108 **Shopping for Clothes**

For Your Information: Florence

Florence is a historic city in the Tuscany region of Italy. It is considered the birthplace of the Renaissance in European culture and played an important role in the development of European art and architecture. Tourists come to visit its Duomo (cathedral) and other magnificent churches and the Ponte Vecchio (Old Bridge), which is lined with many small shops. The city is renowned for its artisans who still work with leather, silk, paper, and other traditional crafts. Modern Florence has a population of about 365,000 people.

After You Watch

- Match students with partners and have them talk about the questions.
- Compare answers with the class.

Communication

- Go over the situation with the class and assign each student a role.
- Have students role-play the situation.
- When all student pairs are finished, ask, *What kind of cloth did you buy? Why?*

4. The silk produced on antique hand looms has _____.
   a. 4,000 threads
   b. 12,000 threads
   c. 3,000 threads
5. Every damask and brocade is _____.
   a. man-made
   b. handmade
   c. custom-made

After You Watch

Discuss these questions with a partner.

1. Why do you think Stefano Benelli is the only man in the video?
2. Are men better at some jobs than women? Why?
3. At which jobs are women better than men? Why?

▲ loom

▲ brocade

Communication

Role-play the following situation.

Student A

You are a sales assistant in a textile shop. Try to sell the handmade silk.

Handmade silk brocade	Machine-made silk	Artificial silk (acetate)
Price: $55-$100 per meter	**Price:** $25-$35 per meter	**Price:** $15-$25 per meter

Student B

You are a customer. You want 5 meters of cloth for some curtains. You can spend about $200.

Teacher Tip: Sharing students' work

There are a number of ways that students can share their work with their classmates:
- give oral presentations in front of the class
- make large posters to display in front of the class (brown wrapping paper for packages is cheap and works well for this)
- tape students' papers around the classroom walls and allow time for students to walk around and read their classmates' work
- have students write or draw on transparencies and show these to the class on an overhead projector
- photocopy students' papers into a class magazine/newspaper and make a copy for each student

- Introduce the theme of the unit. Explain that your lifestyle is your way of living—all the things you do every day.

- Direct students' attention to the pictures. With the class, look at each picture in turn, and have students name things they see in each one.

- Have students work with a partner to discuss the questions.

- Compare answers with the class.

Answers: 1. (left to right) the organic food market, the runner, the woman celebrating her 100th birthday, 2. Answers will vary.

- Follow up with these questions, asking them orally or writing them on the board for students to answer in pairs:

  1. *What are the most important things for a healthy lifestyle?*

  2. *Are our lifestyles healthier now than they were in the past?*

- Go over the Unit Goals with the class, explaining and/or translating as necessary.

LIFESTYLES

1. Which of these photos show a healthy lifestyle?

2. How is your lifestyle? Can you improve it?

UNIT GOALS

Give advice on healthy habits
Suggest ways to improve bad habits
Ask about lifestyles
Evaluate your lifestyle

110

Unit Goals	Grammar	Vocabulary	Listening	Speaking and Pronunciation	Reading and Writing
• Give advice on healthy habits • Suggest ways to improve bad habits • Ask about lifestyles • Evaluate your lifestyle	Modals—*could, ought to, should, must, have to* You **have to** *stop smoking.* Questions with *how* **How** *much exercise do you do?*	Healthy and unhealthy habits Compound adjectives	Listening for general understanding: personal lifestyles	Discussing healthy and unhealthy habits Giving advice for improving habits *Should, shouldn't*	"The Secrets of Long Life" Writing a paragraph about personal lifestyle

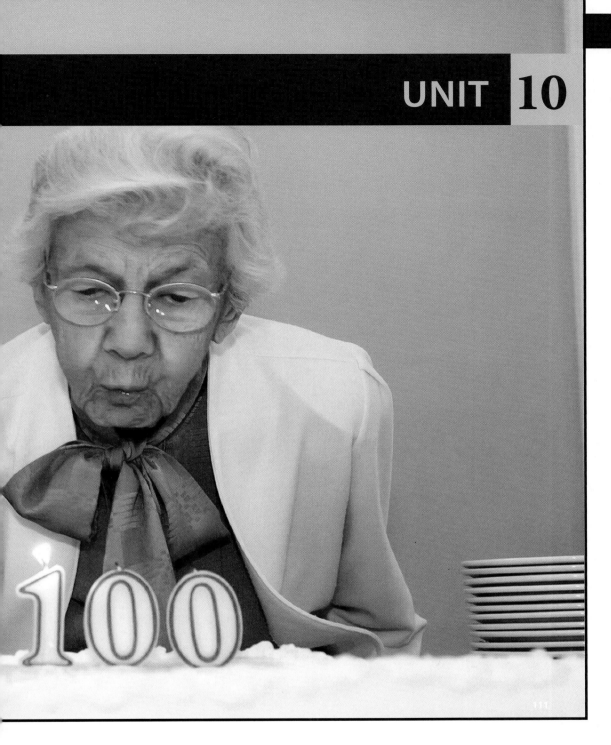

UNIT 10

Unit Theme Overview

- The concept of lifestyle was first developed in 1929 by the psychologist Alfred Adler, but it became popular in the 1970s. The term refers to the overall way that a person lives. A person's lifestyle is made up of a complex collection of personal choices and customs imposed by society. Our environment and our culture limit the range of choices that we can make.

- This unit focuses on one particular aspect of lifestyle: the habits and choices that affect our health. Here, again, lifestyle has both personal and social components. People's choices about food, exercise, and other daily activities have an impact on their health, but there are also cultures in the world where people enjoy unusually long and healthy lives due to culturally imposed customs.

- In this unit, students begin by discussing healthy personal habits and giving advice. They talk about ways to change habits and learn to ask questions to get more details. Finally, they learn about cultural patterns that seem to promote good health—and others that seem to hinder it.

Give Advice on Healthy Habits

Vocabulary

- Go over the sentences with the class, pointing out the expressions in blue and explaining as necessary. Ask questions for further practice: *Are you in good shape or are you unfit? Do you eat a lot of junk food?*

A • Have students work individually to fill in the words.

- Check answers.

Answers: 1. bad shape, 2. healthy, 3. lifestyle, junk food, 4. unfit, 5. works out, good shape

B • Go over the names for the activities in the pictures.

- Have students work individually to classify the activities in the chart.

- Check answers.

Answers: Healthy: cycling, getting eight hours of sleep every night, drinking lots of water, eating a balanced diet; Unhealthy: sunbathing, smoking, watching lots of TV, eating lots of sugar

- Point out that these expressions can also be formed as verbs: *I sunbathe. I drink lots of water.* Ask students to tell you one healthy/ unhealthy thing they do (*I run every day / I eat lots of sugar*).

A GOAL 1 GIVE ADVICE ON HEALTHY HABITS

Vocabulary

Alicia has a **healthy** lifestyle. She's in **good shape** because she **works out** in the gym every day. She eats healthy food, like fruit and fresh vegetables.

Alan doesn't have a good **lifestyle**. He's **unfit** because he never does any exercise. He eats too much **junk food** so he's overweight. He's in **bad shape**.

A. Complete the sentences with the words in **blue**.

1. I need to exercise more. I'm in _____.
2. Helen doesn't have a _____ diet. She eats a lot of junk food.
3. I have a good _____. I don't smoke, I exercise regularly, and I don't eat _____.
4. I need to exercise more. I'm _____, and I'm overweight.
5. Jane is looking great! She _____ and eats healthy food like whole grain bread and lots of fruit. Soon she'll be in _____.

B. Write the activities in the correct column.

▲ sunbathing   ▲ smoking   ▲ watching lots of TV   ▲ cycling

▲ getting eight hours sleep every night   ▲ drinking lots of water   ▲ eating a balanced diet   ▲ eating lots of sugar

Healthy	Unhealthy

Word Bank: Healthy and unhealthy habits

Healthy:
taking vitamins
going for a walk every day
getting fresh air
relaxing
going to the doctor for a checkup
playing tennis/basketball/soccer
avoiding stress

Unhealthy:
staying up late
getting angry often
playing too many computer games
drinking alcohol
eating a lot of salty/fatty food
not wearing a seat belt in the car

Grammar: Modals—*could, ought to, should, must, have to*

Could, ought to, should, must, have to		
Make suggestions	**Give advice**	**Express obligation**
You **could** stop smoking.	You **should/ought to** stop smoking.	You **must/have to** stop smoking.
! gentle	**!!** strong	**!!!** very strong

 A. Take turns. Make suggestions, give advice, or express obligations. Use the activities on page 112.

> You could drink more water.
>
> He ought to stop sunbathing.

B. Give advice for the following situations.

1. Tell your sister to stop smoking. **!!!**

   _____

2. Tell to your father go on a diet. **!!**

   _____

3. Tell your friend to stop watching so much television. **!**

   _____

Conversation

Track 2-16

A. Listen to the conversation. Why does Mia want to lose weight?

Mia: I need to lose some weight. My clothes don't fit anymore. What should I do?

Alex: Well, instead of watching TV all day, you could do more exercise.

Mia: Like what?

Alex: Like cycling, or you could work out at the gym.

Mia: I don't have time. I'm too busy.

Alex: OK, then you could change your diet. Eat something healthier, like fruit.

Mia: You mean no more hamburgers! Oh no!

Alex: OK. Buy some bigger clothes then.

Real Language

We use *like what* to ask for an example. We can use *like* to give an example.

B. Practice the conversation with a partner. Switch roles and practice it again.

 Goal 1 **Give advice on healthy habits**

Take turns. Give a partner suggestions on how to improve his or her health.

Grammar

- Introduce the structures. Tell the class, *Mr. X is a teacher at our school. He smokes forty cigarettes every day, and he coughs all the time. What would a student say to him?* Have students read the chart. Elicit, You could stop smoking. Ask, *What would his friend say to him?* (You should/ought to stop smoking.) *What would his doctor say to him?* (You must/have to stop smoking.)

A • Match students with partners and have them talk about the pictures on the previous page.

- Call on students to tell the class about one of the pictures. They should also say who would say that sentence.

B • Have students work individually to write a sentence for each situation.

- Check answers.

Answers: 1. You have to stop smoking. 2. You ought to go on a diet. 3. You could stop watching so much television.

Conversation

A • Have students close their books. Write the question on the board: *Why does Mia want to lose weight?*

- Play the recording. **(CD2 T16)**
- Check answers.

Answer: Her clothes don't fit.

B • Play or read the conversation again for the class to repeat.

- Practice the conversation with the class in chorus.
- Have students practice the conversation with partners and then switch roles and practice it again.

☑ Goal 1

- Have students work with partners to talk about their habits and give advice for improvement.
- Call on students to tell the class one suggestion that they made to their partner.

Grammar: Modals—*could, ought to, should, must, have to*

Telling other people what to do can be a sensitive situation, and native speakers use modals to make an idea less forceful and more polite, depending on their relationship with the other person.

Grammar Practice: Modals—*could, ought to, should, must, have to*

Have students work with partners to write a letter about a health problem to a newspaper column. Together, they should write a letter. When all student pairs have finished, have them exchange letters with another pair. Tell them that they are now "doctors" and should write a reply.

Suggest Ways to Improve Bad Habits

Listening

A • Tell students they are going to hear three people talking about their lifestyles. Have them look at the pictures and read the question. Have them circle the name of the person they think has the least healthy lifestyle. Tell them to listen and find the answer.

• Play the recording one or more times. **(CD2 T17)**

• Check answers.

Answer: Ben

B • Tell students to listen to the three people again and find the information. Play the recording one or more times. **(CD2 T17)**

• Check answers.

Answers: 1. no, 2. yes, 3. She swims. 4. any two of: whole meal bread, honey, yogurt, high-fiber cereal, 5. from her garden, 6. She drinks a lot of coffee.

C • Have students work with partners to make recommendations for the three people.

• Compare answers with the class.

Pronunciation

A • Tell students to listen to the pronunciations of *should* and *shouldn't* in the sentences. Play the recording one or more times. **(CD2 T18)**

B • Tell students to listen to the sentences and circle the correct word. Play the recording one or more times. **(CD2 T19)**

• Check answers.

Answers: 1. shouldn't, 2. should, 3. should, 4. shouldn't

C • Tell students to repeat the sentences. Play the recording again several times. **(CD2 T19)**

• Call on students to read a sentence to the class.

Listening

Track 2-17

A. Look at the pictures. Who do you think has an unhealthy lifestyle? Listen and check your prediction.

▲ Ben

▲ Maggie

▲ Anita

Track 2-17

B. Listen again and answer the questions.

1. Does Ben exercise every day? _____
2. Does Ben smoke? _____
3. What exercise does Maggie do? _____
4. Name two things that Maggie has for breakfast. _____
5. Where does Anita get her vegetables? _____
6. What is Anita's one bad habit? _____

C. Work with a partner. What advice would you give to Ben, Maggie, and Anita on how to improve their lifestyles?

Pronunciation: *Should, shouldn't*

Track 2-18

A. Listen to the sentences. Notice the difference between *should* and *shouldn't*.

I **should** get more sleep.
They **shouldn't** eat junk food.

Track 2-19

B. Listen and circle the word you hear.

1. You should/shouldn't go to bed at one o'clock every night.
2. You should/shouldn't drink less coffee.
3. Zeta should/shouldn't lose some weight.
4. They should/shouldn't watch so much TV.

Track 2-19

C. Listen again and repeat the sentences.

114   Lifestyles

For Your Information: Components of a healthy lifestyle

Research has found that seven habits are closely linked with a longer life. They are:

1. eating breakfast every day, 2. avoiding snacks between meals, 3. keeping an ideal weight, 4. regular exercise, 5. sleeping 7–8 hours per night, 6. not smoking, 7. drinking two or fewer alcoholic drinks per day.

People aged 55 to 64 who practiced all seven of these habits were found to be as healthy as younger people, aged 25 to 34, who followed only one or two of them.

Communication

Take turns. Talk about these bad habits and give advice.

She's worried that she is gaining weight.

What advice are you going to give her?

Well, she should stop eating junk food. She should . . .

✔ Goal 2 | Suggest ways to improve bad habits

Ask two partners about their bad habits. Give them advice.

Communication

- Go over the photos with the class. What is the problem in each picture?
- Match students with partners and have them discuss each picture, giving advice for each person.
- Compare answers with the class.

✔ Goal 2

- Match students with partners. Tell them to describe their own bad habits and ask for advice. Remind students to be polite and use *could*, *should*, or *ought to* in telling their partners what to do.
- Have students change partners and repeat the exercise.

Expansion Activity

Have students work with partners to prepare a role-play about one of the situations in the photos. One person has a problem, and the other tries to help with it. They should decide who the two people are (for example, two friends, or doctor and patient) and use appropriate language in their role-play. When all student pairs are ready, call on them to present their role-plays to the class.

Ask about Lifestyles

Language Expansion

A • Read through the list of adjectives. Point out that each one is formed from two other words.

• Have students work individually to match the columns.

• Check answers.

Answers: 1. b, 2. h, 3. e, 4. g, 5. c, 6. f, 7. a, 8. d

B • Have students work individually to complete each sentence with compound adjectives.

• Check answers.

Answers: 1. lifelong, 2. homegrown, 3. overworked, 4. homemade, mouthwatering

• Elicit more sentences using these adjectives. Ask, *Do you have a lifelong friend? What kinds of homemade food do you like? Who is overworked?* and so forth.

Grammar

• Go over the information in the box about the formation of these questions. Remind students that they already know questions like *How old (are you)?* and *How much/How many.*

A • Have students work individually to match the columns.

• Check answers.

Answers: 1. e, 2. a, 3. d, 4. b, 5. c

▲ mouth-watering fruit

▲ homemade pie

Language Expansion: Compound adjectives

A. Match the compound adjectives to their meanings.

1.	mouth-watering ___	a.	works too much
2.	homemade ___	b.	delicious
3.	heart-warming ___	c.	without worries or problems
4.	lifelong ___	d.	not high in calories
5.	stress-free ___	e.	makes you happy
6.	homegrown ___	f.	produced in your own garden
7.	overworked ___	g.	all your life
8.	low-calorie ___	h.	not made in a factory

B. Complete the sentences. Use the adjectives from exercise **A**.

1. Kevin and I went to kindergarten together. We are _____ friends.
2. When I was a child, my father had a vegetable garden, so we ate lots of _____ fruit and vegetables.
3. I have to work long hours and I'm always tired. I think I am _____.
4. My grandmother makes the best _____ chicken soup in the world! It's absolutely _____.

Grammar: Questions with *how*

How much exercise do you do?
How many cigarettes do you smoke?
How old is your father?
How long did your grandfather live?
How often do you go to the gym?
*We use **how much** to ask about the quantity of non-countable nouns.
*We use **how many** to ask about the quantity of countable nouns.
*We use **how old** to ask about age.
*We use **how long** to ask about length or a period of time.
*We use **how often** to ask about frequency.

A. Match the questions and the answers.

1.	How often does Ian go swimming? ___	a.	She's about 95.
2.	How old is Akuru's grandmother? ___	b.	Until I'm 80.
3.	How much junk food do you eat? ___	c.	About 15.
4.	How long do you think you will live? ___	d.	Not much.
5.	How many cigarettes does Mario smoke a day? ___	e.	Once a week.

Word Bank: Compound adjectives

middle-aged
left-handed/right-handed
world-famous
fat-free/sugar-free
low-salt/high-protein

Grammar: Questions with *How . . .*

How is used with adjectives (*How old, How long*) and adverbs (*How often*) to make questions. In this lesson, the only adverb presented is *often*, an adverb of frequency. Other adverbs can also be used with this structure, including adverbs of manner (*How <u>well</u> do you speak English?*)

B. Write the questions.

Questions	Answers
1. _____	We go to the gym three times a week.
2. _____	I am 27 years old.
3. _____	I think it will take about two hours.
4. _____	I weigh 168 lbs.
5. _____	We will need another 12 chairs.

Conversation

Track 2-20

A. Listen to the conversation. What's the problem with Mr. Lopez?

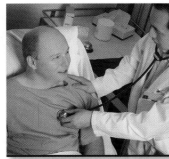

Doctor: Good morning, Mr. Lopez. How can I help you?
Mr. Lopez: Yes, doctor. <u>I'm always tired but when I go to bed I can't sleep.</u>
Doctor: OK, how long have you had this problem?
Mr. Lopez: Since I started my new job.
Doctor: What is your job?
Mr. Lopez: I'm in advertising.
Doctor: How many hours do you work?
Mr. Lopez: I work about 80 hours a week.
Doctor: 80 hours! That's a lot. And how much exercise do you do?
Mr. Lopez: Not much. I don't have the time.
Doctor: OK, it seems to me that you are overworked. You need to work less and find time to do more exercise. Maybe you should look for a more stress-free job.

B. Practice the conversation with a partner. Switch roles and practice it again.

C. Change the underlined problem and practice a new conversation.

✓ **Goal 3** | **Ask about lifestyles**

Ask a partner about his or her lifestyle.

B • Have students work individually to write the question for each answer.
• Check answers.

Answers: 1. How often do you go to the gym? 2. How old are you? 3. How long will it take? 4. How much do you weigh? 5. How many chairs do/will we need?

• Have students practice saying the questions and answers with a partner.

Conversation

A • Have students close their books. Write the question on the board: *What's the problem with Mr. Lopez?*
• Play the recording. **(CD2 T20)**
• Check answers.

Answer: He is overworked; he can't sleep and is always tired.

B • Play or read the conversation again for the class to repeat.
• Practice the conversation with the class in chorus.
• Have students practice the conversation with a partner and then switch roles and practice it again.

C • Have each pair think of a different problem and then make a new conversation, using their own ideas for solving the problem.
• Call on student pairs to present their conversations to the class.

✓ **Goal 3**
• Match students with partners and have them ask each other at least three questions with *How*.
• Call on students to tell you something they learned about their partners.

Grammar Practice: Questions with *How* ...

Have students work with partners to practice a role-play of a reporter interviewing a famous person about his or her lifestyle. The reporter should ask at least three questions with *How*. When all student pairs are ready, call on them to present their role-plays to the class.

OKINAWANS

Since I last visited Ushi five years ago, she's taken a new job, tried to **run away** from home, and started wearing **perfume**. Normal for a young woman, perhaps, but Ushi is 103. When I ask about the perfume, she **jokes** that she has a new boyfriend, then puts a hand over her mouth and gives a long heart-warming laugh.

"Okinawans have one-fifth the heart disease, one-fourth the breast and prostate cancer, and one-third less mental health problems than Americans," says Craig Willcox of the Okinawa Centenarian Study. What's the key to their success? "Ikigai certainly helps," Willcox says. The word translates to "reason for living," and it may help to prevent stress and diseases such as high blood pressure.

Okinawans have a low-calorie diet. "A full plate of Okinawan vegetables, tofu, miso soup, and a little fish or meat contains fewer calories than a small hamburger," says Makoto Suzuki of the Okinawa Centenarian Study. "And it will have many more healthy nutrients."

▲ When she's not watching sumo wrestling on TV, Yasu Itoman, 100, gets her own exercise by growing onions, tomatoes, carrots, and other herbs and vegetables in her garden. Her homegrown vegetables give her natural antioxidants that may help **prevent** cancer.

B. Answer the questions

1. A long, healthy life depends on mainly two things. What are they? _____ _____

2. Why do men live longer in Sardinia than in the United States? _____ _____

3. How old was Ushi the last time the writer visited her? _____ _____

4. How often should you exercise? _____ _____

5. What are the advantages of growing your own vegetables? _____ _____

Writing

Write a paragraph about your own lifestyle. Answer the questions.

1. Do you lead a healthy lifestyle?
2. How often do you exercise?
3. What sort of food do you eat?
4. Do you smoke?
5. Do you get enough sleep?
6. How can you improve your lifestyle?

✓ Goal 4 | Evaluate your lifestyle

Take turns. Discuss with a partner the good habits and the bad habits in your lifestyles. Give each other advice.

B • Tell students to read the article again and answer the questions.
• Check answers.

Answers: 1. genes and good habits, 2. The men have a stress-free life. 3. 98, 4. every day, 5. you get exercise

• Ask students about the oldest people they know. Do the old people follow any of these habits? Is their health good?

Writing

• Tell students they are going to write a composition about their lifestyle. They should answer each question with one or more sentences. Walk around helping as needed while students write their papers.

• Have students exchange papers with partners. Ask students to mark corrections and suggestions for improvements on their partners' papers.

• If desired, have students rewrite their papers, to be collected for marking.

✓ Goal 4

• Have students work with partners to discuss their own health habits and make suggestions.

After Reading

Assign each student to do research online to find three interesting facts about Okinawa or Sardinia and write them down. Then match them with partners who researched the other place and have them exchange information.

Video Journal

Before You Watch

- Introduce the idea of stress. Ask students, *Do you feel stressed today? Why, or why not?*

A • With the class, look at each picture. Discuss whether the situations in the pictures can cause stress. Opinions may differ—some people may find one situation stressful, while others think it's exciting or interesting.

B • With the class, match the words and definitions.

Answers: 1. c, 2. a, 3. b

While You Watch

A • Tell students to watch the video the first time and circle the answers. Play the video.

- Check answers.

Answers: 1. T, 2. T, 3. F, 4. T

E VIDEO JOURNAL *THE SCIENCE OF STRESS*

Before You Watch

A. Look at the photos. Which of these cause stress?

B. Match the words and the definitions.

1. hormones _____   a. stress on your body, like running
2. physical stress _____   b. stress on your mind, like too much work
3. mental stress _____   c. chemical that your body produces

While You Watch

 A. Watch the video. Circle **T** for *true* and **F** for *false*.

1. There are two types of stress: physical and mental.   T F
2. Stress produces hormones.   T F
3. When you exercise, you don't burn all the hormones.   T F
4. Long-term hormones can cause problems.   T F

For Your Information: The effects of stress

Stress is a normal reaction to things that threaten our well-being. When your body senses danger of some kind, it reacts to give you extra strength. But long-term stress every day can cause serious health problems, because it affects all the physical systems of the body. Stress can cause or worsen heart disease, digestive problems, and skin conditions, and can lead to sleep problems and depression. Because stress hormones have such a strong impact on the body, it's important for our health to find ways to lessen stress and deal with it effectively.

B • Tell students to watch the video again and complete the chart. Go over the chart with the class. Play the video.

• Check answers.

Answers: hormones, burns, No, too much work

After You Watch

• Match students with partners and have them answer the questions together.

• Compare answers with the class.

Communication

• Divide the class into groups of three or four students and explain the task. Because stress is bad for your health, your school or office has decided to do an Anti-Stress Campaign to make the students/employees healthier. Give/elicit an example of one way to do this. (For example: Play beautiful music in the halls.)

• Have each group make its list.

• Call on a member of each group to present his or her ideas to the class.

• Discuss which ideas would work best.

B. Write the following words and expressions in the **stress** flowchart.

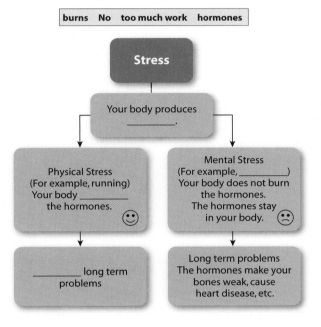

burns   No   too much work   hormones

Stress

Your body produces _____.

Physical Stress
(For example, running)
Your body _____
the hormones. ☺

Mental Stress
(For example, _____)
Your body does not burn
the hormones.
The hormones stay
in your body. ☹

_____ long term
problems

Long term problems
The hormones make your
bones weak, cause
heart disease, etc.

Word Focus

If you feel under **stress**, you feel worried and tense because of difficulties in your life.

After You Watch

👥 Discuss the questions with a partner.

1. What did you learn from this video?
2. Will it change your lifestyle?

Communication

👥 Work in a group of three or four students. You have been assigned to design your school's or office's Antistress Campaign. Make a list of four things you will do.

Teacher Tip: "Fillers"

Here are some activities to "fill in" a few extra minutes at the end of a lesson:

• The Blackboard Game (if you have filled the board with vocabulary and other notes). Have a volunteer sit with his/her back to the board. Students take turns giving definitions of words on the board. When the volunteer says the correct word, you step up and erase it. The game ends when all the words are erased.

• Error Quiz. On the board, write 10 incorrect sentences that you have heard or seen in the students' recent work. Have students work with a partner to correct as many as they can in five minutes. When the time is up, ask the class for corrections and rewrite the sentences on the board.

• Spelling Practice. Dictate 10 to 15 words that students find difficult. Let them compare answers with partners before you give the correct answers.

- Introduce the theme of the unit. Explain that achievements are important things that people have done. Elicit examples using names of famous people: *What was _____'s big achievement? She/He _____.*

- Direct students' attention to the pictures. With the class, look at each in turn and have students name things they see in each one

- Have students work with partners to talk about what the people in the pictures have achieved.

- Compare answers with the class

Answers: 1. (left to right) graduation, landing on the moon, buying a new car, scoring a goal or winning a game. 2. Answers will vary.

- Then have students tell partners about things they have achieved.

- Follow up with these questions, asking them orally or writing them on the board for students to answer in pairs:

  1. *Which achievement in the pictures is the most important?*

  2. *Which achievement in your life is the most important?*

- Go over the Unit Goals with the class, explaining and/or translating as necessary.

ACHIEVEMENTS

1. What have these people achieved?

2. What have you achieved in your life so far?

UNIT GOALS

Talk about today's chores
Interview for a job
Talk about lifetime achievements
Discuss scientific achievements

122

	Unit Goals	Grammar	Vocabulary	Listening	Speaking and Pronunciation	Reading and Writing
	• Talk about today's chores • Interview for a job • Talk about lifetime achievements • Discuss scientific achievements	Present perfect tense ***Have*** you ***finished*** your homework? Present perfect tense vs. simple past tense Alan ***has been*** to many countries. He ***went*** to France last year.	Chores Lifetime achievements	Listening for general understanding and specific details: a job interview	Interviewing for a job Catching up with a friend Reduced form of *have*	"Uncovering the Mysteries of the Universe" Writing an email to catch up

UNIT 11

123

Unit Theme Overview

- Achievements come in all sizes. In the unit opener, students look at global achievements (astronauts walking on the moon or a major victory in sports) and also personal lifetime achievements (buying your first car or completing your education). But there are also small, daily achievements that build up to bigger things: finishing a tough workout in the gym or learning a long list of vocabulary words. This unit covers achievements on all different scales and introduces the language students need to talk about them.

- Students begin by looking at their daily tasks and practicing the present perfect tense to talk about the ones that have been completed. They move on to consider previous experiences and talk about them in the context of a job interview. They consider important milestones in one's lifetime and, finally, look at some of the great achievements of scientists and astronauts. Throughout the lessons, they consolidate their understanding of the present perfect tense and contrast it with the simple past tense.

Talk about Today's Chores

Vocabulary

A • Introduce the idea of chores—things you must do to take care of your home. Go over the expressions in the box. Then have students write each expression under the correct picture.

• Check answers.

Answers: 1. buy the groceries, 2. cut the grass, 3. walk the dog, 4. iron the clothes, 5. pay the bills, 6. sweep the floor, 7. vacuum, 8. put away the clothes

B • Have students work individually to classify the activities in the chart.

• Compare answers with the class and discuss differences of opinion. (Answers will vary.) Ask students to explain why they listed a chore as easy or difficult.

C • Match students with partners and have them answer the question.

• Compare answers with the class. Which chores do students do? How do they feel about these chores?

Grammar

• Introduce the structure. Tell students, *I've played a lot of sports. I've played tennis, soccer, and volleyball.* What about you? What sports have you played? Write on the board, *I've played ____.* Elicit answers around the class. Explain that *I've played* is the present perfect tense of the verb.

• Go over the information in the box.

Vocabulary

A. Label the pictures with phrases from the box.

| pay the bills |
| buy the groceries |
| sweep the floor |
| cut the grass |
| walk the dog |
| vacuum |
| iron the clothes |
| put away the clothes |

1. _____ 2. _____ 3. _____ 4. _____

5. _____ 6. _____ 7. _____ 8. _____

B. Write the activities from exercise **A** in the correct column.

Easy chores	Difficult chores
walk the dog	

C. Discuss with a partner. In your family, who does the household chores?

Grammar: Present perfect tense

Present perfect tense	
Statement	He **has ironed** the clothes.
Negative	I **haven't cooked** lunch yet.
Yes/no questions	**Have you finished** your homework?
Short answers	Yes, I **have**. No, I **haven't.**
Information questions	What **have you done** today?

*The present perfect tense is formed with the verb *has/have* + the past participle of the verb.
*We use the present perfect tense to talk about an action that has just been completed or to talk about an action that happened in the past but will happen again in the present or future.

*Some verbs have regular past participles. They end in *-ed*.		*Some verbs have irregular past participles.	
pass – passed	graduate – graduated	have – had	take – took
clean – cleaned	travel – traveled	go – gone	pay – paid
iron – ironed	visit– visited	be – been	put – put

Word Focus

chore = A *chore* is a task that you must do, but that you find boring or unpleasant.

Word Bank: Chores

wash the dishes

take out the garbage

wash the floor

dust

do/run errands

do the laundry

cook/make breakfast/
    lunch/dinner

clean the bathroom

shovel the snow

Grammar: Present perfect tense

It emphasizes the connection between past and present situations. It is used:

• for situations that began in the past and continue into the present.

• for experience in general, when the specific time is not important.

• for situations that have just finished.

A. Match the past participle forms to the verbs.

1. eaten ____   a. meet
2. drunk ____   b. tell
3. swept ____   c. eat
4. met ____   d. say
5. said ____   e. speak
6. spoken ____   f. drink
7. told ____   g. win
8. won ____   h. sweep
9. bought ____   i. read
10. read ____   j. buy

B. Complete the sentences with the present perfect tense. Use the words in parentheses.

1. Alan _____ (wash) the car.
2. _____ (you, buy) the groceries?
3. I _____ (not, put away) the clothes.
4. _____ (Peter, sweep) the floor?
5. They _____ (not, pay) their telephone bill.

Conversation

Track 2-21

A. Read the note and listen to the conversation. Has Lynn done her chores?

Mom: Hi, honey, I'm home.
Lynn: Hi, Mom.
Mom: Have you walked the dog?
Lynn: Yes, Mom, of course I've walked the dog. And I've vacuumed the living room.
Mom: And have you done your homework?
Lynn: Mom! I've been busy walking the dog and vacuuming. I haven't had time.
Mom: Sorry, honey. It's just I've had a long day myself.

B. Practice the conversation with a partner. Switch roles and practice it again.

C. Write another chore list and practice the conversation again.

Honey, will you please do these things before I come home?
–vacuum the living room
–walk the dog

Thanks,
Mom

> ✓ **Goal 1** **Talk about today's chores**
>
> Talk to a partner about the chores you have done today.

A • Have students work individually to match the columns.
  • Check answers.

Answers: 1. c, 2. f, 3. h, 4. a, 5. d, 6. e, 7. b, 8. g, 9. j, 10. i

B • Have students work individually to fill in the verbs in the present perfect tense.
  • Check answers.

Answers: 1. has washed, 2. Have you bought, 3. haven't put away, 4. Has Peter swept, 5. haven't paid

Conversation

A • Have students close their books. Write the question on the board: *Has Lynn done her chores?*
  • Play the recording. **(CD2 T21)**
  • Check answers.

Answer: No

B • Play or read the conversation again for the class to repeat.
  • Practice the conversation with the class in chorus.
  • Have students practice the conversation with partners and then switch roles and practice it again.

C • Have students work with partners to list three more activities and make a new conversation.
  • Call on student pairs to present their conversations to the class.

✓ Goal 1

• Match students with partners and have them take turns talking about their activities so far today.

Grammar Practice: Present perfect tense

Play "Find Someone Who . . ." Dictate the following phrases for students to write down: *travel to another country/ live in another city/climb a mountain/give a party/see a ghost/find some money/play basketball.*

• Tell students to find a person who has done each of these things by walking around the class asking questions.

• Model the activity by asking a student, *Have you ever traveled to another country? Have you ever lived in another city?* and so on, until the student answers *yes* to a question. Then write the student's name.

• Set a time limit (5 to 10 minutes). After finishing the game, ask the class, *Who has traveled to another country?* and so forth.

Interview for a Job

Listening

- Introduce the idea of a job interview. Ask students if they or someone they know has had one. What happens at a job interview?

A • Tell students they are going to hear two people at an interview for a job. Have them read the ad and go over any unfamiliar words. Talk briefly about a tour guide's job and what is required. Tell students they should listen and decide who is the better person for the job and prepare to explain their reasons.

- Play the recording two or more times. **(CD2 T22)**

- Match students with partners and have them compare and explain their decisions.

- Call on students to tell the class about their opinions and give reasons.

B • Tell students to listen again and fill in the blanks. Play the recording. **(CD2 T22)**

- Check answers.

Answers: 1. graduated, 2. worked, 3. met, 4. passed

C • Tell students to listen again to the interviews and answers the questions.

- Play the recording one or more times. **(CD2 T22)**

- Check answers.

Answers: 1. no, 2. eight, 3. her father, 4. yes, 5. yes

Listening

Track 2-22

A. Read the ad. Listen to Richard and Erin at the interview. Decide who should get the job. Give your reasons.

NEEDED URGENTLY!

TOUR GUIDE
Bermuda

Smart appearance. Good interpersonal skills. Experience an advantage. Driver's license essential. Call 2356 9845.

▲ Erin

▲ Richard

Track 2-22

B. The interviewer asked the following questions. Complete the questions. Listen again to check your answers.

1. Have you _____ from college?
2. Have you ever _____ as a tour guide?
3. Who is the most interesting person you have ever _____?
4. Have you _____ your driving test?

C. Answer the questions.

1. Has Richard ever traveled abroad? _____
2. How many countries has Erin visited? _____
3. Who is the most interesting person Erin has met? _____
4. Has Richard passed his driving test? _____
5. Has Erin graduated from college? _____

126 Achievements

For Your Information: Job interviews

A job interview is a common step in getting a job in most countries, though the form of the interview may differ. Candidates may be interviewed one at a time or in a group. They may speak with only one interviewer or with a whole group of them. There are also differences in the kinds of questions that are asked. In the United States, for example, there are laws against job discrimination by age, religion, and marital status, so interviewers are not allowed to ask questions like *Are you married?* or *Don't you think you're too old to do this job?*

Pronunciation: Reduced form of *have*

Track 2-23

A. Listen to the examples. Notice the pronunciation of the reduced forms.

Full form	Reduced form
I have	I've
have you	/'hav-yə/
you have	you've
has he	/'ha-zē/
she has	she's

Track 2-24

B. Listen to the sentences. Check the correct column.

	Full form	Reduced form
1. **Has she** left?		
2. **Have you** finished?		
3. **Has he** read this book?		
4. **Have you** done your homework?		
5. **I have** never been to the United States.		

Track 2-24

C. Listen again. Repeat the sentences.

Communication

Interview a partner for the following jobs.

WANTED!

Handyman for Kindergarten

Small kindergarten needs a person to help with maintenance— plumbing, carpentry, fixing our vehicles, etc. No experience with children necessary but must enjoy being around kids. Any age. $25 per hour.

SALES ASSISTANT

Fashionable clothes shop is looking for a SALES ASSISTANT 18-30 years old, 2 p.m. to 10 p.m. Experience an advantage. Must have an interest in clothes and fashion. Salary negotiable.

Goal 2 | **Interview for a job**

Think of another job. What's required? Write notes. Interview a partner.

Expansion Activity

Find job ads online for several jobs that would interest your students. Print out copies of the ads for students to read or read them out loud to the class. Discuss the qualifications that are required for each job and ask if students have those qualifications: *Have you worked with computers?*

Pronunciation

- Remind students that many words have a reduced pronunciation in everyday speech.

A • Tell students to listen to the full and reduced forms of the phrases. Play the recording. **(CD2 T23)**

B • Tell students to listen to the recording and check the pronunciation they hear for the phrase in bold. Play the recording one or more times. **(CD2 T24)**

- Check answers.

Answers: 1. full, 2. reduced, 3. reduced, 4. full, 5. reduced

C • Tell students to listen to the recording and repeat the sentences using the pronunciation they hear. Play the recording. **(CD2 T24)**

- Have students read the sentences to a partner, giving both pronunciations.

Communication

- Go over both ads with the class, and explain new vocabulary (**maintenance** = fixing things; **plumbing** = fixing bathrooms and water pipes; **carpentry** = fixing things with wood; **vehicles** = cars and trucks; **negotiable** = we can discuss this). Talk about questions the interviewer might ask.

- Match students with partners and have them role-play the interview for the first job. Then have them change roles and role-play the interview for the second job.

- Ask, *Did you get the job? Why, or why not?*

☑ Goal 2

- Have students work individually to choose another job and think of questions to ask in an interview.

- Match students with partners and have them role-play interviews for the two jobs they've chosen.

Talk about Lifetime Achievements

Language Expansion

A • Go over the phrases in the box. Then have students work individually to write the correct phrase for each picture.

• Check answers.

Answers: 1. graduate from high school/college, 2. buy your own car, 3. pass your driving test, 4. travel abroad, 5. buy a house, 6. run a marathon, 7. get a promotion, 8. get a credit card

B • Have students mark the things in the previous exercise that they have done.

C • Match students with partners and have them ask and answers questions about the achievements in exercise **A**.

Grammar

• Go over the information in the box, contrasting the two tenses.

Language Expansion: Lifetime achievements

A. Label the pictures with phrases from the box.

graduate from high school/ college	travel abroad	pass your driving test	run a marathon
get promotion	buy your own car	buy a house	get a credit card

1. _____ 2._____ 3. _____ 4._____

5. _____ 6._____ 7. _____ 8._____

B. Check the achievements in exercise **A** that you have done.

C. Take turns. Ask a partner what he or she has achieved.

> Have you graduated from college?

Grammar: Present perfect tense vs. simple past tense

Present perfect tense vs. simple past tense	
The present perfect tense is used to show an action that happened at any time in the past. *Alan **has been** to many countries.*	The simple past tense is used to show an action that happened at a specific time in the past. *He **went** to France last year.*
*We often use time expressions with the simple past tense. *We use expressions like *just, never, ever* with the present perfect tense. *Have you **ever** been to another country? Alan has **just** returned from France. I have **never** been there.*	

Word Bank: Personal achievements

win an award	teach a class
have grandchildren	have your name in the newspaper
get a better job	lose weight
give a speech	get fit

Grammar: Present perfect/simple past tense

The present perfect tense is used to connect the past with now. It describes events at any time in the past that have a connection with the present.

I've already graduated from college (so now I have my degree).
I've been to Mexico four times (so I know something about the country).

The simple past describes a completed action at a specific time.
I graduated from college in 2004.
I went to Mexico last summer.

Past **Simple past tense** **Now** **Future**

↓

Present perfect tense

A. Complete the sentences with the correct form of the verb in parentheses.

1. Last summer, we _____ (go) to the Maldives.
2. I _____ (live) in the same house all my life.
3. John _____ (never travel) abroad.
4. Italy _____ (win) the World Cup in 2006.
5. Brazil _____ (win) the World Cup five times.

B. Complete the conversations with the correct form of the verb in parentheses.

1. A: _____ (you pass) your driving test?
   B: Yes. I _____ (take) it in January and I _____
   (pass) the first time.
2. A: _____ (you be) to Europe?
   B: Yes, I have. I _____ (go) to Germany last year.

Conversation

Track 2-25

A. Listen to the conversation. Who has started his own business?

Simon: Hi, Pete. I haven't seen you for a long time. What's new?
Pete: Lots! I quit my job with <u>CompuSoft</u> and I've started <u>my own computer business</u>.
Simon: Congratulations! When did you <u>open the business</u>?
Pete: Eight months ago and it's going well.
Simon: Great.
Pete: And what about you?
Simon: Things haven't changed much. I'm still <u>working at the bank</u>. But I've <u>bought a new house</u>. It's on 5th and Main.
Pete: Wow! Nice <u>neighborhood</u>.
Simon: Yeah. You should come round and visit some time.
Pete: Will do. When I have some time.

B. Practice the conversation with a partner. Switch roles and practice it again.

C. Practice the conversation again. Change the underlined words.

✓ **Goal 3** **Talk about lifetime achievements**

Talk to a partner about your lifetime achievements.

Lesson C **129**

Grammar Practice: Present perfect/simple past tense

Write these questions on the board for students to discuss in groups.

What is the most unusual food you've ever eaten? When/where/why did you eat it? What is the best movie you've ever seen? When/where did you see it?

When groups have finished, ask them for interesting/surprising information they heard from their classmates.

Lesson C **129**

Discuss Scientific Achievements

Reading

- Introduce the topic of the reading. Ask students, *What are some important things that scientists have done in the last 10 years?*

A
- Have students read the question. Point out the vocabulary that is defined in the Word Focus box.
- Have students read the article to check their guesses. Tell them to circle any words they don't understand.
- Check answers.

Answer: yes

- Go over the article with the class, answering any questions from the students about vocabulary.

Additional words:

summit = highest part; **peak** = top of a mountain; **focus** = look clearly; **revolve** = go around in a circle; **expand** = make bigger; **intelligent** = able to think; **high and low** = everywhere; **limit** = a place where you can't go any further; **legend** = old story

---

Reading

A. Are there other planets outside the solar system? Read and check your answer.

▲ In 1996 astronomers discovered a planet orbiting the star Upsilon Andromedae. Recently they have found two more planets **orbiting** Upsilon Andromedae. This is the first evidence of a **solar system** beyond ours.

Word Focus

orbit = to go round and round a planet, moon, or star.
solar system = the sun and all the planets

☐ Uncovering the Mysteries of the Universe

▲ Gary Puniwai is an observing assistant in the Keck Observatory control rooms on Mauna Kea, Hawaii.

GARY PUNIWAI sits at the controls of the Keck 1 telescope, the world's most powerful telescope on the summit of the highest peak in the Pacific. The telescope focuses on objects in space more than 10 billion years old.

Since people started looking at stars we have achieved a lot. The ancient Egyptians believed that the stars were very near—almost close enough to touch. Just a few hundred years ago, in the 16th and 17th centuries, most Europeans thought that the earth was the center of the universe and that the sun revolved

---

For Your Information: Keck Observatory

The Keck Observatory stands on top of a dormant volcano called Mauna Kea on the island of Hawaii. Conditions in that location are excellent for observing the sky. There are few lights nearby, so the sky is very dark, and because it is in the middle of the Pacific Ocean, the weather is clear and calm. The observatory's two telescopes are the largest in the world. Each one is eight stories tall and weighs 300 tons. The mirrors inside each one are 10 meters across, made of 36 six-sided pieces of reflecting glass.

around the earth. But modern science has expanded our understanding, and we know the earth is a small planet that goes around an ordinary star in the Milky Way Galaxy. We also know that there are more than 100 billion galaxies in the universe. We live on a small planet in a very large universe.

But there are many questions we haven't answered yet. For example, are we the only intelligent life in the universe? Scientists have discovered that there are other planets in the universe. However, all the planets that they have found are much bigger than the earth—about the size of Jupiter—and they probably don't have life on them. But who knows?

Also we have discovered that the universe contains something called Dark Matter. We know it is there, but we can't see it and there is a lot of it. Some scientists say that as much as 70 percent of the universe is made from this Dark Matter. They have looked high and low for the missing matter, but they have not found it.

Science has achieved a lot, but there are still some very big questions we need to answer. Or will science reach some limit like the Pillars of Hercules, the classical symbol for what lies at the edge of what we know? On these pillars, according to legend, was written in Latin: "*Ne plus ultra*"—No further. Are there some things we will never understand?

B. Answer the questions.

1. What is Gary Puniwai's job? _____
   _____

2. Are there other planets outside our solar system? _____
   _____

3. Why is Dark Matter difficult to find?
   _____
   _____

4. What have we learned since people started looking at stars? _____
   _____

5. Do you think there are some things that we will never understand? Give your reasons. _____
   _____
   _____
   _____

Writing

Gary is writing to a friend. Answer the email.

Hi Ana

How's life? I haven't heard from you for a long time. What's new?
I've changed jobs three times since we last met. I'm now a technician at the Keck telescopes. I haven't been here long, but I like it. And guess what? I've started an online course in physics. Yes, I'm going to be a scientist.

Anyway, what have you done since I saw you last? Let me know.

Gary

✓ **Goal 4** | **Discuss scientific achievements**

Talk to a partner about other scientific achievements.

B
- Tell students to read the article again and find the information.
- Check answers.

Answers: 1. observing assistant in the Keck Observatory, 2. yes, 3. We can't see it. 4. The earth is a small planet that goes around a star, and there are more than 100 billion galaxies. 5. Answers will vary.

Writing

- Read the email with the class. Tell students to write a reply about things they have done in the last two or three years.
- Have students exchange papers with partners. Ask students to mark corrections and suggestions for improvements on their partners' papers.
- If desired, have students rewrite their papers, to be collected for marking.

✓ Goal 4

- Match students with partners and have them make a list of important scientific achievements (for example, sending astronauts to the moon).
- Compare answers with the class.

After Reading

Have students write a paragraph about a person who has made an important achievement that they admire. Have them share their paragraphs with a partner or a group.

Video Journal

Before You Watch

A • With the class, look at the photos and talk about the activities they show. Ask students why it's dangerous to go outside in space (there's no air; it's hard to move).

B • Go over the words in the box. Then have students work individually to complete the summary. Have them check their work while watching the video.

Answers: oxygen, survive, solar panels, underwater, weightless

E VIDEO JOURNAL *SPACEWALK*

Before You Watch

A. Look at the photos. What are the astronauts doing? Which activity do you think is the most dangerous. Why?

B. Read the summary of the video and fill in the blanks with words from the box. Then watch the video and check your answers.

weightless   survive   underwater   oxygen   solar panels

Video summary

Outside the earth's atmosphere, in space, there is no _____.
It is impossible to breathe. Sometimes astronauts have to make a spacewalk outside the spacecraft. In order to _____, astronauts wear special space suits. They do jobs like repair _____. But it is difficult and dangerous work.

They prepare for their spacewalks _____ in special tanks. It is like being _____ in space but much safer.

For Your Information: Weightlessness

Astronauts experience long periods of weightlessness in space when their spacecraft is not rotating or using its engines. It puts a lot of stress on the human body and causes "space sickness," with nausea and vomiting, in about 45 percent of people who experience it. Spending long periods of time in space can seriously affect people's health, because it weakens muscles and bones. Videos of astronauts often show them enjoying things that they can't do in earth's gravity, such as lifting heavy objects with one finger. But weightlessness also makes their daily work much more difficult, and they spend many hours training to do the simplest tasks.

While You Watch

 A. Watch the video and complete the chart.

On earth	In space
The atmosphere protects us from dangerous radiation.	There is no atmosphere to protect the astronauts from dangerous radiation.
There is oxygen to breathe.	
Temperatures range from −50°C to 50°C.	
Gravity keeps us on the ground.	

 B. Watch the video again and circle **T** for *true* or **F** for *false*.

1. It is always very cold in space.   T   F
2. Space suits are filled with oxygen.   T   F
3. The first person to walk in space was Edward White.   T   F
4. Astronauts fixed the solar panels on the Hubble Space Telescope.   T   F
5. Astronauts practice spacewalking in special tanks.   T   F

After You Watch

 Man's scientific achievements are expensive. The National Aeronautics and Space Administration (NASA) spent $17 billion in 2008. The Large Hadron Collider (a gigantic scientific instrument), which opened in 2008, cost $4.6 billion. Discuss this with a partner. Why do governments spend a lot of money on big science projects?

Communication

Discuss with a partner other ways you could spend NASA's budget (money) to help people. Make a list of specific things you can do. Be prepared to share your list and the reasons for your choices with the class.

Video Journal   **133**

Teacher Tip: Fun with English outside of class

Encourage students to find language activities that they enjoy to get more practice outside of class. Some ideas:

- sing along with English songs on CDs (lyrics can be found on the album liner or on Web sites)
- speak in English with a friend or classmate outside of class time
- read an English comic book or a magazine on a topic that is well-known in the native language (for example, soccer or fashion)
- watch English-language movies with native-language subtitles
- talk to yourself in English!

- Direct students' attention to the pictures. With the class, look at each picture in turn, and have students name things they see in each one (for example, trees, shopping bags).

- Discuss the pictures one by one. Talk about the situation in each one and what some of the results will be. Introduce the idea of *consequences*—the results of things we do.

Answers: 1. (left to right) shopping (over-spending), throwing out garbage carelessly, texting in class, deforestation. 2. Answers will vary.

- Follow up with these questions, asking them orally or writing them on the board for students to answer in pairs:

  1. *When have you made a bad decision?*

  2. *What were the consequences?*

- Go over the Unit Goals with the class, explaining and/or translating as necessary.

CONSEQUENCES

1. What is happening in each picture?

2. What are the possible results, effects, or consequences of these actions?

UNIT GOALS

Talk about managing your money
Make choices on how to spend your money
Talk about how our actions can have positive
  consequences
Discuss ways to prevent habitat destruction

134

Unit Goals	Grammar	Vocabulary	Listening	Speaking and Pronunciation	Reading and Writing
• Talk about managing your money • Make choices on how to spend your money • Talk about how our actions can have positive consequences • Discuss ways to prevent habitat destruction	Real conditionals (or first conditional) **If** they **borrow** some money, they **will be able to** buy a new house.	Personal finances Animal habitats	Listening for specific details: at a travel agency	Making decisions about spending money Talking about important issues Sentence stress	"Habitat Destruction" Writing a letter to the editor

UNIT 12

135

Unit Theme Overview

- Many of the headlines in the news today are about the consequences of past actions. Industrial development and rapid economic growth have increased the production of carbon dioxide and other "greenhouse gases"—the consequences are global warming and severe weather. Old ethnic and national conflicts have never been resolved: The consequences are war and the displacement of millions of refugees. Even in our own lives, we can easily see the pattern of actions and consequences.

- In this unit, students begin examining the topic of consequences on a personal level by talking about money and financial decisions. They examine the possible results of different choices they might make. They move on to talk about consequences on a larger scale, by thinking about how people's actions affect animals. Finally, they look at the human role in habitat destruction. All of these situations involve real possibilities and give students many opportunities to practice the use of the real (first) conditional form.

Talk about Managing Your Money

Vocabulary

A • Introduce the topic of managing your money. Ask students, *How do you manage your money? Do you make a plan? Or do you just spend as much money as you want to?*

• Have students read the article, paying special attention to the words in blue. If necessary, explain that in some countries, studying at a university is very expensive and students must borrow money to pay for things. They usually get all the money at the beginning of the school year.

B • Have students work individually to find the words with the given meanings.

• Check answers.

Answers: 1. expenses, 2. borrow, 3. income, 4. overspend, 5. budget, 6. lend, 7. save

Grammar

• Introduce the structure. Tell students (for example), *I'm going shopping this weekend. I want to buy a lot of things. If I have enough money, I'll buy some new clothes. If I have enough money, I'll buy some CDs.* Ask, *What about you? What will you buy if you have enough money?* Elicit answers from the class.

• Go over the information in the box.

Word Focus

student loan = money that the government lends to students at a very low interest rate

---

Vocabulary

A. Read the article from a student magazine.

> **STUDENT LIFE**
>
> # MANAGE YOUR MONEY
>
>
>
> Congratulations! You have received your first student loan. How are you going to spend it? Are you going to go out and buy that new cell phone or those cool sneakers? Well, don't!
>
> Before you spend a penny, you have to make a budget and plan your spending. First write down your income—how much money you receive. Then calculate your expenses (rent, transportation, food). If your expenses are lower than your income, you are on the right road! Now you know how much money you have left to spend each month. But don't overspend or you will have to borrow money. Borrowing money from the bank is expensive. Interest rates are high. Always check to see if a friend or family member can lend you the money.
>
> You also have to think about the long term. How are you going to pay for that spring break at the beach, or buy your family presents? You will have to save some money every month. So, that new cell phone can wait. Manage your money and maybe you'll be able to take that spring break at the beach–in Mexico!
>
> **21** November 2008

B. Write the words in **blue** next to the correct meanings.

1. the amount of money you spend _____
2. to ask someone to give you money _____
3. the amount of money you receive _____
4. to spend too much money _____
5. a spending plan _____
6. to give someone money _____
7. to put money in the bank for the future _____

Grammar: Real conditionals (or first conditional)

If clause (simple present tense)	Result clause (future tense)
If I **buy** an MP3,	I **will** not **have** enough money to pay the rent.
If they **borrow** some money,	they **will be able to** buy a new house.
*We use real conditional sentences to express possible consequences of choices we make.	
*When the *if* clause comes first, there is a comma between the *if* clause and the result clause.	

136 Consequences

Word Bank: Money

bank

credit card

savings account

checking account

deposit

withdraw

interest rate

Grammar: Real conditionals

English has three types of conditional sentences with *if*.

1. Real situations (sometimes called the first conditional): *If I study hard, I will get a good grade.*

2. Unreal situations (sometimes called the second conditional): *If I studied hard, I would get better grades.* (but I'm lazy)

3. Unreal situations in the past (sometimes called the third conditional): *If I had studied hard, I would have gotten a better grade.* (but I didn't study)

A. Match the *if* clauses to the correct result clauses.

1. If you borrow money from the bank, ___.
2. If you save some money every month, ___.
3. If you lend money to your sister, ___.
4. If your expenses are bigger than your income, ___.
5. If we eat in, ___.

a. she won't return the money until the end of the month
b. you won't have enough money to take a vacation
c. we will have enough money to go to the theater
d. the interest rates will be high
e. you will have enough money to buy a new computer

B. Unscramble the words to write conditional sentences. Don't forget the punctuation.

1. a bigger car / some money / we borrow / If / we can buy
   If we borrow some money, we can buy a bigger car.
   _____

2. a new job / more money / I will have / I get / If
   _____

3. on vacation / we overspend / If / to go / we won't be able
   _____

4. I won't have to / I / use my credit card / If / borrow money
   _____

5. our car / sell / we will be able to rent / If we / a bigger apartment
   _____

Conversation

Track 2-26

A. Listen to the conversation. What choice does Jim have to make?

Jim:	I don't know what to do. I want to take a vacation and I also want to buy a new camera.
Dave:	I see. If you buy the camera, you won't have enough money for the vacation. Is that it?
Jim:	You got it.
Dave:	So, just take the vacation. Don't buy the camera.
Jim:	But if I don't buy the camera, I won't be able to take any vacation photos.
Dave:	OK, just buy the camera.
Jim:	But if I buy the camera, I won't be able to take the vacation and I won't need a camera.
Dave:	Hmm . . . you have a problem

B. Practice the conversation with a partner. Switch roles and practice it again.

✔ **Goal 1**   **Talk about managing your money**

Work with a partner. Discuss how you manage your money.

A • Have students work individually to match the sentence parts.
  • Check answers.

Answers: 1. d, e (both possible); 2. e; 3. a, b (both possible); 4. b; 5. c

B • Have students work individually to write the sentences.
  • Check answers.

Answers: 2. If I get a new job, I will have more money. 3. If we overspend, we won't be able to go on vacation. 4. If I borrow money, I won't have to use my credit card. 5. If we sell our car, we will be able to rent a bigger apartment.

Conversation

A • Have students close their books. Write the question on the board: *What choice does Jim have to make?*
  • Play the recording. **(CD2 T26)**
  • Check answers.

Answer: take a vacation or buy a new camera

B • Play or read the conversation again for the class to repeat.
  • Practice the conversation with the class in chorus.
  • Have students practice the conversation with partners and then switch roles and practice it again.

✔ **Goal 1**
  • Match students with partners and have them talk about their money habits. For example, do they make a budget? Save money to buy things?

Grammar Practice: Real conditionals

Tell students they are going to make their own real conditional sentences about different situations—and then share the sentences with the class. Remind students that the clause with *if* has the verb in the present tense.
Write on the board: *We'll be very happy if _____.* Give students one minute to think of a sentence.
Then go around the class quickly and have each student say his/her sentence.
Continue with: *I'll be very surprised if _____.*

  We'll learn English faster if _____.

  I'll save more money if _____.

Make Choices on How to Spend Your Money

Listening

A • Tell students they are going to hear a conversation in a travel agency. Ask them what people do in a travel agency (plan a vacation, buy plane tickets, etc.).

• Play the recording one or more times. **(CD2 T27)**

• Check answers.

Answer: c

B • Tell students to listen again to the conversation.

• Play the recording one or more times. **(CD2 T27)**

• Check answers.

Answers: 1. yes, 2. she won't see anything, 3. she will get lost, 4. two hours and fifteen minutes, 5. $150

• Ask the class, *How can a train go from London to Paris?* (Through a tunnel.) *If you go from London to Paris, how will you travel—by plane, train, or car?*

Pronunciation

• Remind students that our voices rise and fall when we say sentences. Practicing intonation will help them to sound more like native speakers.

A • Tell students to listen to the sentences and mark the rising and falling intonation they hear. Play the recording one or more times. **(CD2 T28)**

• Check answers.

Answers: 2. ↗bus, ↘cheaper; 3. ↗money, ↘month; 4. ↗now, ↘train; 5. ↗plane, ↘quicker

B • Play the recording again for students to repeat the sentences. **(CD2 T28)**

• Then have students practice reading the sentences to partners. Walk around listening for good intonation.

Listening

 A. Listen to the conversation. Circle the correct answer.

Track 2-27

The travel agent is in ____.

    a. London
    b. Paris
    c. New York

 B. Listen again and answer the questions.

Track 2-27

1. Is this the first time that the woman has visited England? _____
2. Why doesn't she want to take the plane? _____
3. Why doesn't she want to rent a car? _____
4. How long does it take to go from Paris to London by train? _____
5. How much does the train ticket cost? _____

Pronunciation: Intonation

 A. Listen to the sentences. Write the arrows to show rise or fall.

Track 2-28

                ↗   ↘

1. If I buy a car, I won't be able to pay the rent.

2. If you take the bus, it will be cheaper.

3. If we borrow some money, we will repay it in a month.

4. If Sara leaves now, she will catch the seven o'clock train.

5. If we take the plane, it will be quicker.

B. Listen again and repeat the sentences.

Track 2-28

138   *Consequences*

For Your Information: Eurostar

Eurostar is the name of the train service that runs from London to Paris and Brussels through a tunnel under the water of the English Channel. The project was planned in 1986, and service began in 1994. Long trains of 18 carriages run at a speed of up to 185 mph (300 kph). In 2007, more than 8 million passengers traveled between London and Paris on the train. More than ninety-one percent of the trains arrived on time.

Communication

Work with a partner. Plan a six-day visit to California. Each of you has $200 to spend on transportation. You will arrive in Los Angeles. Your airport transfers are paid for. You would like to visit Yosemite, Sea World in San Diego, and San Francisco.

> If we take the Greyhound bus, it will be cheaper.

> If we take the plane, it will be quicker.

> If we take the train, will it be cheaper?

	San Diego	San Francisco	Merced (for Yosemite)
Los Angeles	🚌 $30, 4 hours 🚆 $70, 3 hours ✈ $120, 1 hour	🚌 $50, 6 hours 🚆 $60, 8 hours (3 changes) ✈ $120, 1½ hours	🚌 $70, 7 hours 🚆 No service ✈ No service
San Diego		🚌 $128 return, 12 hours 🚆 No service ✈ $250, 1½ hours	🚌 $82, 10 hours 🚆 No service ✈ No service
San Francisco			🚌 $62, 4 hours 🚆 $53, 3 hours ✈ No service

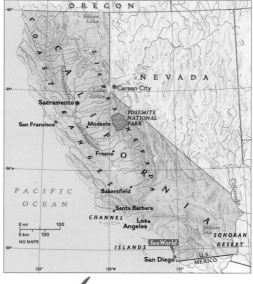

	Itinerary	Transport	Transport costs
Day 1			
Day 2			
Day 3			
Day 4			
Day 5			
Day 6			

✔ Goal 2 — Make choices on how to spend your money

Join another pair of students and explain to them how you decided to spend your transportation money.

Communication

- Introduce the activity. Ask, *What are some famous places in California? Where do visitors like to go?*
- Match students with partners and present the situation. They are going to visit California for six days, and they must decide how to travel to three places they want to visit. Each person has $200 to spend.
- Go over the chart that shows the means of transportation and prices.
- Have students work with partners to make a plan for spending their time and money and complete the chart about their trip.
- Call on student pairs to explain their decisions and reasons to the class.

✔ Goal 2

- Have students join another pair and talk about their decisions on how to spend their travel money.
- Have them take turns asking and answering questions about what they decided and why they did so.

Expansion Activity

Have students work in pairs to make a similar plan for a six-day trip to three places in their country. You can assign three places or let them choose their own destinations.

Talk about How Our Actions Can Have Positive Consequences

- Introduce the idea of habitats: places where animals live in nature. Go over the habitats in the pictures.
- Then go over the names of the animals.

A • Match students with a partner and have them talk about where each animal lives.
- Check answers.

Answers: orangutan/rainforest, camel/desert, shark/coral reef, mountain goat/mountains, zebra/grasslands

B • Have students work individually to fill in the blanks with words from the previous activity.
- Check answers.

Answers: 1. rainforests, 2. Camels, the desert, 3. coral reef, sharks, 4. grasslands, zebras, 5. mountains, mountain goat

Grammar

- Go over the information in the box, reviewing what students learned about real conditionals in Lesson **A**.

A • Have students work individually to match the sentence parts.
- Check answers.

Answers: 1. d, 2. e, 3. a, 4. b, 5. c

Language Expansion: Animal habitats

👥 **A.** Take turns. Make statements about animals and their habitats.

▲ desert ▲ mountains ▲ grasslands ▲ rainforest ▲ coral reef

▲ orangutan ▲ camel ▲ shark ▲ mountain goat ▲ zebra

B. Complete the sentences. Use the habitats and animals in exercise **A**.

1. Many countries near the equator have _____. They contain hundreds of different plants and animals.
2. _____ can live without water for many days. They are perfectly adapted to live in _____.
3. The Great Barrier Reef in Australia is the biggest _____ in the world. It is the home of _____ and many kinds of fish.
4. Kenya is famous for its _____. Tourists come from all over the world to see the animals, like lions, elephants, and _____.
5. The highest _____ in the world are in Nepal. Not many animals live there. If you are lucky, you may see a _____.

Grammar: Real conditionals

Result clause (future tense)	*If* clause (simple present tense)
The climate **will** change	if we **continue** to burn fossil fuels.
We **will** lose many valuable animals	if we **destroy** their habitats.

*Real conditionals can be written with the result clause first.
*These conditionals do not need a comma.

A. Match the result clauses to the correct *if* clauses.

1. Our coral reefs will die ____
2. We will lose many useful plants ____
3. You can rest tomorrow ____
4. It will reduce pollution ____
5. It's starting to rain. You'll get wet ____

a. if you finish your work today.
b. if more people use public transport.
c. if you don't leave now.
d. if ocean temperatures rise.
e. if we cut down all the trees.

Word Bank: Animals and habitats

desert: rat, snake
mountains: mountain lion, wolf
grasslands: lion, elephant
rainforest: gorilla, chimpanzee
coral reef: sea turtle, jellyfish

Grammar: Real conditionals

Look out for common errors including wrong use of tenses (*If I will have enough money . . .*) and use of this structure for situations that are not real or possible (*If I am the president of this country . . .*)

B. Use these cues to write conditional sentences

1. children / suffer / if / don't take care of / animal habitats
   Our children will suffer if we don't take care of animal habitats.

2. fish / die / if / coral reef / die
   _____

3. visitors / not come / if / no / animals
   _____

4. live longer / if / exercise more
   _____

5. go / beach / if / no / rain
   _____

Conversation

 Track 2-29

A. Listen to the conversation. What is John worried about? How can he help?

John: I'm very worried about all we hear and read about habitat destruction. It's important, but how can I help?
Sharon: You go to work by car. Right?
John: Yes.
Sharon: It will help if you go to work by bus.
John: How will that help?
Sharon: Buses carry lots of passengers, that means you use less gasoline per person. Less pollution, less climate change, less habitat destruction. Right?
John: Yes, and I save money as well.
Sharon: Right!

 B. Practice the conversation with a partner. Switch roles and practice it again.

Real Language

You can say *Right* (rising tone) at the end of a statement to check information. You can also use *Right* (falling tone) to show you agree.

 Goal 3 | **Talk about how our actions can have positive consequences**

Work with a partner. Choose an important problem or environmental issue. Make a list of the things you can do to help. Tell your partner what positive consequences your actions will have.

B.
- Have students work individually to write sentences using the given words.
- Check answers.

Answers: 2. Fish will die if the coral reefs die. 3. Visitors won't come if there are no animals. 4. People live longer if they exercise more. 5. I will go to the beach if it doesn't rain. (variations are possible in 4 and 5)

Conversation

A.
- Have students close their books. Write the questions on the board: *What is John worried about? How can he help?*
- Play the recording. **(CD2 T29)**
- Check answers

Answers: habitat destruction; go to work by bus

B.
- Play or read the conversation again for the class to repeat.
- Practice the conversation with the class in chorus.
- Have students practice the conversation with partners and then switch roles and practice it again.

☑ Goal 3

- Match students with partners and have each pair choose one important problem. It can be a personal problem (such as being unfit) or a world problem (such as global warming). Have them brainstorm a list of ways to solve the problem and then talk about the consequences of each action.
- Call on student pairs to present their ideas to the class.

Grammar Practice: Real conditionals

On the board, write, *The population of our city increases to 5 million.* Ask the class, *What will happen if the population of our city increases to 5 million?* Elicit several sentences with consequences (for example, *If the population of our city increases to 5 million, we will build more houses*) and write them on the board, linking them to the original sentence with an arrow. Then ask about the results of these events: *What will happen if we build more houses?* and write the possible consequences, linked to that event with an arrow. Continue in this way to explore the sequence of possible consequences. Then talk about other situations such as *The earth's climate gets warmer; Everyone in this country can have a free education*, and so forth.

Discuss Ways to Prevent Habitat Destruction

Reading

- Introduce the topic of the reading. Ask students if they know any animals that are endangered (for example, polar bears). What is the problem?

A • Match students with partners and have them discuss the questions. Compare answers with the class.

Answers: 1. seal: in the ocean; frog: wetlands; 2. If we don't look after the habitats, the animals will die.

- Point out the vocabulary that is defined in the Word Focus box.
- Have students read the article. Tell them to circle any words they don't understand.
- Go over the article with the class, answering any questions from the students about vocabulary.

Additional words:

reduce = make smaller; **freshwater** = water that we can drink; **saltwater** = water in the ocean; **pollutants** = things that pollute the environment; **convention** = agreement; **estimate** = guess; **continue** = not stop; **increase** = get bigger or more.

B • Have students work individually to find the information in the reading.
- Check answers.

Answers: 1. Fishermen have bigger boats and catch more fish. 2. The number of fish will recover. 3. They remove pollutants and provide habitats for fish, birds, and other animals. 4. can't answer this from the article—it talks about 100 years for wetlands, 50 years for reefs; 5. The water is too hot.

D   GOAL 4   DISCUSS WAYS TO PREVENT HABITAT DESTRUCTION

◀ Hawaiian monk seal

◀ Illinois chorus frog

Reading

A. Discuss these questions with a partner.

1. These animals are in danger of extinction. Where do they live? In what kind of habitat?
2. Why is it important to look after animal habitats?

B. Answer the questions.

1. Why is the number of fish going down? _____

2. If we stop fishing, what will happen? _____

3. Why is it important to look after wetlands? _____

4. Which are we losing more quickly, coral reefs or wetlands? _____

5. Why are coral reefs dying? _____

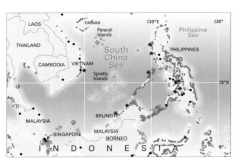

▲ endangered coral reefs

Habitat Destruction

OCEANS

Fish are like money in the bank. If you overspend, soon you will have no money. If we overfish, soon we will have no more fish. Fishermen now have bigger boats than in the past and they can catch more fish, so the number of fish is going down. Many scientists want to reduce or stop fishing completely in many parts of our oceans so the number of fish can **recover**.

WETLANDS

Freshwater and saltwater wetlands remove pollutants and provide habitat for fish, birds, and other animals. Many people, especially in Southeast Asia, depend on wetlands for food.

One hundred thirty-two nations have signed the Convention on Wetlands. However, the results have been **disappointing**. From the Amazon Basin to Iraq, we are **draining** wetlands for agriculture, dams, and development. Scientists estimate that we have lost 50 percent of our wetlands in the last 100 years. If we continue, there will be no wetlands left in 100 years.

For Your Information: Habitat destruction

Habitat destruction means the process in which a natural habitat is changed so that the original plants and animals there can no longer survive. According to experts, agriculture is the biggest cause of this, followed by mining, logging, fishing, and the growth of cities. Habitat destruction is now the most important cause of species extinction around the world. Islands are especially subject to habitat destruction, because the human population has limited land to use. Some of the worst-affected islands are New Zealand, Madagascar, the Philippines, and Japan.

▲ coral reefs of the world

CORAL REEFS

A quarter of all animals that live in the sea live in coral reefs. They are the rainforests of the sea. However, we have lost 27 percent of our coral reefs in the past 50 years according to the Coral Reef Alliance. Why are they dying? Man—sometimes directly, sometimes indirectly—is the problem. Fishermen use **explosives** and **poison** to kill fish. They kill the fish but they also kill the coral. Ocean temperatures have increased due to climate change. Coral needs water to be at exactly the right temperature. If the water is too hot, the coral will die. So man's activities are indirectly killing the coral reefs.

▲ endangered coral reefs

Word Focus

recover = to get back the same amount
drain = to remove water
disappointing = When something is *disappointing* it is not what you wanted or expected.
explosive = like a bomb
poison = a chemical that kills living things

Writing

Complete the letter to a magazine editor. Use the information you have learned in the article and your own ideas.

Dear Editor,

I read your article with interest and I agree with all you say. But what can the individual do?

The answer to the overfishing problem is simple. If everyone stops eating fish, _____ _____

The problem of the wetlands is more complicated because it is political. If people write to their senators, _____ _____ _____

The loss of coral reefs is partly caused by climate change, so if _____ _____ , that will help.

But how can **one** person change everything, I hear you say. Well, if **everyone** does something, _____

Yours sincerely,

Earl B. Butler
Wisconsin

✓ **Goal 4** | **Discuss ways to prevent habitat destruction**

Work with a partner. Talk about the things you will do to prevent habitat destruction.

Writing

- Introduce the idea of letters to the editor of a newspaper or magazine. Why do people write them? Why do people like to read them?
- Tell students to fill in the spaces in the letter with their own ideas and opinions, referring back to the article as needed.
- Have students exchange papers with partners. Ask students to mark corrections and suggestions for improvements on their partners' papers.
- If desired, have students rewrite their papers, to be collected for marking.

☑ Goal 4

- Have students discuss with partners ways to save animal habitats. With the class, compile a list on the board.

After Reading

Choose an English-language newspaper or magazine that students are familiar with. Have them write an actual letter to the editor about a topic that interests them. Collect the letters and mail them to the publication.

Video Journal

Before You Watch

- Introduce the topic of the video. Ask what, if anything, students know about Mt. Kilimanjaro (the highest mountain in Africa).

A • Have students work individually to write the correct words from the box.
- Check answers.

Answers: deforestation, glacier, melt

B • Have students read the iactions and consequences and then number the events in the order they happen.
- Check answers.

Answers: 4, 2, 1, 3

While You Watch

A • Tell students to watch the video the first time and find the numbers. Play the video.
- Check answers.

Answers: 1. four (19,340 feet), 2. 220, 3. 1936, 4. 11,000, 5. 2020

E VIDEO JOURNAL   *THE MISSING SNOWS OF KILIMANJARO*

Kilimanjaro, Tanzania

Before You Watch

A. Label the pictures with words from the box.

    melt   glacier   deforestation

_____   _____   _____

B. Read the chain of actions and consequences. Number the sentences to make a similar chain.

Cars and airplanes produce carbon dioxide. > Carbon dioxide makes the atmosphere hotter. > The glaciers of Kilimanjaro melt.

___ The glaciers of Kilimanjaro get smaller.
___ There is less water in the atmosphere.
_1_ People cut down trees.
___ There is less rain and snow.

While You Watch

A. Watch the video. Fill in the numbers and dates.

1. Kilimanjaro is nearly _____ miles high.
2. It is around _____ miles south of the equator.
3. Ernest Hemingway published "The Snows of Kilimanjaro" in _____.
4. The glaciers on Kilimanjaro are _____ years old.
5. Experts now predict that the mountain's glaciers could completely disappear by the year _____.

144 Consequences

For Your Information: Mt. Kilimanjaro

Kilimanjaro is located in Tanzania in East Africa, near the border with Kenya. It is an inactive volcano, but hot gas still comes out of holes in the rock. The mountain was first climbed by three men in 1889. Because it is one of the "Seven Summits" (the highest mountain on each continent of the world) many people climb it every year. The climb doesn't require great skill, but many people suffer from altitude sickness on the climb, and every year about 10 people die on the mountain.

 B. Answer the questions.

1. Why are the glaciers of Kilimanjaro important for the people who live near the mountain? _____

2. Why are the glaciers of Kilimanjaro important for Tanzania? _____

3. Why are the glaciers disappearing? _____ _____

After You Watch

Discuss this question with a partner. Is there anything that *you* can do to stop the melting of Kilimanjaro's glaciers?

Communication

Choose a photo. Describe it to your partner.
Discuss the different causes of the changes you see.

STUDENT A

▲ the Rhone Glacier in Switzerland, 1849

STUDENT B

▲ the Rhone Glacier today

B • Tell students to watch the video again and answer the questions. Have the students read the questions. Play the video.

• Check answers.

Answers: 1. They are an important source of water. 2. Tourists come to see the mountain, and they bring money. 3. global warming and deforestation

After You Watch

• Match students with a partner and have them brainstorm ways that they can help save the glaciers of Kilimanjaro.

• Compare answers with the class, making a list on the board.

Communication

• Match students with partners and have each student choose a picture to describe.

• Then have student pairs talk about possible causes of the changes between the pictures.

• Compare answers with the class.

Teacher Tip: Self evaluation

At the end of the course, it's useful to have students spend some time reflecting on the progress they've made and their goals for future learning. One way to do this is by having them fill in a questionnaire in English or their own language and then (if time permits) having a brief meeting with each student to discuss his/her answers.

Here are some possible questions you could use:

How much have you improved in these areas? Write "A lot," "Some," or "A little": Speaking/Listening/Writing/ Reading/Vocabulary/Grammar

Which activities in class helped you the most?

Which activities didn't help you?

What will you do differently in your next class?

HOW TO USE THIS SECTION?

These pair and group work activities are intended to take about 5 minutes. They can be used when a lesson finishes early or for a quick break from a lesson.

Students will probably need some help with vocabulary. If a pair of students asks you for a word and you think it is useful for the other students, write it on the board.

Don't worry if the students make mistakes, the idea is to get them to make the best use of their limited English.

After the class has finished you may want to share information about the photo or photos they used.

Activity 1

About the photo

The girl in the photo is Carmen Craig. She is proudly showing a story she wrote for her kindergarten class in Brookline, Massachusetts. Her class is just learning to read.

Activity 2

About the photo

This photo appeared on the cover of National Geographic Magazine, August 1999. The women live in Mumbai (formerly Bombay). They are both well-educated and fluent in several languages. The mother, Nakshatra, is a biochemist married to a prosperous businessman. Her daughter, Meghana, who is wearing a catsuit of her own design, is a model and a former TV host on a music video channel.

Activity 1

 Look at the picture. Discuss the questions.

a. Where is Carmen from?
b. How old is she?
c. Can you read her writing?
d. Are there any mistakes?
e. Is she worried?
f. Do you make mistakes with your English?
g. Are mistakes important?

Activity 2

 Work with a partner.

STUDENT A

Describe Nakshatra's clothes to a partner.

STUDENT B

Describe Meghana's clothes to a partner.

Discuss these questions together.

a. Do you think Nakshatra likes Meghana's clothes? How do you know?
b. Do you think young people should wear traditional clothes? Give your reasons.

▲ Nakshatra Reddy and her daughter Meghana

Activity 3

👥 Work with a partner.

▲ Francine Patterson and Koko

STUDENT A

Describe the picture to a partner. What is Koko doing? What expression does he have on his face? What are Francine's feelings?

STUDENT B

Describe the picture to a partner. What are Jane and Flint doing? Describe their feelings.

Discuss together.
Which picture do you prefer? Why?

▲ Jane Goodall and Flint

Activity 3

About the photo (top)

Dr. Francine Patterson is an American scientist and researcher who taught a simplied version of American Sign Language to the gorilla in this photo, Koko. Francine Patterson is the President and research director of The Gorilla Foundation in California.

About the photo (bottom)

Jane Goodall travelled to Kenya in 1957 at age 23. There she met paleontologist, Louis S.B. Leakey, who put her to work studying the chimpanzees of what is now Gombe National Park in Tanzania. Her patient unobtrusive observation brought her very close to the chimpanzees, including Flint.

Activity 4

About the photo (top)

These children live in Chengdu, China. They have an enormous interest in reading. Here they are all deeply engrossed in books they have rented from a street vendor.

About the photo (bottom)

This movie audience is watching a 3D film. The special glasses enhance the video images so the audience can perceive depth. 3D films which had been popular in the early 50's came back into fashion from 1960-1979 when this photo was taken.

Activity 4

 Work with a partner.

STUDENT A

Describe the photo to a partner. How many children are there? Where are they from? What are they doing? Where are they? Are they bored?

STUDENT B

Describe the photo to your partner. Where are the people? What are they doing? What are they wearing? What are their feelings?

Discuss these questions
a. Do people in your country like to read?
b. Do you prefer to read a book or go to the movies?

Activity 5

👥 Work with a partner. Make a list of all the objects in the picture you can name in five minutes. Read your list to the class.

Activity 6

👥 **A.** Work with a partner. Choose a person from one of the pictures. Describe him or her to your partner. What does the person look like? What is he or she doing? What are his or her feelings? Guess their nationality.

👥 **B.** Look at the people. Discuss these questions with a partner. What is their relationship? Are they friends, brother and sister, husband and wife? Are they happy together? What happened before the photo was taken?

Activity 5
About the photo

This is the work of artist René Milot. His triptych combines scenes of Alexandria, Egypt in A.D. 1; Cordoba, Spain in 1000; and modern day New York City. Students can visit *http://www.nationalgeographic.com/3cities/* for an interactive version of this painting.

Activity 6
About the photo (left)

In this photo two old friends talk while sitting on a park bench in Toronto, Ontario.

About the photo (right)

An elderly Chinese couple watch the modern world pass them by as they spend their days sitting on the pavement outside their house.

SKILLS INDEX

Communication.

See also **Listening; Speaking; Writing**

Grammar

Listening. *See also* **Pronunciation**

Pronunciation

Reading skills,

Readings

Speaking

describing, 7, 16, 25, 81, 145–151
discussing, 103, 146
giving advice, 115
job interviews, 127
naming objects, 149
role-playing, 37, 43, 61, 97, 109
trip planning, 139

Test-taking skills, 37

categorizing, 56
checking answers, 43, 55, 66, 73, 90, 96
circling answers, 9, 16, 18, 25, 37, 66, 78, 85, 100, 108, 114
completing charts, 133, 139
definitions, 24, 136
fill in the blanks, 4, 5, 6, 8, 12, 24, 45, 61, 69, 73, 101, 105, 112, 126, 129, 144
flowcharts, 121
labeling pictures, 16, 52, 76, 124, 128
matching, 5, 45, 48, 60, 64, 69, 84, 89, 96, 100, 102, 108, 116, 120, 125, 137
multiple choice, 18, 25, 66, 85, 108–109, 138
ordering pictures, 28
ordering sentences, 25, 144
rewriting sentences, 93
sentence completion, 17, 20, 28, 29, 32, 41, 65, 68, 69, 81, 92, 100, 101, 105, 116, 125, 126, 129, 140
sorting answers into columns, 8, 13, 41–44, 76, 112, 127
true or false, 10, 13, 22, 30, 35, 37, 48, 59, 61, 66, 73, 84, 90, 104, 108, 120, 133
underlining answers, 59, 61, 70, 94, 100
unscrambling sentences, 9, 21, 65, 77, 89, 137
writing questions, 33, 117

Topics

Achievements, 122–133
Communication, 75–85
Consequences, 134–145
Destinations, 62–73
Food, 38–49
The Future, 86–97
Going Places, 26–37
Lifestyles, 110–121
People, 2–13
Shopping for Clothes, 98–109
Sports, 50–61
Work, Rest, and Play, 14–25

Video Journal

Beagle Patrol, 36–37
Cheese-Rolling Races, 60–61

Dangerous Dinner, 48–49
Hula, 24–25
The Last of the Woman Divers, 12–13
Machu Picchu, 72–73
The Missing Snows of Kilimanjaro, 144–145
The Science of Stress, 120–121
Solar Cooking, 96–97
Spacewalk, 132–133
Traditional Silk Making, 108–109
Wild Animal Trackers, 84–85

Vocabulary

achievements, 128
animal habitats, 140
chores, 124
clothing, 100, 104
communication methods, 76
compound adjectives, 116
countries and nationalities, 4
daily routine, 16
descriptive adjectives, 8
emphatic adjectives, 68
festivals and celebrations, 20
food, 40, 44
healthy habits, 112
money, 32, 136
occupations, 4
party words, 20
people, 4
planning, 88
senses, 80
sports, 52, 56
travel, 28, 32, 64
weather conditions, 92

Writing

answering questions, 23, 47
email, 59, 131
letter to editor, 143
list-making, 13
paragraphs, 11, 107, 119
pictograms, 85
postcards, 71
recipes, 47
statements about the future, 95
text messages, 83
travel tips, 35

TEXT

22-23 Adapted from "The Wild Mix of Trinidad and Tobago," by A.R. Williams: National Geographic Magazine, March 1994, **22-23** Adapted from "Brazil: Moment of Promise and Pain," by Priit J. Vesilind: National Geographic Magazine, March 1987, **22-23** Adapted from "Upbeat, Downbeat, Offbeat New Orleans: The Many Faces of MardiGras," by Priit J. Vesilind: National Geographic Magazine, January 1995, **46-47** Adapted from "Bugs as Food: Humans Bite Back," by Maryann Mott: National Geographic News Public Website, April 16, 2004, **58-59** Adapted from "Scaling the Dragon's Spires of Ha Long Bay, Vietnam," by Lynn Hill: National Geographic Magazine, December 1997, **70-71** "In the Wonderland of Peru," by Hiram Bingham: National Geographic Magazine, April 1913, **82-83** Adapted from "The Secret Language Dolphins," by Crispin Boyer: National Geographic Kids Magazine, June/July 2007, Issue 371, **94-95** Adapted from "Powering the Future," by Michael Parfit: National Geographic Magazine, August 2005, **106-107** Adapted from "Silk: The Queen of Textiles," by Nina Hyde: National Geographic Magazine, November 2005, **118-119** Adapted from "New Wrinkles on Aging," by Dan Buettner: National Geographic Magazine, October 1999, **130-131** Adapted from "Unveiling the Universe" by Kathy Sawyer: National Geographic Magazine, October 1999, **142-143** Adapted from "State of the Planet" by Michael Kelsius: National Geographic Magazine, September 2002.

ILLUSTRATION

vi-vii: National Geographic Maps; **4:** National Geographic Maps; **5, 7, 8:** Nesbitt Graphics, Inc.; **10, 11, 12 :** National Geographic Maps (all); **17, 19:** Nesbitt Graphics, Inc.; **22, 24:** National Geographic Maps; **32:** (t to b) photos.com, Nesbitt Graphics, Inc., Scott Espie/istockphoto, Scott Rothstein/Shutterstock, Hu Xiao Fang/Shutterstock; **36:** National Geographic Maps; **40:** Keith Neely/illustrationOnLine.com; **41,42,44:** Nesbitt Graphics, Inc.; **48:** National Geographic Maps; **49, 53:** Nesbitt Graphics, Inc.; **58:** Phil Howe/illustrationOnLine.com; **59:** (l) National Geographic Maps, (r) Nesbitt Graphics, Inc.; **60:** National Geographic Maps; **67:** Nesbitt Graphics, Inc.; **68:** (l to r) Ralph Voltz/illustrationOnLine.com, Keith Neely/illustrationOnLine.com, Ralph Voltz/ illustrationOnLine.com (2), Keith Neely/illustrationOnLine.com; **69:** Ralph Voltz/ illustrationOnLine.com; **70:** Phil Howe/illustrationOnLine.com; **72:** National Geographic Maps; **80:** Nesbitt Graphics, Inc. (all); **84:** (l) National Geographic Maps, (r) shutterstock (all); **92, 94:** Nesbitt Graphics, Inc. (all); **100:** Ted Hammond/illustrationOnLine.com (all); **103:** Nesbitt Graphics, Inc.; **108:** National Geographic Maps; **118:** (l) Nesbitt Graphics, Inc., (r) National Geographic Maps; **119:** National Geographic Maps.; **121, 125, 126, 127, 136:** Nesbitt Graphics, Inc. (all); **139, 142, 143, 144:** National Geographic Maps (all).

PHOTO

Cover photo: Colin Monteath/Minden Pictures/National Geographic Image Collection. **vi–vii:** (t) Press Association via AP Images, (ml) Jose Gil/Shutterstock, (mr) Richard Olsenius/National Geographic Image Collection, (b) Ralph Lee Hopkins/National Geographic Image Collection; v: (tl) Jodi Cobb/National Geographic Image Collection, (tr) Paul Chesley/National Geographic Image Collection, (b) Mark C. Ross/National Geographic Image Collection; **2-3:** (l to r) Creatas/AGE Fotostock, Atlantide Phototravel/Corbis, Raul Touzon/ National Geographic Image Collection, Tim Pannell/Corbis; **4:** (1) Raul Touzon/ National Geographic Image Collection, (2) Jack Fletcher/National Geographic Image Collection, (3) Robert Sisson/National Geographic Image Collection, (4) Christian Ziegler/National Geographic Image Collection, (5) Ed Kashi/National Geographic Image Collection, (6) Winfield Parks/National Geographic Image Collection, (7) W. Robert Moore/National Geographic Image Collection, (8) Jason Edwards/National Geographic Image Collection; **5:** Mironov/istockphoto; **6:** (t to b) Peter Close/istockphoto, Simon Jarratt/Corbis, D Barton/Shutterstock, istockphoto; **7:** Alaska Stock Images/National Geographic Image Collection; **8:** (top, l to r) Nicole S. Young /istockphoto, photos.com, Carmen Martínez Banús/istockphoto, Monkey Business Images/Shutterstock, (bottom, l to r) H-Gall/istockphoto, Louis Michaud/ Shutterstock, Rhienna Cutler/istockphoto, David Freund/istockphoto; **9:** Aldo Murillo/istockphoto; **10:** (t) Ivars Silis/National Geographic Image Collection , (b) Kevin Fleming/National Geographic Image Collection; **11:** (tl) Joel Sartore/National Geographic Image Collection, (tr) William Albert Allard/National Geographic Image Collection, (m) William Albert Allard/National Geographic Image Collection, (b) Robert Essel NYC/Corbis; **12-13:** (l to r) Jung Yeon-Je/AFP/Getty Images (2), Stanislav Komogorov/Shutterstock, David White/Alamy, Andre Seale/Peter Arnold, photos.com, Stanislav Komogorov/Shutterstock, Jung Yeon-Je/AFP/Getty Images; **12:** (m) H. Edward Kim/National Geographic Image Collection, (b) Atlantide Phototravel/ Corbis; **13:** (m) Dennis Sabo/Shutterstock, (b) H. Edward Kim/National Geographic Image Collection; **14-15:** (l to r) Rich Iwasaki/age fotostock, David Young Wolff/ PhotoEdit, William Albert Allard/National Geographic Image Collection,

ANA/The Image Works; **16:** (1) mayamaya/Shutterstock, (2) Justin Horrocks/istockphoto, (3) Orange Line Media/Shutterstock, (4) PhotostoGo.com, (5 to 7) photos.com, (8) Paul Kim/Shutterstock, (9) photos.com, (10) PhotostoGo.com, (11, 12) istockphoto; **18:** Imageshop/SuperStock; **19:** Paul Kim/Shutterstock; **20:** (tl) photos.com, (tr) istockphoto, (bl) Sam Abell/National Geographic Image Collection, (br) Joanna B. Pinneo/National Geographic Image Collection; **22:** (tl) Dudley M. Brooks/National Geographic Image Collection, (ml) Stephanie Maze/National Geographic Image Collection, (br) Tyrone Turner/National Geographic Image Collection; **23:** Michael Nichols/National Geographic Image Collection; **24-25:** (l to r) Scott Leigh/istockphoto, Steve Raymer/National Geographic Image Collection, Mike Brake/Shutterstock, Steve Raymer/National Geographic Image Collection, Jose Gil/Shutterstock (2), Steve Raymer/National Geographic Image Collection, Scott Leigh/istockphoto; **24:** (ml) Syracuse Newspapers/L. Long/The Image Works, (mr) Shutterstock, (bl) Bruce C. Murray/Shutterstock, (br) K. & H. Benser/zefa/Corbis; **25:** (m) Ted Spiegel/National Geographic Image Collection, (b) Antonio Jorge Nunes/Shutterstock; **26-27:** (l to r) sinopictures/Peter Arnold, Oote Boe Photography/Alamy, Creatas/age fotostock, Justin Sullivan/Getty Images; **28:** (top, l to r) Eliza Snow/istockphoto, PhotostoGo.com, Digital Vision/Getty Images, James Steidl/Shutterstock, Stockbyte/Getty Images, (bottom, l to r) Galyna Andrushko/Shutterstock, photos.com, Bruno Domingos/ Reuters/Corbis, sinopictures/Peter Arnold, Timur Kulgarin/Shutterstock; **29:** photos.com; **30:** (t) Jacom Stephens/istockphoto, (m) Justin Sullivan/Getty Images, (b) Jon Feingersh/zefa/Corbis; **31:** (left, t to b) Oote Boe Photography/Alamy, photos.com, James Steidl/Shutterstock, PhotostoGo.com, (right, t to b) Galyna Andrushko/ Shutterstock, Justin Sullivan/Getty Images, Bruno Domingos/Reuters/Corbis, Stockbyte/Getty Images, Digital Vision/Getty Images; **32:** (tl) Elena Kalistratova/Shutterstock, (tr) Oleksiy Maksymenko/Alamy, (bl) Elwood Chu/Shutterstock, (br) Tom Young/istockphoto; **34:** Stockbyte/Getty Images; **35:** (l) Max Rossi/Reuters/Corbis, (r) Aleksander Bochenek/ istockphoto; **36-37:** (l to r) Richard Olsenius/National Geographic Image Collection (2), Karen Kasmauski/National Geographic Image Collection, Richard Olsenius/National Geographic Image Collection, Joseph H. Bailey/National Geographic Image Collection, Brandon Baker/Alamy, Richard Olsenius/National Geographic Image Collection (2); **36:** (ml) Boris Djuranovic/Shutterstock, (mr) vera bogaerts/Shutterstock, (bl) Jan Tyler/ istockphoto, (br) Lisa F. Young/Shutterstock; **37:** (b) Richard Olsenius/National Geographic Image Collection; **38-39:** (l to r) K Ovregaard/Cole Grou/age fotostock, Christopher Pillitz/Getty Images, david sanger photography/Alamy, David Coleman/ Alamy; **41:** (tl) bramalia/Shutterstock, (tr) Laurent Renault/Shutterstock, (bl) Martin Firus/istockphoto; **42:** Catherine Karnow/National Geographic Image Collection; **43:** (t) Cultura/Corbis, (b) Chris Howes/Wild Places Photography/Alamy; **44:** (top, l to r) Shutterstock (all), (bottom, l to r) istockphoto, Elena Schweitzer/Shutterstock, dyoma/ Shutterstock, Graca Victoria/Shutterstock; **45:** Lee Snider/The Image Works; **46:** (l) Kevin Foy/Alamy, (r) Melba Photo Agency/Alamy; **47:** (tl) Arco Images GmbH/ Alamy; (bl) Hans-Peter Moehlig/Alamy, (bm & br) istockphoto; **48-49:** (l to r) Paul Chesley/National Geographic Image Collection, Joe Scherschel/National Geographic Image Collection, Paul Chesley/National Geographic Image Collection, photos.com, Joe Scherschel/National Geographic Image Collection (3), Paul Chesley/National Geographic Image Collection; **48:** (middle, l to r) Keith Flood/istockphoto, photos.com, Achim Prill/istockphoto, Peter Heiss/istockphoto, Brian J. Skerry/National Geographic Image Collection; **49:** (middle, t to b) Gallo Images/Alamy, Joe Scherschel /National Geographic Image Collection, istockphoto, (mr) photos.com, (br) George Grall/National Geographic Image Collection; **50-51:** (l to r) Tyler Olson/Shutterstock, Shawn Pecor/ Shutterstock, Workbook Stock/JupiterImages, Buzz Pictures/SuperStock; **52:** (tl) Rob Marmion/Shutterstock, (1) Anthony-Masterson/JupiterImages, (2) Pete Saloutos/Shutterstock, (3) Andreas Gradin/Shutterstock, (4) Gordon Wiltsie/National Geographic Image Collection, (5) Edward Bock/Corbis, (6) Phase4Photography/ Shutterstock, (7) alysta/Shutterstock; **53:** PhotoDisc/Getty Images; **54:** (top, l to r) Bull's-Eye Arts/Shutterstock, Nick Free/istockphoto, Diego Cervo/Shutterstock, (bottom, l to r) Nicholas Moore/Shutterstock, Nicholas Moore/istockphoto, Eric Renard/ istockphoto; **56:** (tl) Mayskyphoto/Shutterstock, (tr) Tony Tremblay/istockphoto, (bl) Westend61/JupiterImages, (br) nikolpetr/Shutterstock; **57:** Jimmy Chin/National Geographic Image Collection; **58:** (t) Henrik Trygg/Corbis, (b) Daniel Attia/zefa/ Corbis; **59:** Christoph Papsch/Peter Arnold; **60-61:** (l to r) Carl De Souza/AFP/Getty Images, Peter Macdiarmid/Getty Images, Press Association via AP Images, istockphoto, Press Association via AP Images, PA/TopFoto/The Image Works, Kheng Guan Toh/ Shutterstock, Press Association via AP Images; **60:** (ml) Ng Han Guan/AP Images, (mr) Robb Kendrick/National Geographic Image Collection, (bl) Tom Uhlman/AP Images, (br) Carl De Souza/AFP/Getty Images; **61:** (m) Peter Macdiarmid/Getty Images, (b) istockphoto; **62-63:** (l to r) Alison Wright/National Geographic Image Collection, age fotostock/SuperStock, Richard Nowitz/National Geographic Image Collection, David Evans/National Geographic Image Collection; **64:** (tl) Christine Pemberton/The Image Works, (1) Konstantin Sutyagin/Shutterstock, (2) PhotostoGo.com, (3) J. D. Heaton/age fotostock, (4) istockphoto, (5) PhotostoGo.com, (6) istockphoto, (7) Max Alexander/Getty Images; **65:** Michael J. Doolittle/The Image Works; **66:** istockphoto; **67:** (t): Medford Taylor/National Geographic Image Collection, (middle, l to r) Robert Sisson/ National Geographic Image Collection, Specta/Shutterstock, Dan Westergren/National Geographic Image Collection, ratluk/Shutterstock, (m) photos.com, (bottom, l to r) istockphoto, gary yim/Shutterstock, nfsphoto/Shutterstock, Roberto Romanin/ Shutterstock; **70-71:** Hiram Bingham/National Geographic Image Collection (all); **72-73:** (l to r) Thomas Barrat/Shutterstock, Ralph Lee Hopkins/National Geographic Image Collection, Gina Martin/National Geographic Image Collection, Joel Shawn/Shutterstock, Ralph Lee Hopkins/National Geographic Image Collection, Gina Martin/ National Geographic Image Collection, Joel Shawn/Shutterstock, Ralph Lee Hopkins/ National Geographic Image Collection; **72:** (m) jan kranendonk/Shutterstock, (b) Ersler Dmitry/Shutterstock; **73:** (m) Thomas Barrat/Shutterstock; **74-75:** (l to r) The Art Archive/Musée du Louvre Paris/ Gianni Dagli Orti, Justin Guariglia/National Geographic Image Collection, Photononstop/SuperStock, Corbis RF/Photolibrary; **76:** (1) photos.com, (2, 3) istockphoto, (4 to 6) photos.com, (7) forest badger/Shutterstock, (8) Mischa/Shutterstock; **78:** Stepanov/Shutterstock; **79:** (t) istockphoto, (b) photos.com; **80:** (top, l to r) istockphoto (2), HomeStudio/Shutterstock, Monkey Business Images/Shutterstock, (bottom, l to r) Edyta Pawlowska/Shutterstock, photos.com, istockphoto (2) ; **81:** istockphoto; **82:** (tl) Albert Gea/Reuters/Corbis, (br) Flip Nicklin/Minden Pictures/National Geographic Image Collection; **83:** Franco Banfi/Peter Arnold; **84-85:** (l to r) Michael and Patricia Fogden/Minden Pictures/National Geographic Image Collection, Roy Toft/National Geographic Image Collection, Chris Johns/National Geographic Image Collection, Michael Nichols/National Geographic Image Collection, Tim Fitzharris/Minden Pictures/National Geographic Image Collection, Gerald Hinde/Getty Images, Chris Johns/National Geographic Image Collection, Tim

Fitzharris/Minden Pictures/National Geographic Image Collection; **85:** (m) Roy Toft/ National Geographic Image Collection; **86-87:** (l to r) istockphoto, Joel Sartore/ National Geographic Image Collection, Bruce Dale/National Geographic Image Collection, PhotoDisc/SuperStock; **88:** (top, l to r) istockphoto (all), (bottom, l to r) istockphoto, Chris Rose/Getty Images, Thomas M Perkins/Shutterstock, istockphoto; **89:** David Young Wolff/PhotoEdit; **90:** Tim Pannell/Corbis; **91:** (t) istockphoto, (b) Digital Vision/Getty Images; **92:** (t to b) istockphoto (2), Nikolay Postnikov/Shutterstock, Despot/Shutterstock, istockphoto, PhotoPips/Shutterstock, Salima/ Shutterstock, istockphoto; **93:** Corbis RF/SuperStock; **94, 95:** Sarah Leen/National Geographic Image Collection; **96-97:** (l to r) Gina Sanders/Shutterstock, istockphoto, Christopher Pillitz/ Getty Images, Lynsey Addario/Corbis, Falk Kienas/Shutterstock, John Stanmeyer/ National Geographic Image Collection, istockphoto, Lynsey Addario/Corbis; **96:** (middle, l to r) Kateryna Potrokhova/Shutterstock, Alex Kuzovlev/ Shutterstock, istockphoto, Steve and Donna O'Meara/ National Geographic Image Collection, Medford Taylor/National Geographic Image Collection; **97:** (m) Falk Kienas/ Shutterstock; **98-99:** (l to r) PhotostoGo. com, A. Ramey/PhotoEdit, Justin Guariglia/ National Geographic Image Collection, Chris Morris/PYMCA/ Jupiter Images; **101:** Andresr/Shutterstock; **102:** Bill Aron/PhotoEdit; **103:** (tl) Aflo/Corbis, (tr) STOCK4B GmbH/Alamy, (bl) PhotostoGo.com, (br) Fancy/Veer/ Corbis; **104:** (top, l to r) istockphoto (2), Tiziana and Gianni Baldizzone/Corbis, image100/Corbis, istockphoto, photos.com; **106:** Cary Wolinsky/ National Geographic Image Collection (both); **107:** (tl) Luis Marden/National Geographic Image Collection, (tr) Cary Wolinsky/National Geographic Image Collection, (bl) istockphoto, (br) J. Baylor Roberts/National Geographic Image Collection; **108-109:** (l to r) Jodi Cobb/National Geographic Image Collection, Lee Prince/Shutterstock, istockphoto, Luis Marden/National Geographic Image Collection, istockphoto (2) Luis Marden/National Geographic Image Collection, Lee Prince/Shutterstock; **108:** istockphoto; **109:** (m) July Flower/Shutterstock, (b) istockphoto; **110-111:** (l to r) Randy Faris/Corbis, PhotostoGo.com, Jeff Greenberg/Peter Arnold, Jim West/The Image Works**; 112:** (tl) Jamie Grill/Getty Images, (bl) Leila Cutler /Alamy, (middle, l to r) Alice/ Shutterstock, istockphoto, PhotostoGo.com, istockphoto, (bottom, l to r) PhotostoGo.com,

istockphoto, Maximilian Stock Ltd/PhotoCuisine/ Corbis, istockphoto; **113:** altrendo images/Getty Images; **114:** (l & m) istockphoto, (r) Jeff Greenberg/ The Image Works; **115:** (tl) Radius Images/ Photolibrary, (tr) istockphoto, (mr) Blend Images/Getty Images, (bl) Gregor Kervina/Shutterstock, (br) Ieva Geneviciene/Shutterstock; **116:** (t) Ellen B. Senisi/The Image Works, (b) istockphoto; **117:** PhotostoGo.com; **118, 119:** David Mclain/National Geographic Image Collection; **120-120:** (l to r) image100/Corbis, istockphoto (3), Suzanne Tucker/ Shutterstock, Dex Images/Corbis, istockphoto (2); **120:** (ml) Joel Sartore/ National Geographic Image Collection, (mr) Mark C. Ross/National Geographic Image Collection, (bl) Lorraine Swanson/Shutterstock, (br) John Burcham/ National Geographic Image Collection; **122-123:** (l to r) Annie Griffiths Belt/National Geographic Image Collection, NASA/National Geographic Image Collection, Monkey Business Images/Shutterstock, Jerry Lampen/Reuters/Corbis; **124:** (1) Monkey Business Images/Shutterstock, (2) katja kodba/ Shutterstock, (3) sonya etchison /Shutterstock, (4) Anne Kitzman/Shutterstock, (5 to 7) istockphoto, (8) David Young-Wolff/ PhotoEdit; **126:** (tl) istockphoto, (all others) Shutterstock; **128:** (1) Andresr/ Shutterstock, (2) Juriah Mosin/Shutterstock, (3) istockphoto, (4) koh sze kiat/ Shutterstock, (5) photos. com, (6) Chunche/Dreamstime.com, (7) istockphoto, (8) Andresr/Shutterstock; **129:** istockphoto; **130:** (tl): ESA and NASA/National Geographic Image Collection; (tr) Joe McNally/Getty Images; **132-133:** (l to r) ESA and NASA/ National Geographic Image Collection, NASA (7); **132:** (middle, l to r) NASA/ National Geographic Image Collection (2), NASA; **133:** (m) ESA and NASA/National Geographic Image Collection, (b) Peter Ginter/National Geographic Image Collection; **134-35:** (l to r) PhotostoGo.com, Ron Giling/Peter Arnold, Bob Daemmrich/PhotoEdit, Gerry Ellis/Minden Pictures/National Geographic Image Collection; **136:** (l) Schaefer Elvira/Shutterstock, (r) David Young-Wolff/PhotoEdit; **137:** photos.com; **138:** (l) Image Source/JupiterImages, (m) O. Louis Mazzatenta/National Geographic Image Collection, (r) Nicole Duplaix/National Geographic Image Collection; **140:** (top, l to r) Carsten Peter/National Geographic Image Collection, Michael Melford/ National Geographic Image Collection, Tui De Roy/ Minden Pictures/National Geographic Image Collection, Michael and Patricia Fogden/Minden Pictures/National Geographic Image Collection, Chris

Newbert/Minden Pictures/National Geographic Image Collection, (bottom, l to r) Konard Wothe/ Minden Pictures/National Geographic Image Collection, Richard Nowitz/National Geographic Image Collection, Norbert Wu/ Minden Pictures/ National Geographic Image Collection, Michael S. Quinton/National Geographic Image Collection, Gerry Ellis/Minden Pictures/National Geographic Image Collection; **142:** (t1) Bill Curtsinger/National Geographic Image Collection, (t2) Suzanne L. & Joseph T. Collins/Photo Researchers, (m) Alaska Stock Images/National Geographic Image Collection, (b) Tim Fitzharris/Minden Pictures/National Geographic Image Collection; **144-145:** (l to r) Ralph Lee Hopkins/National Geographic Image Collection, Mark C. Ross/National Geographic Image Collection, David Pluth /National Geographic Image Collection, Kondrachov Vladimir/ Shutterstock, David Pluth / National Geographic Image Collection, emin kuliyev/ Shutterstock, Ralph Lee Hopkins/National Geographic Image Collection, David Pluth /National Geographic Image Collection; **144:** (middle, l to r) Gerry Ellis/ Minden Pictures/National Geographic Image Collection, istockphoto, Paul Nicklen/National Geographic Image Collection; **145:** (bl) Science Museum/SSPL, (br) James Balog/National Geographic Image Collection; **146:** (t) Cary Wolinsky/National Geographic Image Collection,(b) Joe McNally/ National Geographic Image Collection; **147:** (t) Gorilla Foundation/AP Images, (b) Hugo Van Lawick/National Geographic Image Collection; **148:** (t) Cary Wolinsky/ National Geographic Image Collection, (b) Ed Bock/ Corbis; **149:** (t) René Milot/National Geographic Image Collection, (bl) Robert Madden/National Geographic Image Collection, (br) G P Bowater/Alamy

T194: (tl) Jason Stitt/Shutterstock, (tr) iStockphoto, (bl) iofoto/Shutterstock, (br) Joseph/Shutterstock; **T196:** Darren Baker/Shutterstock; **T198:** Pete Saloutos/ Shutterstock; **T199:** iStockphoto; **T200:** (1) Yobidaba/Shutterstock, (2) Cynthia Lindow/ iStockphoto, (3) Miguel Angel Salinas Salinas/ Shutterstock, (4) iStockphoto, (5) Yobidaba/ Shutterstock, (6) iStockphoto; **T201:** PhotostoGo. com; **T202:** (tl) photos.com, (ml) Skip ODonnell/ iStockphoto, (mr) Jani Bryson/iStockphoto, (bl) photos.com, (br) iStockphoto; **T203:** Winston Davidian/iStockphoto; **T204:** (tl) iStockphoto , (tr) John Wollwerth/Shutterstock, (bl & br) PhotostoGo. com; **T205:** PhotostoGo.com.

UNIT 1

Track 1-3

LESSON B, LISTENING

TV Game Host: Hi, can you tell me something about yourself?

Kyoko: Sure. My name is Kyoko, and I'm from Japan. Actually, I'm from Tokyo.

Host: And what do you do?

Kyoko: I'm an engineer.

Host: Thank you, Kyoko. And here is our next contestant. Can you introduce yourself?

Luis: Yes. My name is Luis, and I'm a doctor. I'm from Bogota in Colombia.

Host: Thank you, Luis. And welcome to tonight's show.

Contestant Number 3, can you tell us something about yourself?

Jim: Yes, my name is Jim, Jim Waters. I'm a farmer.

Host: And where are you from?

Jim: I'm from a small town in Canada called Coldstone.

Host: Thank you, Jim. And welcome. And now our last contestant for tonight's show.

Silvia: Hello. My name is Sylvia and, as you can see, I'm a musician. I'm from Rio de Janeiro in Brazil.

Track 1-5

LESSON B, PRONUNCIATION

1. I am a teacher.

2. He's an engineer.

3. She's a nurse.

4. They are interesting.

5. You're welcome.

UNIT 2

Track 1-8

LESSON B, LISTENING

Helen: Good evening, everyone. Welcome to *Sunday with the Stars*. You all know tonight's guest—it's Bob Hardy the star of *Life on the Run*. Great to have you here, Bob.

Bob: Thanks, Helen. Great to be here.

Helen: OK, Bob. So, we know what you do during the week. You're a star! But on *Sunday with the Stars* we want to find out what you do in your free time. So, Bob, what do you do on Sundays?

Bob: Well Helen, the simple answer is that I do nothing.

Helen: Nothing! Come on, Bob.

Bob: Nothing. I don't play sports, I don't do any exercise. I just chill out.

Helen: OK, but what time do you get up?

Bob: I get up at about 9 o'clock and have breakfast around 10. In the week I don't have time for breakfast, so on Sunday I have a big breakfast.

Helen: Do you eat in or do you have breakfast in a restaurant?

Bob: I like cooking so I eat at home. Eggs, bacon, sausages—the works!

Helen: And then?

Bob: Then I read the Sunday newspaper and I often take a nap at about 1 o'clock. In the afternoon, I sometimes watch sports on TV.

Helen: Do you like sports?

Bob: Yes. Basketball is my favorite—but I don't play—I just watch.

Helen: OK. So you don't leave the house at *all* on Sundays.

Bob: Oh yes. In the evening, I often go to the movies with my girlfriend or we go out for dinner together. But I always try to go to bed early. I need to be ready for Monday morning and work.

Helen: OK, we'll go to a commercial break and when we come back, I'm going to find out more about this girlfriend. Back in a minute.

UNIT 3

LESSON B, LISTENING

Track 1-12   **Conversation 1**

Check-in clerk: Good morning. Can I see your ticket and passport, please?

Traveler: I have an e-ticket. Here is the confirmation number.

Check -in clerk: Thank you. Can I see your U.S. visa please?

Traveler: Here it is.

Check in clerk: Window or aisle?

Traveler: Excuse me?

Check in clerk: Would you like a seat next to the window or one next to the aisle?

Traveler: Oh, I see. A window seat, please.

Check in clerk: Do you have any bags to check in?

Traveler: Yes, this one's mine.

Check-in clerk: OK, here's your boarding pass. Your seat number is 18A. We will be boarding at gate number 5 at 2:30. Have a nice trip.

Traveler: Thank you.

Conversation 2

Officer: Good morning. Can I see your passport please?

Traveler: Good morning. Here it is.

Officer: Is this your first time in the United States?

Traveler: Yes it is.

Officer: What is the purpose of your visit?

Traveler: I'm here on vacation.

Officer: How long are you staying?

Traveler: For 2 weeks.

Officer: Where are you staying?

Traveler: I'm staying with friends in Los Angeles.

Officer: Place your left index finger here. Now, the right one. Thank you. Now please, look into the camera. Thank you. OK, that's fine. I hope you enjoy your vacation.

Traveler: Thank you.

Conversation 3

Receptionist: Good evening, sir. Can I help you?

Guest: Yes, I have a reservation. My name is Ken Lee.

Receptionist: Ah yes, Mr. Lee. Just for one night?

Guest: Yes, that's right. Just tonight.

Receptionist: Very good. Could you fill out this form, please?

Guest: Yes, of course.

Receptionist: OK, you have a single room. Number 303, on the third floor. Here is your room key.

Guest: Thank you.

Receptionist: Are those your bags?

Guest: Yes, and they are heavy.

Receptionist: Let me get a bell boy to help you.

Guest: Thank you.

Receptionist: You're welcome. Have a nice stay.

Guest: Thank you

UNIT 4

 LESSON B, LISTENING

Track 1-16

Waiter: Good evening, sir. My name is Walter and I am your waiter this evening.

Man: Good evening, Walter.

Waiter: Are you ready to order, sir?

Man: Can we order drinks first?

Waiter: Yes, of course.

Man: I would like a glass of red wine.

Woman: Do you have any mineral water?

Waiter: Yes, we do.

Woman: OK, I'll have a bottle of mineral water.

Waiter: And would you like an appetizer, madam?

Woman: No thank you, I'll just have a main dish. What would you recommend?

Waiter: The butter-baked chicken is excellent

Woman: OK, I'll take the chicken.

Waiter: Butter-baked chicken. And for you, sir?

Man: Mmm let me see. Does the filet mignon come with salad?

Waiter: Yes, it does, sir.

Man: OK, I'll have the fillet mignon and the French dressing on my salad.

Waiter: Filet mignon. And how do you like your steak, sir?

Man: Medium, please.

Waiter: Anything else?

Man: No, I don't think so. Thank you

LESSON B, PRONUNCIATION

Track 1-18

1. /djə æv/ a pen?

2. Would you like some more bread?

3. Do you have any paper?

/wʊd dʒə/ like some coffee?

/djə æv/ any change?

UNIT 5

LESSON B, LISTENING

Track 1-21

Conversation 1

Jean: Hi, Karen. What are you doing?

Karen: Hi! You'll never guess. I m ice skating with Alan.

Jean: Ice skating! Wow! Alan doesn't like sports. You guys always go to the movies on Fridays.

Karen: Not today!

Conversation 2

Steve: Hi, Dave. How's the studying going?

Dave: I'm not studying.

Steve: What! You always study in the evening.

Dave: No, today I'm having a rest. I'm playing basketball with some friends. Hey, can I call you back?

Steve: Sure. Enjoy your game.

Conversation 3

Grant: Hi, Robin. What's up?

Robin: Hi, Grant. I'm fixing the roof.

Grant: You're fixing the roof! But you always go to the ball game on Sundays.

Robin: Yes, but it's raining and the roof is leaking. So, no ball game this week.

Grant: Oh, well. Good luck.

LESSON B, PRONUNCIATION

Track 1-23

1. What are you reading?

2. /wætʃə/ thinking?

3. /wætʃə/ playing?

4. What are you cooking?

5. /wætʃə/ writing?

UNIT 6

LESSON B, LISTENING

Track 1-26

Mick: Hey, Glenn. How was Orlando?

Glenn: Great.

Mick: Come on then, tell me all about it! How many theme parks did you visit?

Glenn: Mm, three I think. Let me see. First we went to Disney World and then Universal Studios. Yes, and then Sea World. Yes, three.

Mick: Come on. Tell me more!

Glenn: Well, Disney World was OK. I liked the Downtown Disney show; that was cool. But I didn't like Sea World. Fish, fish and more fish.

Mick: But what about Universal Studios. Did you see the Harry Potter exhibition?

Glenn: Harry Potter. No, thanks. That's for kids. But I went to the Islands of Adventure. Now that was something. We took a ride called the Incredible Hulk Coaster. I can't describe it. You have to try it for yourself.

Mick: Oh, I would love to. You lucky, guy.

UNIT 7

LESSON B, LISTENING

Track 2-3

Radio presenter: So that's it for today, folks. It was great to hear your views on the new traffic system in town. Next week's guest is John Parsons, the new chief of police and he'll be talking about his ideas on reducing crime. So why not call us on thirty-four, thirty-six, twenty-nine, eighteen, thirty-four. Do you want to write that down? Got a pen? Here we go—thirty-four, thirty-six, twenty-nine, eighteen, thirty-four.

You can also send us a fax on thirty-four, thirty, fourteen, seventy-six, twenty-two. One more time. That's thirty-four, thirty, fourteen, seventy-six, twenty-two.

We love to get your emails. Send us your views to Kingstownradio@coolmail.com. I'll say it again. It's Kingstownradio, that's all one word at coolmail dot com. OK one more time. Kingstownradio at coolmail dot com.

Send an SMS to 333 317 3476. That's three, three, three, three one seven, three, four, seven, six.

And that old snail mail still works. Our address is Kingstown Radio, 25 Main Street, Kingstown. Again, Kingstown Radio, 25 Main Street, Kingstown.

So, remember next week we'll be talking to the chief of police. I know he'll want to hear your views.

That's all for today from Community Call In. And it's back to the studio.

LESSON B, PRONUNCIATION

Track 2-4

thirty, fourteen, fifty, sixteen, seventeen, eighty, nineteen

UNIT 8

LESSON B, LISTENING

Track 2-8

Warren: Hi, Pete. Great to see you. Welcome to the show.

Pete: Good to be on your show, Warren.

Warren: So, how's it going? Your last album was a big success. Do you have any plans for another album?

Pete: Sure. I'm going to record a new album in January.

Warren: Great. We're all looking forward to that. And then?

Pete: And then I'm going to have a break.

Warren: So, you're not going to do another world tour?

Pete: No, not this year. Babs is going to have a baby in March.

Warren: Congratulations! So, you're going to be a father.

Pete: Yeah. But it's not going to change my life. I'm still going to be recording and touring.

Warren: A baby is not going to change your life? Just wait, Pete. Just wait.

Pete: Yeah, maybe you're right.

Warren: And I hear you're going to make a film. Is it true?

Pete: I think we're going to start filming at the end of the year.

Warren: So, you're already a pop star, and you're going to be a film star and a father. Nice going.

LESSON B, PRONUNCIATION

Track 2-10

1. When are you /gənə/ finish?

2. They're not going to like it.

3. We're going to leave at three thirty.

4. I'm /gənə/ take a shower.

5. Are you /gənə/ take a taxi?

UNIT 9

Track 2-13

LESSON B, LISTENING

Shop attendant: Can I help you?

Shopper: Yes, I'd like some blue shoes to go with these pants.

Shop attendant: Blue. Let me see. What about these?

Shopper: Do you have anything less formal?

Shop attendant: Yes, these are more casual.

Shopper: I like these. Can I try them on?

Shop attendant: Yes, of course. What size are you?

Shopper: I usually wear a 7 or 7 ½.

Shop attendant: Here we are.

Shopper: Ooo! They're a little tight. Do you have a bigger size? An 8?

Shop attendant: Yes. How about these? Are they looser?

Shopper: Yes. They're perfect. How much are they?

Shop attendant: They are $150.

Shopper: Mmm. Do you have anything a little less expensive?

Shop attendant: Something cheaper? Let me see. No, not in blue. What about black?

Shopper: Yes, black might be OK.

Shop attendant: What about these? They're on sale --- $75.

Shopper: Mmm. I'm not sure.

Shop attendant: We have some white ones at $80. They'll go with your pants.

Shopper: White. No, I don't like white. I think I'll take the blue ones.

Shop attendant: Fine. Cash or charge?

Shopper: I'll put it on my card.

UNIT 10

LESSON B, LISTENING

Track 2-17

Ben: Hi. My name is Ben, I'm 22 years old and I live and work in Los Angeles, California. I'm a very busy real estate agent. Sometimes clients want to see a house at 7 o'clock in the morning and sometimes at 10 o'clock at night, so I can never plan my meals. I just grab a hamburger or hot dog whenever I can and then run off to see the next customer.

I try to go to the gym on Sundays, but sometimes I don't make it. I know I should get more exercise, but I never have the time. And then of course, I smoke. I know I shouldn't and I keep trying to stop, but it's difficult.

Maggie: Hi, my name's Maggie and I'm 70 years old and I come from Winchester in England. In Britain, on your hundredth birthday, the Queen sends you a telegram. That's my ambition, to get a telegram from the Queen. So, I get up early, usually around 6 o'clock and I go to the pool. I love swimming. It's good exercise, but it also helps me to relax. I can plan my day and think through problems as I'm swimming. Then I come home and eat a big breakfast. I think breakfast is the most important meal of the day and I try to eat healthy foods, like whole meal bread, honey, yogurt, high fiber cereal.

The rest of the day I visit friends and take my dogs for long walks. However, I do have one bad habit. I love chocolate. I eat at least one chocolate bar every day. And then there's chocolate cake - mmm I love chocolate.

Anita: Hi, my name's Anita, I'm 35 years old and I have three kids. Bringing up three young kids is a lot of work and I also have a big garden where I grow organic vegetables to sell in the local market. With three kids and a big garden I don't have time to get any regular exercise. But of course, the work in the garden keeps me fit.

Needless to say, we eat a lot of fruit and vegetables from the garden and although we all eat meat, we don't eat much red meat, mainly chicken.

All in all, I think I have quite a healthy lifestyle. However, I do have one bad habit. I drink about 20 cups of coffee a day! I even drink coffee when I'm working in the garden. My husband says I'm just a machine for converting coffee into carrots. Well, at least the carrots are healthy even if the coffee isn't.

LESSON B, PRONUNCIATION

Track 2-19

1. You shouldn't go to bed at one o'clock every night.

2. You should drink less coffee.

3. Zeta should lose some weight.

4. They shouldn't watch so much TV.

UNIT 11

LESSON B, LISTENING

Track 2-22

Interview 1

Interviewer: Good morning Miss Harmon . Thank you for coming to the interview.

Erin: My pleasure.

Interviewer: OK, let's begin. First, have you graduated from college?

Erin: Oh, yes. I studied English and History.

Interviewer: English and History. Very good. OK. Have you ever traveled abroad?

Erin: Yes, I think I have visited about 8 different countries.

Interviewer: Eight! What is the most interesting place you have visited?

Erin: Venice! I love Venice. I've been there three times and I never get tired of it -- the churches, the museums, the canals, the sense of history. It's amazing!

Interviewer: Very good. Have you worked as a tour guide before?

Erin: No, not really. I have taken friends around museums that I know well, but I haven't had a paid job as a tour guide.

Interviewer: OK. That's not a problem. Now a practical question: Have you passed your driving test?

Erin: No, but I've taken driving lessons. I'm going to take my test next month.

Interviewer: OK, and one final general question: Who is the most interesting person you have met?

Erin: Mmm, that's tricky. I've met a lot of interesting people. Possibly, my father.

Interviewer: Your father! Can you explain?

Erin: Well, he's worked in so many different places and he's read so much. I really admire him. But then I of course I would—he's my father!

Interviewer: Indeed. OK, thank you very much, Erin. We will get back to you on Tuesday. Thank you for coming.

Erin: Thank you.

Interview 2

Interviewer: Good morning, Mr. Reed. Thank you for coming to the interview.

Richard: Sure. Nice to meet you.

Interviewer: OK. So, let's begin. Have you graduated from college?

Richard: Sure. I majored in Chemistry.

Interviewer: Chemistry. OK. Now, have you ever worked as a tour guide?

Richard: Sure. I worked in Disneyland last year. I was one of the guides on the Jungle Book tour. That was cool. I really liked meeting all those people.

Interviewer: Disneyland. Right. Speaking of people, who is the most interesting person you have ever met?

Richard: The most interesting person I have met. Well, I once met Earle Grave, you know the quarterback for the Bulls. Great guy. I really admire him.

Interviewer: Earle Grave. OK. And have you ever travelled abroad?

Richard: Er. Abroad? No, it's kind of expensive. But I'd like to.

Interviewer: OK. Have you passed your driving test?

Richard: Sure.

Interviewer: OK, thank you very much. We'll contact you next Tuesday. Thank you for coming.

Richard: Sure thing.

LESSON B, PRONUNCIATION

Track 2-24

1. Has she left?

2. /ævjə/ finished?

3. /æz iː/ read this book?

4. Have you done your homework?

5. I've never been to the USA.

UNIT 12

LESSON B, LISTENING

Track 2-27

Travel Agent: Good morning, can I help you?

Businesswoman: Yes. I'm going to Paris on business next month and when I'm there, I would like to visit some friends in London.

Travel Agent: OK, do you have your flight from New York to Paris? If we book both flights New York to Paris and Paris to London together, we can get you a better price.

Businesswoman: No, thank you. I have the New York to Paris flight. And I don't want any more planes! I've never been to England before and if I take a plane, I won't see anything. Just more airports.

Travel Agent: Well, you could rent a car or take the train.

Businesswoman: If I rent a car, I know I'll get lost. No, the train sounds better.

Travel Agent: OK. There are trains leaving Paris every hour.

Businesswoman: If I take the 6 p.m. train, what time will I arrive in London?

Travel Agent: Let me see. You'll arrive in London at 8:15 p.m.

Businesswoman: That sounds great. And how much will it cost?

Travel Agent: Hmm. That will be $175. But if you buy the ticket 2 weeks in advance, there is a discount. It will only cost $150.

Businesswoman: Great. I'll buy the ticket now. Thank you.

Travel Agent: OK, that will be $150.

UNIT 1

VIDEO JOURNAL *THE LAST OF THE WOMEN DIVERS*

NARRATOR: The island of Cheju off the coast of South Korea is famous for its natural beauty. It's also known for a group of women divers called *haenyos.*

These women dive into the sea every day to look for seafood. It's their job, and it's difficult and very dangerous work. They do not use oxygen tanks. They can hold their breath and stay underwater for up to five minutes!

For hundreds of years, the women of Cheju have made their living from the sea. They dive into the cold waters and catch octopus, abalone, and sea urchins. However, these women divers on Cheju may be the last. Things on this small island are changing.

Sunny Hong is different. She isn't a diver. She is a tour guide. She doesn't catch fish. She helps tourists that come to the island.

SUNNY HONG, Cheju tour guide: "I wanted to find some kind of job which I can use my English, and also this kind of job is (how can I say) fit my aptitude."

NARRATOR: Sunny speaks English. She doesn't have to dive. However, all the other women in her family are divers.

HONG: "This is my aunt, Ms. Hong. She's 63 years old and she started diving when she was thirteen, so almost fifty years now."

NARRATOR: Sunny's aunt and her friends have been diving nearly all of their lives!

HONG: "They didn't have a choice. Also, they were born in sea village, so they had to be a woman diver, and there's nothing they can do except woman diver."

NARRATOR: The job is very dangerous. In Cheju, all the divers are women. Men are not divers.

The youngest diver on the island is 45 years old. The oldest is 75. These women dive for five to six hours every day! But, why do they keep diving?

The answer is easy. Sixty-year-old Song Ho has had a good day. She can make up to 300 U.S. dollars in a day! Diving is still a big business in Cheju. The women can use the money to educate their children.

HONG: "I don't want to be a woman diver. I think I am lucky."

NARRATOR: The young people of Cheju have more opportunities. Sunny's aunt and her friends may just be the last of the Cheju women divers.

UNIT 2

VIDEO JOURNAL *HULA*

NARRATOR: Welcome to the beautiful islands of Hawaii. Hawaii is a land of legends. There is a very old legend about a dance called the hula. The hula started about 300 years ago.

A hula teacher tells us about the legend. She says, "In the legend a girl called Hi'iaki and her friend Hopoe go to the beach one day. They look at the sea and the waves and they start to copy the waves. They move their hands like the waves and they move their bodies like the waves. This is the start of the hula dance."

Then in 1820, missionaries from Western countries came to Hawaii. They were surprised by the hula—the dancers did not wear many clothes! The missionaries were so surprised, that they asked the queen of Hawaii to stop the dance.

After that, most Hawaiians were not allowed to dance the hula for almost sixty years. But the Hawaiians still danced the hula but in secret.

Today, there is a new interest in Hawaiian culture. People want to study the culture and learn how to dance the hula.

More and more people go to *halaus. Halaus* are schools that teach the dance in the traditional way.

The dancers have to work very hard to learn the dance. They have to practice for many hours before they can dance the hula for other people.

Kumano Palini Kulala is a hula teacher. For him, the dance is a way of bringing the best of ancient Hawaiian culture to people today.

KUMANO PALINI KULALA: "…the hula is more…not so much a physical thing, but more of a mental and a spiritual thing. For them the dancing means very little because for Hawaiians today, many of them don't speak the [Hawaiian] language. So, what I try to do is to bring to mind the reality that they see today."

NARRATOR: Every year, there is a hula competition in Hilo, Hawaii. Dancers from all the Hawaiian Islands come to the festival. In the competition, judges look at more than just the dance. They also look at the dancers' costumes and style . . . the way the person wears a skirt, the color of their costume, even their flowers.

Today in Hawaii, the hula is once again part of everyday life. Many people hope that this will save one of Hawaii's most ancient traditions for the future.

UNIT 3
VIDEO JOURNAL *BEAGLE BRIGADE*

NARRATOR: At the National Detector Dog Training Center in Orlando, Florida, every day has a noisy start.

BRENT HELDT: "Hey Guys! Hey Guys! Hey!"

NARRATOR: This is especially true for canine instructor Brent Heldt. A half a dozen beagles are waiting for their morning run. The first lucky dog is a beagle called Stockton.

HELDT: "Go on, go get it! Go get it!"

NARRATOR: Stockton is learning to become a detector dog. Before Heldt and Stockton start work, it is time for play.

HELDT: Come on get some! Come on! Come on!
Their personalities are all very different. That's what makes this job so cool. I mean, every time I train these guys, I learn something different . . . every time.
We're going to work, Come on, Hoss. You big hoss!"

NARRATOR: Detector dogs work in international airports and look for illegal imports like citrus fruits, mangoes, and apples that may carry diseases.

They also sniff for meat products that may carry diseases. At twenty-one international airports around the United States every day, dogs help to find this food. But the dogs have to to do this without bothering passengers who are bringing home safe and legal gifts for their friends and family. That's where the National Detector Dog Training Center comes in.

HELDT: "What we got here is a target box, it's called mixed. The reasons we call it that is because that's exactly what it is. It's mixed odor. We have some beef jerky. I have the beef odor, we have my apple odor, we have a citrus odor, and I have my mango odor. So should we try the bags now? Let's go try the hand bags. Come on.

What we want the dogs to do, is work the seam of the suitcase because the odor comes out from the seam. What we teach the canine officers and the dogs, when we breathe the bag, odor is coming out of the bag.

What have you got? Have you got something Stockton? Good boy! You found it, you found the meat! That's a good boy!"

NARRATOR: Things don't always go so smoothly for Stockton though. On the next test he lies down when he is supposed to sit. On another, he gets too far ahead of Heldt.

HELDT: "Where you going? Wait for me! Stockton, wait for me, Bud! You've got to work with me, I'm your partner remember?"

NARRATOR: Even though it's serious work, it always has to be fun for the animal. So what does it take to be a detector dog?

HELDT: "Obviously, number one, they have to be great with people and children, because when we work them in the airports, that's what we're working with---the public coming from foreign countries. They've got to have real good food drive because they work for food. Anybody knows . . . who has a beagle . . . they love food. Even after they eat a big dinner, they're still ready to eat some more."

NARRATOR: However, even after all that training, not all of the dogs are good enough to become detector dogs.

HELDT: "For some reason if they don't work out, we place them in homes. They stay with us until we can find a home that suits them and we have applicants on our adoption list all the time. And we screen them to make sure they're also a good fit for the dog that we have."

NARRATOR: But Stockton is learning quickly. Stockton's chances of becoming a detector dog look very good.

HELDT: "His demeanor is really meek, he just rolls along kind of like a tortoise. Nothing kind of fazes him. He loves working. It's a game to him, which is really important.
Good job! Good job, very good!"

NARRATOR: But when these two partners are working together, it's easy to see that it's not only Stockton who loves his work.

UNIT 4

VIDEO JOURNAL *DANGEROUS DINNER*

NARRATOR: Japanese people eat a lot of fish. Every morning many people go to Tsukiji Seafood Market in Tokyo. The most expensive fish, and the most dangerous, is the puffer fish, or as the Japanese call it—*fugu*.
Parts of the puffer fish are poisonous. People who eat the poisonous parts of the fish can die.
However, you can find *fugu* on more than 80 menus in the Asakusa restaurant area of Tokyo. Although it is dangerous, people like to eat *fugu*.
Tom Caradonna is visiting Tokyo because he wants to try *fugu*. Tom and his friend Aki are eating at the Matsumoto restaurant. This famous restaurant is 120 years old. Everyone knows that the restaurant prepares the fish very carefully.

TOM: I've heard stories about people dying you know, trying the *fugu* but it hasn't really concerned me.

NARRATOR: Tom isn't worried but many have died because they ate the puffer fish.
At the Matsumoto restaurant, Chef Hayashi prepares the *fugu*.

CHEF HAYASHI: "It'll be fine, don't worry. I've been doing this for 53 years. I took the exam in 1949 and passed it, This is my *fugu* chef license."

NARRATOR: After World War II, many people died from eating *fugu*. Many Japanese people were very hungry, and some looked for food in restaurant trash cans. Sometimes these people found pieces of *fugu*. They cooked the *fugu* and some of them died.
It was a serious problem. So, American General Douglas MacArthur, who led the U.S. forces in Japan, introduced a test. The *fugu* chefs had to take the test and get a license. Chef Hayashi took the test in 1949 and he still has his license.
Nevertheless, *fugu* killed 2,500 Japanese people between 1945 and 1975.

HIDENORI KADOBAYASHI, Tokyo Health Department: "About 70 percent of the poisonings happen in private homes, where people catch and prepare *fugu* on their own and get poisoned. That's most common."
At the Tokyo University of Fisheries, Nagashima Tuji studies *fugu* poison carefully. He hopes to develop an anti-toxin, which is a medicine that will stop people from dying because of *fugu* poisoning.

NAGASHIMA: "A tiger *fugu* has enough poison to kill 30 people. The poison itself, to give you an idea, is 1,000 times stronger than cyanide."

NARRATOR: *Fugu* toxin is a very strong poison. In fact, one milligram of the toxin is strong enough to kill a person. It kills by paralyzing people's nerves. This means that the person who has been poisoned can't move. It also paralyzes the lungs so that the person can't breathe.

Back in the Matsumoto restaurant kitchen, Chef Hayashi is preparing the *fugu* for Tom and Aki.

HAYASHI: "These are the gills. They're poison," he warns.

NARRATOR: Chef Hayashi carefully cuts away the poisonous parts of the fish and throws them out. Then, he cuts the remaining flesh very thinly. Finally, he places the *fugu* on a plate and puts it in the shape of a chrysanthemum. The chrysanthemum is a beautiful flower that's popular in Japan.

At the table, Aki and Tom are ready to try the *fugu*.

AKI: "Still breathing?"

TOM: "I can still breathe!" replies Tom and he continues his meal.

NARRATOR: A *fugu* meal is usually eight different dishes. These dishes feature *fugu* that is prepared in different ways.

TOM: "And I still feel fine."

NARRATOR: Tom's favorite course is the grilled *fugu*, and Aki agrees. At the end of the meal, Tom smiles; he's happy that he's still healthy and breathing.

UNIT 5

VIDEO JOURNAL *CHEESE-ROLLING RACES*

NARRATOR: Around the world there are many unusual sports but cheese rolling is one of the most unusual. Cheese rolling started about 200 years ago in the English town of Brockworth.

First, the competitors come together at the top of Cooper's Hill. Then someone pushes a very large wheel of cheese down the hill. And after that? The competitors run after it! The cheese rolls down the hill at more than 60 kilometer per hour. The competitors go pretty fast, too! The first person to arrive at the bottom wins. What's the prize? The wheel of cheese—of course! The first winner of the day is Craig Brown, a pub worker. Craig's plan was simple.

CRAIG BROWN, Pub Worker: "Keep going…and try to get your balance back. It's steeper than you could ever think. You would have to run down there to really believe how steep it is!"

NARRATOR: Many people enjoy the cheese rolling races, however they can be dangerous. A few years ago, 30 people were injured in an accident at a race. One of the cheeses rolled down the hill and went into the spectators. It's not just spectators who get injured, competitors do as well- especially when it's cold or there hasn't been much rain.

CHEESE-ROLLING SPECTATOR: "It's when the ground is really hard . . . that's when the injuries are going to happen."

NARRATOR: So, why do people enter the race? Are they crazy? One cheese runner thinks they may be.

CHEESE RACER: "It is dangerous. If I'm running down . . . must be crazy. Yeah, I must be crazy…."

NARRATOR: These cheese racers may be crazy. But every year the crowds keep on cheering, and the competitors keep on running. Is it for the fame? Is it for the fun? We may never know, but it's that more than just cheese that makes people want to win Brockworth's annual cheese rolling race!

UNIT 6

VIDEO JOURNAL *MACHU PICCHU*

NARRATOR: This beautiful, quiet place is covered in sunshine and has mountains all around it. Its name is Machu Picchu. It's sometimes called the lost city of the Inca, and it's nearly 8,000 feet up in the Andes.

JULIO, Tour guide: It's a magic attraction that you can feel here. It's known all over the world that Machu Picchu is one of the magnetic centers of the ancient world.

NARRATOR: Machu Picchu is more than 500 years old. Today, it's a favorite place for visitors from all over the world.

Even in the rain and fog, it's wonderful to walk through the ruins.

When the Inca civilization ended, few people knew Machu Picchu existed. For a long time it was lost to the outside world. Then, in 1911, an explorer named Hiram Bingham found it again.

At first, very few people visited Machu Picchu. But now, hundreds of tourists come here every day. They walk up the steps of the ancient city and climb over the ruins. Machu Picchu is no longer quiet. It's full of the sounds of tourists.

Some people in Peru hope that more tourists will come here. They think it will mean more business and money for the country.

However, some conservationists worry that more visitors won't be good for Machu Picchu. They say that tourism might not be good for the environment.

Jose, a local hotel owner says Machu Picchu and Peru can take a few more visitors.

Jose, Hotel owner: Why not be like the rest of the world? Why not expose and show Machu Picchu to the rest of the world? It's such a wonderful place, why keep it to a few?

NARRATOR: The truth is that parts of Peru are very poor, and tourists bring money to these communities.

Aguas Calientes is a town that grew suddenly near an area where visitors get on buses to get to the summit of Machu Picchu. The people here live completely on money from tourism. The town is just a group of stalls where local people sell art and things they have made to visitors

The Lost City is no longer lost. Tourists have found it. The modern world is coming closer to this ancient world every day.

Time may be running out for the Lost City of the Inca. More and more people are discovering it. In the end, it may be the modern world that forever changes this ancient city.

UNIT 7

VIDEO JOURNAL *WILD ANIMAL TRACKERS*

NARRATOR: In parts of South Africa, there are still big herds of wild animals like zebras, elephants, and giraffes. But today many of these animals are in danger because people are taking the land that animals need.

Conservationists are people who protect wildlife and nature. And many of them are now leading a fight to save these animals.

Louis Liebenberg is one of these conservationists.

LOUIS LIEBENBERG, Cyber Tracker Inventor: "The most important thing is to try and get an understanding of what's happening out there."

NARRATOR: Liebenberg reports that people need to know more about animals. He says that people need to understand what happens to plants and animals over time. Are they increasing or decreasing in numbers? What plants are the animals eating?

For hundreds of years, African Bushmen have been very good wild animal trackers.

They know what the animals eat, where they go, and where they sleep. But, they don't always speak the same language as the conservationists so it can be difficult to communicate

Now, Liebenberg has brought an invention to the Karoo National Park. It's called the Cyber Tracker. He hopes that together, the Cyber Tracker and the Bushmen can help protect the animals.

Liebenberg explains that the Cyber Tracker is a small computer that helps collect information about animals with pictures, called icons, instead of words. That way, the Bushmen can record what they see even without words.

According to Liebenberg, the Cyber Tracker can collect very detailed and complicated information. And it can do it very quickly.

The Cyber Tracker also contains a global positioning device. Each time a Bushman sees something interesting about an animal or plant, he pushes a button. The Cyber Tracker records exactly where the man is. That way, even if the man can't read or write, he can record what he sees and where.

Liebenberg explains that the Cyber Tracker uses icons, or pictures, to communicate. There are pictures for drinking, walking, fighting, sleeping, eating, and other things. The user can report whether an animal is sick or dead, too. The Bushman can also record other meanings by pushing different buttons. With this option, they can name about 50 different plants.

BUSHMAN: "Three females, three youngsters and one male."

NARRATOR: Liebenberg adds that the human factor is very important. A big part of using the Cyber Tracker is the Bushman's ability to understand and record what he sees.

When the trackers return to their base, they connect the Cyber Tracker to a personal computer. Then, Liebenberg uses the information to make maps. These maps show where the animal herds are, what they are eating, and what their health is like.

The Cyber Tracker project started five years ago. At first, the idea was to help a few animals in danger. Now, more and more people have started using the Cyber Tracker in African parks, and with different animals.

Recently, Liebenberg put the Cyber Tracker software on the Internet. Many conservationists around the world have started adding the technology to their conservation programs. Soon, the Cyber Tracker may be able to help wild animals everywhere!

UNIT 8

VIDEO JOURNAL *SOLAR COOKING*

NARRATOR: It's a cool, sunny day in Borrego Springs, California and Eleanor Shimeall is cooking food. She isn't using electricity, gas, charcoal, or wood to cook her food. Instead, Shimeall is using the sun to make her lunch.

ELEANOR SHIMEALL, Solar Cook**:** "I'm going to check on this chicken and rice and see how it's cooking. Ah, it's doing a good job."

NARRATOR: In fact, she's made this entire delicious meal with solar power. A solar cooker needs only the light from the sun to cook meat, fish, grains, and vegetables—even if the air temperature isn't very hot. This method is popular with people who are worried about the environment. Solar cooking does not use fossil fuels and it does not cause pollution.

However, in developing countries, solar cookers can save lives.

DR. BOB METCALF, Solar Cookers International**:** "With sunshine you have an alternative to fire. And that's important for two and a half billion people to learn about because they're running out of traditional fuels."

NARRATOR: Dr. Bob Metcalf is a microbiologist and a founding member of Solar Cookers International. Solar Cookers International promotes solar cooking worldwide, especially in the developing countries of Africa. Their goals are to stop deforestation and to make women's lives easier.

METCALF: "They have to walk about two to three miles or so to collect wood. And then they have to tend the fire. And the smoke from that fire, it burns their eyes and chokes their lungs."

NARRATOR: According to the World Health Organization, smoke from wood fires causes the deaths of two million women and children each year. More than 22,000 families now cook traditional foods with the sun.

WENDY, Solar Cook: "Oh, this is good. It's very good! The consistency is good; the texture is fine. No problem!"

SCI WORKSHOP PARTICIPANT: "We're all amazed that a cardboard box can cook."

NARRATOR: After each workshop, attendees get their own portable solar cook kits. The simple cookers cost about five dollars and last almost two years.

METCALF: 'Shiny things direct the sunshine onto a dark pot that then absorbs the sunshine, and changes that light energy into heat energy. And heat energy doesn't get out of the clear plastic bag; it doesn't get out of the window.'

NARRATOR: SCI reports that solar cooking is also an effective way to make water pure and safe to drink.

METCALF: "Six thousand people a day are going to die of waterborne diseases in developing countries. If you heat water to 65° Celsius, 149° Fahrenheit, you can pasteurize water and make it safe to drink."

NARRATOR: Solar Cookers International has developed a useful measuring tool that helps people to know when water is safe to drink.

METCALF: "If the water gets hot enough to melt this wax, the water has reached pasteurization temperatures."

NARRATOR: From Nepal to Nicaragua, solar cooking projects are helping people in nearly every country in the developing world. Solar Cookers International's goal is to increase the use of solar cookers everywhere.

METCALF: "Science is supposed to help and benefit all of mankind, and you've got something that is good science that could help two and a half billion people in the world. There's a great need for information that these things work."

SCI WORKSHOP PARTICIPANT: "OK, solar cooker!"

UNIT 9

VIDEO JOURNAL *TRADITIONAL SILK MAKING*

NARRATOR: In this ancient city, change comes slowly. Narrow stone streets are almost the same as they were when the Medici family ruled more than 500 years ago. The Industrial Revolution, world wars and a flood forced change but one factory , has not changed.

At the *Antico Setificio Fiorentino* or The Antique Silk Factory of Florence the sounds of mechanical looms remind us of the past. These noisy 19th century looms create some of the world's finest silk fabrics for drapery and upholstery. But here they are the new machines. On the other side of the factory are the real pieces of history. Stefano Benelli weaves silk fabric that machines cannot create. And he does it slowly and carefully, one thread at a time. These looms were built in 1780 and they use the same principles of weaving used for centuries before that.

SABINE PRETSCH, Factory director: Everything is done like it was done in the ancient time. But we continue to do an evolution, continuously. We invent and we create continuously but using the old looms.

NARRATOR: All the other factories threw away their old hand looms after World War II. Only the Setificio now uses hand looms.

Usually silk has 3 to 4 thousand threads running in one direction, but the silk produced on the antique hand looms has 12,000 threads. It is much stronger and more beautiful.

Fabric from the Setificio cannot be found in stores and catalogues—it is custom made.Some people may think that making silk on a hand loom is difficult and boring but Benelli enjoys it.

STEFANO BENELLI, Silk craftsman: To the mind, is OK. Not stressful, yes.

NARRATOR: Perhaps no other city on earth has preserved the grandeur and the grace of the renaissance as well as Florence. It is appropriate then that here, at the *Antico Setificio Fiorentino* style and tradition are woven together.

UNIT 10

VIDEO JOURNAL *SCIENCE OF STRESS*

ALYSSA: "Hello, good morning . . . how was your sleep?"

NARRATOR: Six o'clock in the morning and the stress of everyday life begins . . . Family . . . Home . . . Work . . . Over and over again . . . This kind of stress actually gives us energy to get through the day.
But doing it day after day can damage our bodies.
To find out what all that stress is doing to a body . . . let's go to the Neuro-endocrinology lab at Arizona State University.
Kathy Matt and her team of researchers are trying to find out what stress does to our bodies.

DR. KATHY MATT, Arizona State University: "Stress good or bad is not just psychological, it's physiological as well."

NARRATOR: So, your body produces chemicals, called hormones, when you feel stress.

MATT: "In these samples, we are measuring cortisol which is a stress hormone."

NARRATOR: The hormones that your body produces give you energy so that you can manage the stress.
Dr. Matt explains that there are two types of stress. Physical stress, like running and mental stress, like too much work. In physical stress your body burns the hormones. In mental stress your body doesn't burn all the hormones.

TECHNICIAN: "Put this over your head"

NARRATOR: The effects of physical stress on the body are easy to measure . . .

TECHNICIAN: "I'm going to take you up 2 ½ percent . . . ok?"

NARRATOR: As the speed of the treadmill goes up, so does the heart rate and breathing.

TECHNICIAN: "All right here we go. . . "

NARRATOR: Right now the hormones in the blood are rising higher and higher.

TECHNICIAN: *"Here you go all you got . . ."*

NARRATOR: This woman is releasing many hormones and using all of the energy they create.

TECHNICIAN: "Good job, way to go!"

NARRATOR: So she passes the first test. Her body deals with physical stress pretty well. But what about mental stress?

TECHNICIAN: "It's vital that you perform at your highest level for each of the tests."

NARRATOR: With the pressure on . . .

TECHNICIAN: "Come on Alyssa as fast as you can . . . "

NARRATOR: The heart races . . . The blood pressure soars . . .

TECHNICIAN: "God I hate the 8s. I can't do the 8 times table. "

NARRATOR: Again those stress hormones are kicking in.

ALYSSA: "eight . . . "

NARRATOR: When you are under long term mental stress, your body produces hormones all the time, but it doesn't burn the extra fuel . . . and that leads to all sorts of problems.

ALYSSA: "I want you to put your fingers straight down."

TECHNICIAN: This machine checks if your bones are in good shape. If you have too many hormones in your blood, you can have problems with your bones.
Other studies show that long term stress can lead to diabetes, heart disease and neurological diseases.

TECHNICIAN: "Here's your bone density. So you're really right on this norm."

NARRATOR: So far so good. She shows no long-term effects from mental stress . . . yet. But that doesn't mean she can just ignore it . . .

This means that if you do lots of exercise it will burn up the hormones and your body won't have so many problems from mental stress. And remember, not all stress is bad. Every now and then we need a good dose of those hormones to help us get to the end of the day.

UNIT 11

VIDEO JOURNAL *SPACEWALK*

NARRATOR: From inside a spacecraft, the Earth and space look beautiful. But outside the spacecraft—in space—it is a different and far more dangerous world. There is no oxygen to breathe and there is dangerous radiation. Also temperatures can drop to minus 120 degrees Celcius and rise to 120 degrees Celsius. But man has conquered this environment.

In order to survive in space, astronauts have to wear space suits. The space suits are made from a very strong material and it is filled with oxygen so the astronauts can breathe.

The first person to leave a spacecraft and "walk" in space was Soviet Cosmonaut, Alesksy Leonov, in 1965. He "walked" in space for 12 minutes. A few months later, astronaut Edward White became the first American to walk in space during the Gemini IV mission.

These early spacewalks were intended to discover if it is possible for man to survive in deep space. They were successful—man *can* survive in space. Now spacewalks are an everyday part of the space shuttle missions.

Astronauts take spacewalks in order to do jobs that they can't do from inside the shuttle. For example, they have fixed the solar panels on the Hubble Space Telescope and they are the construction workers for the International Space Station.

But still, spacewalks are dangerous. Astronauts work in pairs so if one astronaut has problems, the other astronaut can help. They are connected to the spacecraft so that they cannot float off in to space and lose contact with the spacecraft.

It is not easy to work in a space suit. It is difficult to hold tools in the big gloves. Also the astronauts are weightless and this makes it difficult to work as well.

So, how can the astronauts practice their spacewalks on Earth before they go into space?

The answer is—underwater. At NASA's Neutral Buoyancy Laboratory, the astronauts can practice jobs that they will later do in space. Their space suits are adjusted so that they do not sink to the bottom of the tank or float to the top of the water—they are weightless. They spend a lot of time practicing in the tank. For every hour that they will spend walking in space, they spend 10 hours practicing underwater.

As NASA moves forward on the maintenance and construction of the International Space Station, spacewalks will continue to be important.

UNIT 12

VIDEO JOURNAL *THE MISSING SNOWS OF KILIMANJARO*

NARRATOR: Mount Kilimanjaro is often called the roof of Africa. It rises 19,340 feet, or nearly four miles, into the sky and is the highest point on the African continent. Kilimanjaro is in northeastern Tanzania in East Africa. It lies almost exactly between the cities of Cairo, Egypt, to the north and Cape Town, South Africa, to the south. It's around 220 miles south of the equator, in a hot, tropical region of the world.

The impressive snow-covered peaks of Kilimanjaro have been an inspiration to visitors for a very long time. Over the years, thousands of people have traveled to Tanzania to climb this majestic mountain. Many others have come to view its famous glacier-covered peak. One of these visitors was an American writer named Ernest Hemingway. He wrote a story about the mountain that made it famous. The story, first published in 1936, is called 'The Snows of Kilimanjaro'. In the story, Hemingway describes the mountain's glaciers as "wide as all the world," "great," "high," and "unbelievably white in the sun."

Although the ice cap is fantastic to see, it does in fact have a much more important purpose. The glaciers were formed more than 11,000 years ago. They have become an important source of water for drinking and farming for people who live near Kilimanjaro. Unfortunately, for the last 100 years the snows of Kilimanjaro have been disappearing.

Since 1912, Kilimanjaro's glaciers have gotten more than 80 percent smaller. A NASA satellite has been taking pictures of the mountain's ice cap for more than 15 years. The pictures that were taken in 1993 are very different from those taken only seven years later, in the year 2000.

There are many ideas about why Kilimanjaro's snow is melting so quickly. For one thing, the mountain is in a tropical region, so the glaciers are at risk for the negative effects of climate change. One type of climate change that may be directly affecting Kilimanjaro is called global warming. This worldwide problem is causing a gradual increase in the earth's temperature. As the world's temperatures rise, the snows melt.

Deforestation is another possible reason why Kilimanjaro's glaciers are melting. When trees are cut down in large numbers, the effects can cause changes in the atmosphere and the climate. Trees keep the air cooler and help maintain the water levels in the atmosphere. This helps to create clouds and rain and snow. Less rain and snow and increased temperatures can cause the glaciers to melt.

Whatever the causes may be, the snows of Kilimanjaro are continuing to melt at a very fast rate. Experts now predict that the mountain's glaciers could completely disappear by the year 2020. The loss of Kilimanjaro's glaciers would likely cause many problems for the area around the mountain. It would remove an important source of water for the people who live on or near the mountain. It could also reduce the number of tourists who come to Tanzania to see the mountain, and the money that they bring to the country.

The missing snows of Mount Kilimanjaro may be a warning. They definitely show people all over the world the dangers of climate change and deforestation. Hopefully people will learn from the loss of Kilimanjaro's glaciers. Sadly, the majestic snows of Kilimanjaro may not be around forever for people to enjoy.

UNIT 1 PEOPLE

Lesson A

A. 2. a dancer 3. an engineer 4. a doctor 5. a police officer 6. a travel agent 7. a pilot 8. a teacher

B. 2. Jordanian 3. Bahraini 4. Thai 5. Australian 6. Peruvian 7. Mexican 8. Answers will vary

C. 2. I am from 3. you are 4. Are you 5. Are you 6. I am not 7. I am 8. are you 9. I am 10. That is *OR* Rio de Janeiro is

Lesson B

A. 2. Yes 3. Are you 4. I'm not 5. I am 6. years old *OR* blank 7. your name 8. I am 9. Are you 10. I'm not 11. Are you 12. it is

B. 2. she's 3. it's 4. you're 5. isn't 6. he's 7. they're 8. we're 9. aren't

Lesson C

A. 2. d 3. f 4. e 5. c 6. a

B. Answers will vary.

C. 1. My 2. Her 3. Their 4. your 5. His 6. his 7. my

D. 1. What is your name? 2. Where are you from? 3. What do you do? 4. Is your work interesting? 5. Is your work easy? Answers to the questions will vary.

Lesson D

A. 1. F 2. T 3. F 4. T 5. T

B. 1. Natsuko Mori 2. Moses Agba 3. Natsuko Mori 4. Michael Murphy 5. Shaukat Ali 6. Moses Agba

C. Answers will vary.

REVIEW

Across 4. dangerous 7. rich 8. Canadian 11. Mexican 14. difficult 15. boring 17. are

Down 1. French 2. Korean 3. His 5. occupation 6. Thai 9. am 10. teacher 11. my 12. pilot 13. from 16. is

UNIT 2 WORK, REST, AND PLAY

Lesson A

A. 2. f 3. d 4. h 5. i 6. b 7. l 8. g 9. e 10. k 11. a 12. c

B. Answers will vary.

C. 1. at, in 2. in 3. on 4. on *OR* at 5. at, in 6. on

D. Answers will vary.

Lesson B

A. *Unscramble* 2. What do you do in the evening? 3. Do you have dinner in a restaurant? 4. What do you do in your free time? 5. What do you do on Saturdays? 6. Do you like sports? 7. What do you do on Sundays? 8. Do you go to the movies? Answers to the questions will vary.

B. Answers will vary.

Lesson C

A. 1. fireworks 2. present 3. decorate 4. costume 5. celebrate 6. mask

B. never, sometimes, often, usually, always

C. 1. I usually eat breakfast at home. 2. American Independence Day is always on July 4. 3. We never work on New Year's Day. 4. It is usually cold at Christmas. 5. We often give presents to our friends.

D. Answers will vary.

Lesson D

A. 1. The Netherlands, Iran, China 2. The Netherlands, China 3. The Netherlands, Iran, China 4. Iran, China 5. China 6. The Netherlands 7. The Netherlands, Iran, China

B. Answers will vary.

C. Answers will vary.

REVIEW

Across 3. goes 6. takes 7. catch 9. presents 11. in 12. free 13. eat 15. mask 16. on

Down 1. visits 2. watch 4. take 5. decorate 7. costume 8. festival 10. out 12. fun 14. at

UNIT 3 GOING PLACES

Lesson A

A. 1. buy 2. pack 3. take 4. check 5. go 6. buy 7. check 8. claim 9. go 10. go

B. Answers will vary.

Lesson B

A. 1. d 2. e 3. g 4. a 5. c 6. f 7. b

B. 1. Torres 2. Claudia 3. July 1, 1988 4. Buenos Aires 5. Argentinean 6. Argentina 7. Metro City 8. Metro City

C. 2. passport, visa, and ticket. 3. get up, take a shower, and read the newspaper. 4. China, Japan, Korea, and Thailand 5. coffee, tea, milk, or juice. 6. I eat dinner, do my homework, and watch TV.

Lesson C

A. 1. passport 2. credit card 3. visa 4. airline ticket 5. traveler's checks 6. international driver's license 7. cash 8. travel insurance 9. check

B. Answers will vary.

C. 1. Should I rent a car? 2. Should I take a warm coat? 3. Should I get travel insurance 4. Should I take lots of money? Answers to these questions will vary.

Lesson D

A. 1. F 2. F 3. T 4. T 5. F

B. 1. good idea 2. good idea 3. good idea 4. bad idea 5. bad idea 6. good idea 7. good idea 8. good idea

C. Answers will vary.

REVIEW

Across 2. them 3. pack 9. him 10. immigration 11. should 13. yours 14. Whose

Down 1. visa 2. take 3. passport 4. credit 5. through 6. mine 7. license 8. insurance 12. Don't 15. ours

UNIT 4 FOOD

Lesson A

A. 1. coffee 2. apples 3. fish 4. tea 5. eggs 6. chicken 7. steak 8. tomato 9. bananas 10. milk 11. lettuce 12. orange juice 13. potatoes 14. cheese 15. onions 16. shrimp

B. 1. some 2. any 3. any 4. a 5. any 6. some 7. any 8. some

C. Answers will vary.

Lesson B

A. 1. Are you ready to order? 2. What would you recommend? 3. The chicken is excellent. 4. Does the chicken come with salad? 5. Yes, it does. 6. I'll have the chicken and a baked potato. 7. Would you like anything else? 8. I would like a glass of mineral water.

B. Answers will vary.

Lesson C

A. 1. popcorn 2. bagel 3. broccoli 4. hamburger 5. cereal 6. nuts 7. hot dog 8. radish

B. Answers will vary.

C. Possible answers: 2. How many books do you have? 3. How much money do you have? 4. How much time do you have? 5. How many good friends do you have?

D. Answers will vary.

Lesson D

A. 1, 2, 5, 3, 4

B. 1. F 2. T 3. T 4. F 5. T

C. Answers will vary.

REVIEW

Across 1. much 4. little 6. meat 7. some 10. dairy products 11. waiter 13. matter 14. diet 15. lots of 16. many

Down 2. customer 3. few 5. vegetables 8. fruit 9. protein 10. drinks 12. any 16. mind

UNIT 5 SPORTS

Lesson A

A. 1. rappelling 2. climbing 3. taking a break 4. swimming 5. playing soccer 6. jogging 7. lifting weights

B. Possible answers: 2. What are they doing? / They're playing soccer. 3. What is she doing? / She's rock climbing. 4. What is he doing? / He's jogging. 5. What are they doing? / They are watching television. 6. What is she doing? / She is lifting weights.

C. Answers will vary.

Lesson B

A. 1. play basketball 2. ice skate 3. watch a ball game 4. study 5. watch a movie 6. fix the roof

B. 2. On Mondays, Eric goes to his office. Today he is sleeping late. 3. On Monday's Ms. Tyson teaches classes. Today, she is swimming at the Sports Center. 4. On Monday's, Yuki and Yoko are studying English. Today, they are taking a break. 5. On Monday's, Mr. Kim drives a bus. Today, he is watching a ball game.

C. 1. am sitting 2. see 3. is working 4. am visiting 5. are looking 6. talking 7. is cooking 8. go

Lesson C

A. 1.football 2.volleyball 3. ice hockey 4. baseball 5. golf 6. gymnastics 7. diving 8. skateboarding

B. 2. am watching 3. do you like 4. don't know 5. are running 6. is throwing 7. are shouting 8. cost 9. don't want 10. hate 11. prefer 12. are you doing 13. am sitting 14. (am) listening

C. Answers will vary.

Lesson D

A. *Row 1.* Soccer; of all ages, a ball, a place to play, an international
Row 2. Canada; ice hockey, drink hot chocolate, famous hockey teams on TV.
Row 3. Baseball; slow, interesting, friends, hot dogs
Row 4. China, Volleyball; school, offices, volleyball indoors or outdoors, expensive equipment

B. Answers will vary.

REVIEW

Across 2. break 3. go 5. cook 6. too 7. swimming 9. neither 13. indoor 15. climbing 16. am studying 17. know

Down 1. weights 4. team 5. costs 8. individual 10. equipment 11. prefers 12.jogging 14. play

UNIT 6 DESTINATIONS

Lesson A

A. 1. visit 2. take a 3. check in 4. rent 5. take 6. unpack 7. buy

B. 2. helped 3. took 4. asked 5. needed 6. flew 7. said 8. went 9. bought 10. traveled 11. knew 12. left 13. played 14. told 15. agreed 16. learned

C. 2. We went to India. 3. Where did you fly to? 4. We Flew to New Delhi. 5. Then we took a train to Agra. 6. What did you do in Agra? 7. We visited the Taj Majal. 8. Did you like it? 9. We went to some great restaurants.

Lesson B

A. 1. went to the hotel. 2. On Tuesday, I visited the Eiffel Tower. 3. On Wednesday, I saw all the famous paintings in the Louvre Museum. 4. On Thursday, I took a boat trip on the Seine River. 5. On Friday, I watched artists in Montmartre and had dinner in a French restaurant. 6. On Saturday, I went shopping at a famous department store and bought souvenirs. 7. On Sunday I went to the airport. Then returned home.

B. Possible answers: 1. Where did you go? 2. How long did you stay? 3. What did you visit (or see) and eat? 4. What did you buy? 5. Did you like Buenos Aires?

Lesson C

A. 2. fascinating 3. horrible 4. spotless 5. exhausting 6. filthy 7. huge

B. Answers will vary.

C. 2. weren't, was 3. was, were 4. was, weren't 5. were, weren't 6. was, were

D. 1A. Was 1B. wasn't, was 2A. Were 2B. I wasn't, I was 3A. Was 3B. he wasn't, He was 4A. Were 4B. they weren't, They were 5A. Was 5B. she wasn't, She was

Lesson D

A. 1. b 2. b 3. a 4. b

B. 1. ☺ 2. ☹ 3. ☺ 4. ☺ 5. ☺ 6. ☹ 7. ☺

C. Answers will vary.

REVIEW

Across 3. went 5. take 6. horrible 8. visit 11. huge 12. amazing 14. spotless 15. saw 16. said 17. filthy 18. fascinating

Down 1. left 2. rent 4. flew 7. exhausting 9. souvenirs 10. took 13. bought

UNIT 7 COMMUNICATION

Lesson A

A. 1. email 2. text message 3. phone 4. fax 5. letter 6. BlackBerry 7. newspaper ad

B. Answers will vary.

C. 1. me 2. her 3. them 4. him 5. it 6. you 7. us

D. Answers will vary.

Lesson B

A. 2. eighty-four 3. twenty-three 4. ninety 5. forty-one 6. twelve 7. fifty-six 8. thirty-five 9. sixty-eight 10. eighteen 11. seventy 12. forty-three

B. 1. email address 2. phone number 3. mailing address

C. Answers will vary.

Lesson C

A. 1. smell 2. taste 3. sight 4. hearing 5. touch

B. 1. g 2. c 3. d 4. e 5. f 6. b 7. h 8. a

C. 1. sounds 2. tastes 3. look 4. smells 5. feels 6. looks

D. Answers will vary.

Lesson D

A. They hear messages: dogs, cats, people, birds They see messages: bees They smell messages: wolves, dogs, cats They touch messages: horses, chimpanzees

B. 1. flowers and other places with food 2. smell 3. cats 4. friends 5. sound

C. Answers will vary.

REVIEW

Across 5. bought 7. text 8. taste 10. sound 14. mailing 15. her 17. phone 18. look

Down 1. sent 2. wrote 3. found 4. got 6. hearing 9. touch 11. smell 12. him 13. sight 16. feel

UNIT 8 THE FUTURE

Lesson A

A. 1. h 2. f 3. c 4. a 5. d 6. g 7. e 8. b

B. 2. They're not going to stay home. 3. They're going to pack their suitcases 4. They're not going to get to the airport late. 5. They're going to take an important test. 6. They're going to study very hard. 7. They're not going to play computer games. 8. They're not going to see his friends.

C. 1. What are you going to have for dinner? 2. Where are they going to be? 3. When is she going to leave? 4. Who is going to help you?

Lesson B

A. Possible answers: They are going to take a bath. I am going to eat breakfast. I am going to go shopping. They are going to watch TV. We are going to have a party.

B. Possible answers: Questions: 2. Are you going to do anything special this weekend? 3. What are you going to do Saturday? 4. Who are you going to see this weekend? 5. What are you going to watch on TV? 6. Are you going to spend time with your family? 7. Are you going to study English this weekend?

C. Answers will vary.

D. Answers will vary.

Lesson C

A. 1. sunny, hot 2. it will be raining, windy 3. it will be overcast, cold

B. White Beach: sunhat, sun glasses, swimsuit. Metro City: umbrella, rubber boats, raincoat. Martinville: sweater, scarf.

C. 1. Will it be warm on your birthday? 2. No, it will be cold. 3. Then, you will not have your birthday party outdoors. 4. Of course, we will be outdoors. We will wear sweaters and scarves.

D. Answers will vary.

Lesson D

A. homework, universities, classrooms, computers, jobs, lessons, tests

B. 1. No 2. Yes 3. Yes 4. No 5. No 6. Yes 7. Yes 8. Yes

C. Answers will vary.

REVIEW

Across 3. overcast 5. laundry 8. cold 10. going to 12. rubber boots 13. swimsuit 15. sweater 18. raincoat

Down 1. won't 2. wet 4. sunglasses 6. short-term 7. fluently 9. umbrella 11. long-term 14. will 16. windy 17. hot

UNIT 9 SHOPPING FOR CLOTHES

Lesson A

A. 1. pajamas 2. parka 3. flats 4. scarf 5. sweater 6. hat 7. loafers 8. boots 9. robe 10. slippers 11. stilettos 12. gloves

B. 1. new 2. cheap 3. thick 4. light 5. formal 6. good quality 7. hand-made 8. cool

C. 2. Flats are more comfortable than stilettos. 3. These jeans are more informal than a suit. 4. A raincoat is better than an umbrella. 5. A shirt is thinner than a sweater. 6. This dress is prettier than that dress. 7. The black coat is cheaper than the blue coat. 8. Leather shoes are more expensive than plastic shoes.

Lesson B

A. 1. Can I help you? 2. What size are you? 3. What about this sweater? 4. How much is it? 5. Do you have anything a little less expensive? 6. Can I try it on?

B. 2. easier 3. more casual 4. larger 5. more interesting 6. more handsome 7. worse 8. more expensive 9. heavier 10. thinner 11. warmer 12. nicer

C. Answers will vary.

Lesson C

A. 1. wash 2. bleach 3. dry 4. iron 5. dry clean

B. Answers will vary.

C. 1. the easiest 2. the coldest 3. the most expensive 4. the most exciting 5. the best 6. the most comfortable 7. the worst

D. 1. I think it is the most beautiful place in our country. 2. It is the best restaurant in our city. 3. He/She is the best athlete in the world. 4. It is the most interesting program on TV now. 5. It is the biggest problem in the world today.

Lesson D

A. 1. see pictures of t-shirts 2. words and pictures 3. Customers 4. six 5. a week

B. 1. $22, 2. $18, 3. $14, 4. $28

C. Answers will vary.

D. Answers will vary.

REVIEW

Across 10. cotton 11. pajamas 12. most beautiful 14. bigger 16. better 17. thick 18. gloves

Down 1. best 2. nicest 3. worst 4. boots 5. handmade 6. expensive 7. prettiest 8. casual 9. hat 13. slippers 15. silk

UNIT 10 LIFESTYLES

Lesson A

A. 1. f 2. a 3. b 4. d 5. g 6. e 7. c

B. 1. suggestion 2. obligation 3. suggestion 4. advice 5. obligation 6. advice

C. Answers will vary.

D. Answers will vary.

Lesson B

A. 1. go, unhealthy 2. go, healthy 3. eat, healthy 4. lose, healthy 5. work, healthy 6. drink, unhealthy 7. watch, healthy

B. Answers will vary.

Lesson C

A. 1. mouth-watering 2. home-made 3. heart-warming 4. life-long 5. stress-free 6. over-worked 7. low-calorie

B. 1. How old are you? 2. How many brothers and sisters do you have? 3. How long will you study English today? 4. How much junk food do you eat? 5. How often do you exercise? Answers to these questions will vary.

C. 1. often do you 2. How much do you play basketball every day? 3. Do you spend much time at home? 4. How old are you? 5. How many are in your family?

Lesson D

A. 1. good 2. no information 3. no information 4. good 5. bad 6. good 7. no information 8. bad

B. Answers will vary.

C. Answers will vary.

REVIEW

Across 4. could 6. long 8. lifelong 9. workout 11. stress-free 13. improve 14. must 15. often 16. much

Down 1. overworked 2. balanced 3. junk food 5. lifestyle 7. homegrown 10. unfit 12. should 15. ought 16. many

UNIT 11 ACHIEVEMENTS

Lesson A

A. 1. pay 2. cut 3. put away 4. buy 5. walk 6. iron 7. vacuum, sweep

B. 2. won 3. had 4. meet 5. go 6. swept 7. been 8. buy 9. taken 10. tell 11. pay 12. drunk 13. put 14. said 15. read 16. spoken

C. 1. haven't finished 2. Have you cleaned 3. I've vacuumed 4. haven't washed 5. haven't swept. 6. Have you done 7. I have 8. haven't walked

Lesson B

A. 2. Have you taken classes in business administration? 3. Have you had experience working in hotels? 4. Have you traveled to other countries? 5. Possible answer: Have you gotten (got) a driver's license?

B. 2. She hasn't taken any classes in business administration. 3. She has worked as a secretary. 4. She has lived in Italy for 5 years. 5. She has failed the driver's license test. 6. He has been a student at Eastern University. 7. He has majored in business administration. 8. He has worked in a restaurant. 9. He has traveled to Japan, Korea, and China. 10. Possible answer: He has gotten (got) his driver's license.

C. Answer will vary.

Lesson C

A. 1. c 2. h 3. f 4. d 5. a 6. b 7. e 8. g

B. 1. has traveled, went 2. has finished 3. was 4. has met 5. have known 6. started 7. has written 8. ate

C. Answer will vary.

Lesson D

A. 1. scientist 2. ALS 3. wheelchair 4. computer 5. the beginning of the universe

B. 1. famous books/ scientific papers 2. the greatest scientist in the world 3. many important 4. prizes 5. been in 6. on television 7. traveled to countries 8. in space

C. Answer will vary.

REVIEW

Across 2. went 6. spoken 7. have seen 9. marathon 11. interview 13. groceries 15. graduate 16. promotion

Down 1. have had 3. taken 4. drunk 5. been 8. achievement 10. ever 12. eaten 14. abroad 15. gone 16. put

UNIT 12 CONSEQUENCES

Lesson A

A. 1. expenses 2. budget 3. lend 4. save 5. overspends 6. income 7. borrow

B. 1. eat, will lose 2. lend, won't (will not) get 3. will, read 4. will get, work out 5. buy won't (will not) have 6. won't (will not) be, doesn't save

C. 1. If I study hard I'll get a good grade. 2. If I go to bed late, I'll feel tired tomorrow. 3. If I buy a new computer, I won't have money for a vacation. 4. If I don't eat more, I'll be very unhealthy.

Lesson B

A. 1. $1,185, 2. His income is less than his total budget. 3. rent, food in restaurants, and movies, concerts, and clubs. 4. Movies, concerts, clubs, and food in restaurants

B. Answer will vary.

C. Answer will vary.

Lesson C

A. 1. camel, desert 2. zebra, grasslands 3. shark, coral reef 4. mountain goat, mountains 5. orangutan, rainforest

B. 2. If you travel in the desert, you won't need a raincoat. 3. If we cut down the rainforests, orangutans won't have a home. 4. If people use the grasslands for farms, zebras will have to live in zoos. 5. If you go to the mountains, you will see mountain goats.

C. 2. You won't need a raincoat if you travel in the desert. 3. Orangutans won't have a home if we cut down the rainforests. 4. Zebras will have to live in zoos if people use the grasslands for farms. 5. You will see mountain goats if you go to the mountains.

D. Answers will vary.

Lesson D

A. 1. Rainforest Hotel, Coral Reef Ship, Mountain Camp 2. Coral Reef Ship 3. Rainforest Hotel 4. Mountain Camp 5. Rainforest Hotel, Coral Reef Ship, Mountain Camp

B. Answers will vary.

C. Answers will vary.

REVIEW

Across 3. save 4. lend 5. will 7. consequence 14. grassland 15. shark 16. decide 18. transportation

Down 1. overspend 2. coral reef 6. income 8. expenses 9. habitat 10. borrow 11. budget 12. desert 13. zebra 17. If

Reasons for Writing

The Writing Program reinforces and complements the lessons in the Student Book. Writing gives students a chance to reflect on the English they've learned and to develop an indispensable academic skill.

The Writing Syllabus

The Writing Activities help students to develop all the building blocks of good writing: words, logical connectors, sentences, transitions, paragraphs, and short essays. As students progress through the levels of the **World English** series, the Writing Activities progress from the word and sentence level to the paragraph and composition level, allowing students to master the basics before they're asked to do more complex writing tasks.

The Writing Activities help students move from sentences to paragraphs as they show relationships between ideas and add detail and precision to their writing with descriptive adjectives.

Writing from Models vs. Process Writing

When students are provided with writing models–examples of completed writing tasks–they have a clear idea of what is expected from them as well as a model on which to base their own writing. Such models give students confidence and a sense of direction and can be found at all levels of the Writing Worksheets.

On the other hand, writers must also learn the writing process. They must generate ideas, plan their writing, perform the writing task, then polish their writing by revising and editing. The Writing Worksheets support process writing by providing activities to stimulate thinking, useful topics and vocabulary, graphic organizers for planning, and opportunities for students to share and refine their writing.

Ways to Use the Writing Program

In general, the Writing Activities are designed to be used after the class has covered all or most of a unit in the Student Book. The Writing Activities often contain grammar, vocabulary, and ideas from the units, which give students solid linguistic and conceptual ground to stand on.

On the other hand, it's not necessary to complete the Lesson D Writing task in the Student Book before using the Writing Activity for that unit. The worksheets complement the writing lessons in the Student Book, but can be used independently.

- **In-Class Discussion**

  Discussion is an important way to stimulate thinking and to help students generate ideas they can use in their own writing. When an activity contains a preliminary matching or listing activity, for example, ask students to share and explain their answers. Ask specific questions about the writing models in order to check comprehension and to elicit opinions about the topics. And be sure to take advantage of opportunities for students to discuss their writing with you and their classmates.

- **Homework**

  Most of the Writing Activities are appropriate for self-study as long as follow-up discussion and feedback are provided later.

- **Vocabulary Practice**

  Many of the Writing Activities contain target vocabulary from the corresponding unit in the Student Book. Ask students to locate vocabulary from the unit in the writing models, or check comprehension by asking students to explain vocabulary words in the context of the worksheet.

- **Grammar Reinforcement**

  Many of the Writing Activities require the use of grammar points found in the Student Book units, and using the grammar in context supports real language acquisition.

- **Pronunciation Practice**

  Although oral skills are not the focus of the Writing Activities, you can do choral repetition of the word lists in the worksheets or use the writing models to practice pronunciation points from the Student Book. Students can also do read-alouds of their finished writing in pairs or small groups while the teacher monitors their pronunciation.

- **Personalization**

  When students complete unfinished sentences, paragraphs, and essays, or when they do less controlled original writing, they bring their personal thoughts and experiences into the classroom and take ownership of the writing task as well as the language they are learning.

- **Real Communication**

  Since the real-world purpose of writing is to communicate, be sure to respond not only to linguistic and technical aspects of student writing, but also to students' ideas. Make comments and ask questions that show genuine interest, either in class or when you collect and give written feedback on the worksheets.

	Writing Tasks	Language Focus
UNIT 1 Email Message	• Use *be* in statements and questions • Identify countries, nationalities, and occupations • Use descriptive adjectives	*Are you a new student?* *I'm Chilean.* *Is this class interesting?*
UNIT 2 Describe a Celebration	• List daily activities • Use the simple present tense with *first, next, then,* and *finally* • Write about a celebration	*On my day off, I usually visit friends.* *In the evening, we watch fireworks.*
UNIT 3 Travel Tips	• Practice using pronouns to show possession • Use *should* and other expressions to give travel tips	*These are my keys. They belong to me.* *When you visit my country, you should always …*
UNIT 4 Restaurant Menu	• Use *some* and *any* to talk about eating habits • Answer questions with *How much?* and *How many?* • Create a restaurant menu	*In the morning, I usually eat some eggs.* *How much should the appetizers cost?*
UNIT 5 What Are They Doing?	• Use the present continuous and stative verbs to write about what people are doing	*Haley is walking on the beach. She prefers not to play sports.* *Jim is probably talking on the phone right now.*
UNIT 6 Describe a Place	• Write about your childhood • Describe a favorite childhood place	*When I was a child, I went to Cairo with my family.* *My favorite place was the park near our house.*
UNIT 7 Chain of Events	• Use verbs with direct and indirect objects to describe a chain of events • Use linking verbs to give your opinion	*Tara sent an email to Brian.* *To me, violin music sounds wonderful.*
UNIT 8 Plans and Predictions	• Use *be going to* to write about short-term and long-term plans • Use *will* to make predictions	*This afternoon, I'm going to write some emails.* *She will probably look for a job.*
UNIT 9 Similarities and Differences	• Compare clothing styles in the present and the past • Write a conversation about shopping for clothes	*My father wore tighter jeans than I do.* *Let's get Henri a sweater.*
UNIT 10 Lifestyle Advice	• Answer *How…?* questions • Write about ways to make your lifestyle healthier	*How much junk food do you eat?* *I should walk to school more often.*
UNIT 11 Bullet-Point List	• Write about past achievements • List the steps to a future goal • Use the present perfect tense to chart your progress	*My team won first place in a math competition.* *I have already applied to three universities.*
UNIT 12 Cause and Effect Story	• Write sentences using the real conditional • Use *so* to describe cause-and-effect relationships	*If you buy a camera, you won't be able to buy a plane ticket.* *Mike didn't want to rent a car, so they took the train.*

UNIT 1 PEOPLE
AN EMAIL MESSAGE

A. Read and complete the conversation.

Miguel: Hi, _____I'm_____ Miguel.
Jean: Hi, Miguel. I'm _____.
Miguel: Nice to meet you, Jean.
Jean: Nice to meet you, too. _____ you a new student?
Miguel: Yes, I am. I'm from Mexico.
Jean: Oh, you're _____! I'm from here. I'm Chilean.
Miguel: I see. Tell me, _____ this class interesting?
Jean: Yes, it is, and the teacher is nice.
Miguel: Oh, good. _____ is the teacher from?
Jean: Mr. Ortiz? He's _____ Argentina.

✔ Read the conversation again and complete the chart.

Name	Miguel		Mr. Ortiz
Country			Argentina
Nationality	Mexican	Chilean	
Occupation		student	teacher

✔ Write sentences about these people. Give the information in parentheses.

1. (occupation) This is Mr. Ortiz. _____He's a teacher_____.

2. (nationality) This is Jean. _____.

3. (country) This is Miguel. _____.

4. (name) _____. She's from Chile.

5. (occupation) This is Miguel. _____.

6. (name) _____. He's Argentinean.

B. Complete the email message. Choose any descriptive adjective from the box.

happy	interesting	boring	good	difficult	dangerous	bad

From: Miguel Hernandez
To: Alberto Ochoa
Subject: my new home

Hi Alberto,

Well, I'm in Chile, and I'm very _____! I really like the place and the people. On the first day of class, I talked to Jean. She's very _____. She knows a lot about my new school. We have a/n _____ teacher named Mr. Ortiz. His class is _____, but I like it. On the other hand, my sister doesn't like our new home. According to her, life here in Chile is _____. I hope she changes her opinion soon!

Your friend,

Miguel

UNIT 2 WORK, REST, AND PLAY
DESCRIBE A CELEBRATION

A. What do you do on a work day? What do you do on your day off when you have free time? Use phrases from the box and some of your own phrases.

get up	go to school	take a nap	do homework	visit friends
catch the bus	go to work	go to bed	go to class	go shopping

On a work day . . .	On my day off . . .
• I get up at _____. • • •	• • • •

✓ Take turns. Ask a partner these questions. Answer with information from the chart.

1. What do you usually do on a work day?

2. What do you usually do on your day off?

✓ Write about your usual work day OR your usual day off.

On my usual (work day/day off), I do several things. First, I _____.

Next, I _____. Then, I _____. Finally, I

_____.

B. Which festival or celebration do you enjoy? Answer these questions.

1. What's the name of the festival or celebration? (my birthday, Songkran, etc.)

   _____

2. What do you usually do during that festival or celebration . . .

   in the morning? _____

   in the afternoon? _____

   in the evening? _____

✓ Write about the festival or celebration.

One of my favorite things to celebrate is _____. In the morning,

_____. Then, in the afternoon, _____.

Finally, in the evening,_____.

It's a lot of fun!

UNIT 3 GOING PLACES

TRAVEL TIPS

A. Fill in each blank with the correct pronoun. Use the information from the chart.

me	you	Bob	you and me	Melissa	Lynn and Steve
keys	a camera	a passport	plane tickets	a purse	a suitcase

1. These are __my__ keys. They're __mine__. They belong to __me__.
2. This is _____ camera. It's _____. It belongs to _____.
3. This is _____ passport. It's _____. It belongs to _____.
4. These are _____ plane tickets. They're _____. They belong to _____.
5. This is _____ purse. It's _____. It belongs to _____.
6. This is _____ suitcase. It's _____. It belongs to _____.

✓ Read the paragraph below and fill in each blank with the correct pronoun.

B. Write a list of travel tips for someone who wants to visit your country.

When you visit my country

- You should always _____
- You should never _____
- It's a good idea to _____
- While you're here, you will need _____
- And don't forget to bring your _____
- Most importantly, you should _____

UNIT 4 FOOD

RESTAURANT MENU

A. List some things you might eat and drink in one day.

morning	
afternoon	
evening	
night	

✔ Write sentences about your daily diet. Use the information from the chart.

1. In the morning, I usually eat some _____, and I usually drink some _____.
2. In the morning, I never eat any _____, and I never drink any _____.
3. In the afternoon, I usually eat some _____, and I usually drink some _____.
4. In the afternoon, I never eat any _____, and I never drink any _____.
5. In the evening, I usually eat some _____, and I usually drink some _____.
6. In the evening, I never eat any _____, and I never drink any _____.
7. At night, I usually eat some _____, and I usually drink some _____.
8. At night, I never eat any _____, and I never drink any _____.

B. Imagine you are going to open a new restaurant. Answer these questions, then create a menu.

1. How many appetizers should be on the menu? _____
2. How much should the appetizers cost? _____
3. How many main dishes should be on the menu? _____
4. How much should the main dishes cost? _____
5. Should your menu have a few dishes for people on special diets? _____
6. Should your menu have a few desserts? _____

Menu

UNIT 5 SPORTS

WHAT ARE THEY DOING?

A. What do you think the people are doing? Write a name next to each activity.

| Haley   Scott   Alejandro   Lucy   Aimi   Yi-Chen |

_____ is walking on the beach.   _____ is playing soccer.

_____ is doing gymnastics.   _____ is taking a break.

_____ is swimming in the pool.   _____ is playing tennis.

✓ Write sentences about the people above. Use stative verbs and some of the words and phrases from the box. Use some of your own ideas, too.

stative verbs	**likes** (to be outdoors/indoor sports/quiet activities)
	has (a lot of sports equipment/a lot of free time)
	prefers (outdoor sports/individual sports/not to play sports)
	thinks (sports are wonderful/it's the best sport)
	seems (happy/tired/relaxed)
	feels (terrific/energetic/exhausted)

1. Haley _thinks_ _____

2. Scott _____

3. Alejandro _____

4. Lucy _____

5. Aimi _____

6. Yi-Chen _____

✓ Put your sentences together. For example, write:

Haley is walking on the beach. She prefers not to play sports.

B. Make a list of important people in your life. What is each person probably doing right now? Then complete the journal entry below.

Today is _____. I'm writing in my journal and thinking about people in my life. First, there's _____ (He/She) is probably _____ right now. Next, there's _____

Finally, there's _____ _____

I think _____

UNIT 6 DESTINATIONS

DESCRIBE A PLACE

A. How was your life when you were a child?

When I was a child . . .

1. I wanted _____

2. I didn't want _____

3. I went _____

4. I didn't go _____

5. I learned _____

6. I didn't learn _____

✓ Take turns. Ask a partner questions about the sentences above.

> What did you want when you were a child?

> What did you not want when you were a child?

B. When you were a child, what was your favorite place to be? (e.g. your family's kitchen; a park near your house; your grandmother's farm; etc.) Answer these questions about that place.

1. What was your favorite place? _____

2. Why did you like that place? _____

3. How did you get there? _____

4. What did you do there? _____

5. What did you see, hear, and feel in your favorite place? _____

✓ Write about your favorite place when you were a child. Use some of the information above.

My Favorite Childhood Place
When I was a child, my favorite place was _____. I liked it because
_____. I usually went there _____.
While I was there, I usually _____.
I could (see/hear/feel) _____
and _____ . It was wonderful to be there!

UNIT 7 COMMUNICATION

CHAIN OF EVENTS

A. Look at the diagram below. How did Sanjay hear the news? Write sentences with indirect objects. (In 1-4, write each sentence two different ways.)

Tara sent an email	→	Brian sent a text message	→	Daniel wrote a letter	→	Sophia told Melanie the news	→	Melanie gave a phone call	→	Sanjay heard the news!

1. a. _Tara sent Brian an email._

   b. _Tara sent an email to Brian._

2. a. _____

   b. _____

3. a. _____

   b. _____

4. a. _____

   b. _____

5. a. _____

✓ Ask a partner questions about the sentences above. How did each person get the news?

How did Brian get the news?

Tara sent him an email.

✓ Write a paragraph with the title: *How Sanjay heard the news.* Use these sequence words: *First, Next, Then, After that, Finally.*

B. What's your opinion? Use adjectives from the box or your own ideas. Then write two new sentences.

wonderful   sweet   horrible   salty   bad   delicious   interesting   nice   terrible

1. To me, pizza tastes _____.

2. To me, running for an hour feels _____.

3. To me, violin music sounds _____.

4. To me, some modern art looks _____.

5. To me, gasoline smells _____.

6. To me, learning a new language feels _____.

7. To me, _____.

8. To me, _____.

UNIT 8 THE FUTURE
PLANS AND PREDICTIONS

A. What are your plans? Use some of the words from the box and some of your own ideas.

| graduate | eat lunch | buy a car | write some emails |
| do homework | get married | travel | go shopping |

my short-term plans	my long-term plans

✓ Write sentences about your plans. Use *be going to* and future expressions such as *Tonight, Next week, In two years, When I'm thirty*, etc.

I have several short-term plans. _This afternoon, I'm going to_ _____

_____

_____

I also have some long-term plans. _Next year, I'm going to_ _____

_____

_____

B. What will probably happen? Make predictions using *will*.

1. Muriel needs some money. She knows how to program computers, and she's a very good cook. _What will she do? She will probably look for a job. Computer programmers make more money than cooks, so she probably won't look for a restaurant job._

2. Tony lives in London, but his girlfriend lives in Rome. They want to get married. What will they do? _____

_____

3. It's winter and you're in Antarctica. A major storm is moving across the ocean. What will happen when the storm hits? _____

_____

4. Paula is going to play soccer this afternoon. Last night, she didn't sleep. What will happen?

_____

_____

UNIT 9 SHOPPING FOR CLOTHES
SIMILARITIES AND DIFFERENCES

A. What do you usually wear? What did your parents wear at your age?
Draw two pictures—one of you, and one of your mother or father at your age.

✓ Write sentences about the clothes in the pictures. What's the same? What's different?
Use some of the words from the box and some of your own ideas.

shorter	less expensive	more colorful	more old-fashioned	tighter
less formal	lighter	more modern	more beautiful	longer

1. My father wore tighter jeans than I do. I prefer looser jeans. _____

2. _____

3. _____

4. _____

5. _____

6. _____

B. Henri's birthday is next week. Gina and Tom are shopping for a gift. Finish their conversation.

Gina: Let's get Henri a sweater. He's always cold.

Tom: I don't know. These sweaters are expensive. Let's _____.

Gina: That's a good idea, but _____.

Tom: You're right. How about some _____?

Gina: Hmmm. I don't really like those.

Tom: Oh! Let's get him _____.

Gina: That's a great idea!

Tom: Henri will love (it/them) because _____.

Writing Activity 9   **T-189**

UNIT 10 LIFESTYLES

LIFESTYLE ADVICE

A. Answer these questions about your lifestyle.

Your Diet

1. How much junk food do you eat? _____

2. How often do you eat fruits and vegetables? _____

Your Exercise Habits

3. How much walking do you do? _____

4. How often do you do exercises or play sports? _____

Your Health Habits

5. How well do you handle stress? _____

6. How often do you spend time with family and friends? _____

B. How could you improve your lifestyle? Write down some ideas.

suggestions (just ideas)	advice (recommendations)	obligation (necessities)
I could . . .	I should . . . I ought to . . .	I must . . . I have to . . .

C. Write a page in your journal. Use the modals and some of your ideas from the chart in exercise **B**.

> Dear diary,
>
> I really want to make my lifestyle healthier, and I've thought of some things I can do.
>
> First, I _____.
>
> Second, I _____.
>
> In addition, I _____.
>
> Most importantly, I _____.
>
> These lifestyle changes will make me a healthier person, and they might help me live longer, too.

✓ Read your journal page to a partner. Then give each other suggestions for other lifestyle changes.

Those are great ideas!

You could also eat breakfast every day.

UNIT 11 ACHIEVEMENTS

BULLET-POINT LIST

A. Write about your achievements. What are you proud of? When did these things happen?

Example: *In the 6th grade, my team won first place in a math competition.*

1. _____
2. _____
3. _____
4. _____
5. _____

B. Check the things you hope to do in the future.

____ buy a house   ____ get a credit card   ____ graduate from a university

____ travel abroad   ____ have children   ____ start my own business

____ get a job   ____ run in a marathon   ____ (other) _____

✓ Choose one of your goals from the list above. Make a bullet-point list of things you must do in order to achieve that goal.

> **Goal:** _____
>
> **Things I must do to achieve my goal:**
>
> • _____
> • _____
> • _____
> • _____
> • _____

✓ Make a bullet-point list to show your progress. What have you already done to achieve your goal? What do you still need to do? Use the present perfect tense.

I have already . . .	I haven't yet . . .
• _____	• _____
• _____	• _____
• _____	• _____
• _____	• _____

UNIT 12 CONSEQUENCES
CAUSE AND EFFECT

A. What will (or won't) happen? Finish the sentences.

   Example: *If you buy a camera, you won't be able to buy a plane ticket.*

   1. If you save your money now, you _____

   2. If you take the train, you _____

   3. If you argue with your friend, _____

   4. If you eat a sandwich now, _____

   5. If people continue to overfish, _____

   6. If the number of people in the world continues to increase, _____

B. We can use *so* to show causes and effects.

   Example: <u>Riley bought a camera</u>, so <u>he doesn't have enough money for a plane ticket</u>.
                 cause   **effect**

✓Complete the sentences. Use *so* to show the effects.

   1. Susan has a lot of money in the bank, so _____

   2. We're going to take the train, so _____

   3. I argued with my best friend, so _____

   4. I ate a sandwich a few minutes ago, so _____

   5. People are continuing to overfish, so _____

   6. The number of people in the world is continuing to increase, so _____

C. Write a story about two friends who took a vacation together. What did they do? Where did they go? Use your imagination, and use *so* to show causes and effects.

   Example: *Mike didn't want to rent a car, so they took the train.*

	Goals	Language Focus
UNIT 1 People	• Talk about people	*Her/his name is ____ .* *S/he's from ____.* *S/he's a(an) ____.*
UNIT 2 Work, Rest, and Play	• Describe an unusual celebration • Share your ideas with the class	*It's called ____. It's for ____.* *People always . . . on ____.*
UNIT 3 Going Places	• Deciding what to take on a trip • Limiting travel needs to one suitcase	*I think we should take . . .* *Don't take . . .*
UNIT 4 Food	• Completing a menu • Ordering meals at a restaurant	*Do you have . . .* *Would you like . . .*
UNIT 5 Sports	• Planning a sports center • Organizing activities at a new sports center	*I think . . .* *I prefer . . .* *We need . . .*
UNIT 6 Destinations	• Improving a TV travel commercial with emphatic adjectives • Developing a TV travel commercial	*. . . was outstanding!* *. . . was fascinating/amazing enormous!*
UNIT 7 Communication	• Interpreting symbols • Creating signs from symbols	*What does this mean?* *It looks like a sign for . . .*
UNIT 8 The Future	• Making predictions about the future • Choosing the best predictions	*____ is going to . . .* *____ will . . .*
UNIT 9 Shopping for Clothes	• Shopping for clothes in a store • Shopping for clothes online	*I'm looking for . . .* *This is ____ than that one.* *Are these ____?*
UNIT 10 Lifestyles	• Forming opinions about lifestyle habits • Sharing opinions about lifestyle	*I agree that . . .* *I disagree that . . .*
UNIT 11 Achievements	• Selecting a person for an achievement award • Explaining reasons for a choice	*I chose ____ because s/he has . . .* *____ is a better choice because s/he has . . .*
UNIT 12 Consequences	• Considering consequences in planning a project • Offering different alternatives	*If we . . . we will . . .* *If we . . . we will be able to . . .*

UNIT 1 PEOPLE

A. Talk about the people in the pictures. Write your ideas.
What are their names? How old are they? Where are they from? What do they do?

1. _____

_____

_____

_____

2. _____

_____

_____

_____

3. _____

_____

_____

_____

4. _____

_____

_____

_____

B. Get together with another pair of students. Share your ideas. Are they the same or different?

UNIT 2 WORK, REST, AND PLAY

A. Look at these unusual celebrations. What do you think people do on these days?

September 5

Be Late for Something Day

July 20

National Ice Cream Day

January 3

Festival of Sleep

May 6

INTERNATIONAL NURSES' DAY

B. Think of a new celebration. Answer the questions.

1. What is the name of your celebration? _____
2. Who is your celebration for? _____
3. When is your celebration? _____
4. What are three things people do for this celebration? _____
   _____
5. What are three things that people eat or drink for this celebration? _____
   _____
6. Why is your celebration fun? _____
   _____

C. Tell the class about your celebration.

UNIT 3 GOING PLACES

A. You and your partner are going on a trip for one week. Choose the place you will go to.
Destination: _____

B. Work alone. Look at this list and circle the things you want to take along.

sweaters	your passport	a swimsuit	a jacket	sunglasses
books to read	your camera	jeans	t-shirts	nice clothes to go out at night
a dictionary	credit cards	a video camera	lots of CDs	cookies and candy
dishes	an umbrella	a coat	boots	three pairs of shoes
magazines	a radio	skis	a tennis racquet	a laptop computer
cash	a driver's license	a guitar	a pillow	photos of your family
sandwiches	perfume	DVDs	_____	_____

C. Now work with a partner. The airplane is very small, so you can only take one suitcase—together! Which things on the list will you take? Remember, all the things must fit into one suitcase! Write your list.

_____
_____
_____
_____
_____

D. Share your list with the class.

Photocopiable © 2010 Heinle, Cengage Learning

UNIT 4 FOOD

A. Read the menu. Fill in the spaces with foods you like.

Amy's Family Restaurant

Main Dishes	**Desserts**
Fried chicken … $5.95	Ice cream … $1.50
Baked fish … $7.95	Fruit plate … $2.00
Italian spaghetti … $6.95	_____
_____	_____
_____	
Side dishes	**Drinks**
Salads: green, tomato, mixed … $1.95	Mineral water, iced tea, coffee … $1.50
Soups: chicken, _____,	_____, _____
_____ … $2.50	

B. Practice this conversation with a partner.

Waiter:	Good evening. My name is Andy, and I'll be your waiter today. Are you ready to order?
Julie:	Yes, I am. I'd like the fried chicken, please.
Waiter:	OK . . . And would you like french fries or a baked potato with that?
Julie:	Hmm . . . I'll have french fries. And what kind of salad do you have?
Waiter:	We have green salad, tomato salad, and mixed vegetable salad.
Julie:	I'd like a green salad.
Waiter:	And what would you like to drink?
Julie:	Do you have iced tea?
Waiter:	Yes, we do. Small, medium, or large?
Julie:	Medium, please.

C. Look at the menu and make a new conversation with foods you like. Then change roles and make another conversation.

D. Present your conversation to the class.

UNIT 5 SPORTS

You and your group are going to plan a new sports center for all the people in your city. People can go there to play their favorite sports, and learn to play new sports. Talk together and decide about these things.

A. What are five sports people can do or play in your sports center?

1. _____
2. _____
3. _____
4. _____
5. _____

B. What are five things that people can learn at your sports center?

1. _____
2. _____
3. _____
4. _____
5. _____

C. What are five special rooms in your sports center?

1. _____
2. _____
3. _____
4. _____
5. _____

D. Give your sports center a name. _____

E. Tell the class about your Sports Center!

UNIT 6 DESTINATIONS

A. Read this TV commercial for a travel destination out loud.

Actor #1: Wow, you look so relaxed! How was your vacation at White Beach?
Actor #2: Oh, it was very good.
Actor #1: Tell me about your hotel!
Actor #2: It was nice. Our room was big, and the view from the window was good.
Actor #1: Did you like the beach?
Actor #2: It was big and clean. We went swimming every day, and we took an interesting boat tour.
Actor #1: Were you happy with your trip?
Actor #2: Yes! White Beach is a good place for a vacation, and the weather there is nice every day.
Actor #1: I should call my travel agent today—and take my next vacation at White Beach!

B. Make the commercial in exercise **A** more interesting. Cross out some of the adjectives and use emphatic adjectives from the box.

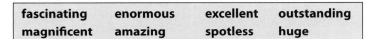

fascinating	enormous	excellent	outstanding
magnificent	amazing	spotless	huge

C. On another sheet of paper, write your own TV commercial for a place in your country. Use emphatic adjectives. Then practice your commercial with your partner.

D. Present your commercial to the class.

UNIT 7 COMMUNICATION

A. People use symbols to communicate without words. Look at the signs. What do these symbols mean in English?

1. _____ 2. _____ 3. _____

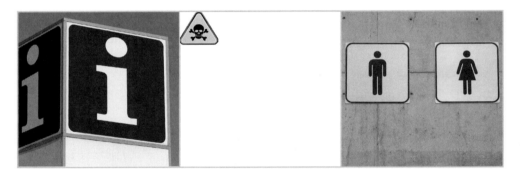

4. _____ 5. _____ 6. _____

B. Think of two new symbols for useful signs. Draw them on another sheet of paper.

C. Show your signs to other students. Can they understand them?

UNIT 8 THE FUTURE

▲ A fortune teller can see the future! He or she makes predictions to help people.

👥 **A.** You are fortune-tellers. Make predictions for ten years in the future, like the example.

1. your school <u>Our school is going to have a big, new building. It will be beautiful!</u>

2. your city _____

3. your teacher _____

4. a classmate _____

   Name: _____

5. a classmate _____

   Name: _____

6. your country _____

7. a sports team _____

8. a famous person

   Name: _____

👥👥 **B.** Get together with another pair. Share your predictions.

👥👥 **C.** Choose the three best predictions from your group. Read them to the class.

UNIT 9 SHOPPING FOR CLOTHES

A. Read the conversation and fill in the words. Then practice the conversation with your partner.

looking	take	on sale	price	fitting room

Clerk: May I help you?

Customer: Yes. I'm _____ for a warm sweater.

Clerk: These sweaters are _____ this week. They're only $18.

Customer: What are they made of?

Clerk: They're 100% wool.

Customer: $18 is a good _____ for a wool sweater. Do you have any in medium?

Clerk: This green one is medium.

Customer: Can I try it on?

Clerk: Yes, the _____ is in the back of the store.

– – – –

Customer: It's very warm. Do you have any other colors?

Clerk: Let's see . . . We also have blue, brown, and black.

Customer: Great! I'll _____ a green one and a black one, too.

B. Look at the advertisement and make two new conversations. Take turns buying things.

Gracy's Department Store

Big Winter Sale!

Leather jackets— only $125! Black, brown, or tan

Fashion jeans— just $40! 100% cotton denim in dark blue, light blue, or black

Winter ski parkas— $89! Warm, 100% man-made fiber, in red, blue, green, gold, or purple.

Snow boots— $35! Made of nylon in HOT colors to keep your feet warm. Blue, orange, green, or red

Cotton t-shirts— $10 In ten different colors

| XS extra-small |
| S small |
| M medium |
| L large |
| XL extra-large |

Photocopiable © 2010 Heinle, Cengage Learning

UNIT 10 LIFESTYLES

A. Read the opinion survey and mark your answers.

> **Lifestyle Survey**
>
> 1. Most people today don't sleep enough.
>   ☐ I agree.　　☐ I disagree.　　☐ I don't know.
>
> 2. Traditional food in our country is healthier than modern food.
>   ☐ I agree.　　☐ I disagree.　　☐ I don't know.
>
> 3. You can be healthy even with no exercise.
>   ☐ I agree.　　☐ I disagree.　　☐ I don't know.
>
> 4. People must take vitamin pills to be healthy.
>   ☐ I agree.　　☐ I disagree.　　☐ I don't know.
>
> 5. Life in the past was healthier than life today.
>   ☐ I agree.　　☐ I disagree.　　☐ I don't know.
>
> 6. Eating a lot of junk food is worse than smoking.
>   ☐ I agree.　　☐ I disagree.　　☐ I don't know.
>
> 7. Working too much is very bad for your health.
>   ☐ I agree.　　☐ I disagree.　　☐ I don't know.
>
> 8. For good health, your genes are more important than your habits.
>   ☐ I agree.　　☐ I disagree.　　☐ I don't know.
>
> 9. Most people worry about their health too much.
>   ☐ I agree.　　☐ I disagree.　　☐ I don't know.
>
> 10. I eat a very healthy diet.
>   ☐ I agree.　　☐ I disagree.　　☐ I don't know.

B. Discuss your opinions with a group. Explain your reasons.

C. Compare your answers with the whole class.

UNIT 11 ACHIEVEMENTS

A. Your city is giving an Achievement Award to the person who has the most important achievements. Read about the four candidates.

Candidate 1: Alicia

Alicia got married after she graduated from high school, and had two children. Her husband died in a car accident. She went back to school and became a teacher. She teaches in a school for children with learning problems. She has helped more than 100 children learn to read and write.

Candidate 2: Jacob

Jacob can't walk. He has used a wheelchair since he was a little boy. He always loved his science and math classes. He is now studying to be a doctor, and he is the top student in his classes. He wants to help other people who can't walk.

Candidate 3: Kyra

Kyra's family had to leave their home country because of a war. When she was in high school, she worked at night to earn money for her family. After she graduated from high school, she started her own business. Her business has given jobs to more than 30 poor women.

Candidate 4: Rick

Rick is the oldest of ten brothers and sisters. He loves art, and he made beautiful drawings and paintings as a child. His parents didn't have money to pay for his education, so he worked in a factory for five years to study at an art school. He has given more than 100 paintings to hospitals to put in sick people's rooms.

B. Talk with your partner. Choose two people to recommend for the award.

C. Get together with another pair. Choose one person for the award, and make notes of your reasons.

D. Tell the class about your decision. Explain your reasons.